THE LITERARY
HERITAGE
OF CHILDHOOD

Recent Titles in
Contributions to the Study of World Literature
Series Adviser: Leif Sjoberg

THE LITERARY HERITAGE OF CHILDHOOD

An Appraisal of Children's Classics in the Western Tradition

CHARLES FREY and JOHN GRIFFITH

CONTRIBUTIONS TO THE STUDY OF WORLD LITERATURE
NUMBER 20

GREENWOOD PRESS
NEW YORK • WESTPORT, CONNECTICUT • LONDON

Library of Congress Cataloging-in-Publication Data

Frey, Charles H.
    The literary heritage of childhood.

    (Contributions to the study of world literature,
0738-9345 ; no. 20)
    Bibliography: p.
    Includes index.
    1. Children's literature—History and criticism.
I. Griffith, John W.   II. Series.
PN1009.A1F74   1987   809'.89282   87-266
ISBN 0-313-25681-0 (lib. bdg. : alk. paper)

British Library Cataloguing in Publication Data is available.

Copyright © 1987 by Charles H. Frey and John W. Griffith

Library of Congress Catalog Card Number: 87-266
ISBN: 0-313-25681-0
ISSN: 0738-9345

First published in 1987

Greenwood Press, Inc.
88 Post Road West, Westport, Connecticut 06881

Printed in the United States of America

The paper used in this book complies with the
Permanent Paper Standard issued by the National
Information Standards Organization (Z39.48-1984).

10 9 8 7 6 5 4 3 2 1

Copyright Acknowledgments

We are grateful for permission to use materials previously published in the
following: *Children's Literature, Classics of Children's Literature* and accompanying material (New York: Macmillan, 1981 and 1987), *The Jack London
Newsletter, Kansas Quarterly, The Lion and the Unicorn,* and *The Southern
Humanities Review.*

CONTENTS

PREFACE

The Literary Heritage of Childhood freshly interprets famous works in the western tradition by twenty-eight authors, enduring works read to and by successive generations of children. Through these works, the authors provide a reading of children and of childhood, a reading of what children and childhood have signified in our culture. Most children in our culture who are given books to read (or to listen to) are exposed to many or all of the books we consider here, and adults often re-read them, once again reading a meaning out of or into the children and childhoods addressed by the works. The works we discuss thus speak to and mediate between our child and grown-up states. They both define and measure our sense of maturation. They provide one crucial reading of where we have come from and of what paths we are traveling.

The classics of children's literature are thus an unusually fertile and many-sided subject for contemplation. They connect to so many different parts of life and literature that to begin thinking about them—about their sources and their intrinsic natures and their moral and philosophical implications—is to pick up threads leading inward and outward toward uncountable insights and realizations. The classics for children are a rare thing in the modern world's canon of literature: They are acknowledged literary masterpieces that people buy and read not merely because some teacher or professor has instructed them to, but willingly and with joy. A major reason for this, we believe, is that the great literature for children is about so many things of fundamental concern to us—to us as children, as adults, as readers, as decision-makers, as seekers. It is about freedom and coercion, play and duty, desire and fear, innocence and experience, parents and children, ambition and humility, dream and reality, sex and violence, mortality and immortality—all seen under the aspect of the nursery, the schoolroom, the bedtime ritual, the lark. The more one advances "inside" the great and famous stories and poems for children, the deeper one goes into our childhoods, our culture, our literary history, and our spiritual, moral, and emotional constitutions.

Children's classics stand in a reciprocal relation to the rest of life: they draw from experience, and they provide experience. They are formed out of the lives of the people who created them, and they extend the possibilities of life for those who read or hear them. These works reveal the world as it has been revealed to imaginative geniuses—sensitive, passionate, righteous, troubled, articulate poets and storytellers, artists giving creative order to their personal preoccupations and the challenges of the cultures in which they matured.

That books read both in childhood and adulthood must play a crucial role in our cultural life may seem obvious enough, but the dynamics of the interplay between our reading the works as children and our reading the works as adults deserves consideration. Children who are reading both about themselves and forward into life may not find quite the same meanings in what they read as would be found by grown-ups who are reading to or about children, retrospectively, through the same works. Children, for example, may not observe the same note of pathos that adults are likely to find in Alice's thought that to be a grown-up queen must be all "feasting and fun" or in Mowgli's "spring running" out of the jungle and past his boyhood friends, forever. Children may be relatively insensitive, moreover, to the deep ambivalence expressed in many children's classics toward the rewards and pains of our sexual maturation. That not only *Alice's Adventures in Wonderland* and *The Jungle Books* but also *Peter Pan*, *The Wind in the Willows*, *Pinocchio*, the tales of Hans Christian Andersen, and many other children's readings may reveal to observing adults a distinct anxiety, if not a lament, concerning the ending of childhood and beginning of adulthood, is a speculation to be reckoned with and even carefully explored. In our readings of children's reading we have sought to remain sensitive to this issue and to other, similar margins between early and later interpretations of great writings for children.

That post-adolescents probably will not view some parts of life quite in the way that pre-adolescents are likely to view them does provide a simple but basic quandary for the authors of children's books. Such authors are themselves grown-ups. When grown-up authors imagine themselves back toward childhood, they rarely seem to shed altogether the genuine sophistication maturity has brought them. The full dimensions of Lewis Carroll's sense of humor, or of Mark Twain's or A. A. Milne's or E. B. White's, for example, remain unexplored by most children. One reason for the double-layering of adult and child perspectives in so many of the works discussed here is that many authors for children know very well that their works will be read by adults to children as well as by children to themselves. The author's audience becomes, then, significantly split, divergent, incongruent, so that it becomes specially relevant, when interpreting children's books, to consider the background and possible aims of the author. Again, we have sought in the chapters that follow to appreciate the relevance, finally limited as it always is, of author's lives to their meanings. Occasionally, our interpretations of the relations between the life of an author (such as Hans Christian Andersen, Robert Louis Stevenson, James Barrie, or Laura Ingalls Wilder) and his or her works may appear somewhat stricter or darker than the heretofore prevailing view, but we have sought in each case to provide the evidence both from the life and the work upon which our interpretations rest. We are of course engaged, as all interpreters are, with a community of past and present commentators, and we seek no more than that our contribution to the ongoing dialogue be considered with the same openness we have tried to bring to the contributions of others.

One way of suggesting what we take to be the drift of our interpretations is to say that we often find less prettiness or innocence or even conventional happiness in children's readings than we find disruptive energy, rapid and shocking experience, and persistent revelations of contradictions and strangeness at the core of personal, familial, and social life. We see in children's books much of the grotesqueness, metamorphosis, seeming illogic, and teasingly veiled insights that we associate with dreams. To us, great writing for children often tends to hover over the glowing border between good dream and nightmare, between cosy domesticity and sharp family struggle, between edenic nostalgia and sobering maturity. As swiftly becomes plain, we do not discount the reading of children. Far from it. We find the authors and works we interpret here to be deeply affecting, engaged with crucial life themes, wrestling over and over with the most protean and firmly insinuated forms of our growth process.

The creative order of children's reading has been achieved, we note, through the shaping and liberating conventions of the folk tale, the fairy tale, the nursery rhyme, the quest-romance, the domestic novel, the moral fable, the talking-animal story, the semi-biographical account, the nonsense poem—an exceedingly wide range of styles and genres. There is that about children's genres, moreover, which makes them more telling in some ways than other literary types. While some kinds of censors swing into place when an adult turns to write for children, some other kinds of censors are dismissed, and we are treated to a view of the imagination at play or on vacation, as it were, releasing deeper and more basic impulses through the apparently carefree forms of fancy, adventure, whimsy, and dream.

The authors chosen for discussion here are those judged to be most securely representative of our own culture's classic tradition in readings for children. We know that additional authors could easily be nominated for inclusion among those we treat, but we think also that we give a generous and varied array of the historical and generical traditions central to children's fiction in the English-speaking west. It is our hope and belief that readers of this book will find in its pages new, sometimes surprising, but generally persuasive readings of, to use Stevenson's phrase, "all the old romance." Our methods and themes are somewhat eclectic in that we vary our focus from, say, Calvinist issues in *Treasure Island*, to small-town mores in *Tom Sawyer*, to grown-up baiting in *Alice's Adventures in Wonderland*, to psycho-sexual readings of Andersen and Barrie, to character analysis in *A Christmas Carol*, to comparisons of tales by the Grimms and Perrault, to consideration of Kipling's ethos, to grappling with Jack London's contradictions, to bio-graphical interpretation of *Little House on the Prairie*, and so on through the kaleidoscopic and brilliantly varied authors whom we interpret. If we have often taken these readings for children quite seriously, we have always done that to deepen the reader's enjoyment and to inform the reader's evaluations.

We have tried to follow our understanding of these works and their authors wherever it has led us. The fundamental spirit in which we approach our project is one of celebration; we believe that the immortal literary works have earned their immortality as unique and valuable products of the imag-ination. At some level, art is always essentially joyous; its making is as much play as work, and this is particularly true of children's literature. But it is also true that the wellsprings of the imagination more often flow from pain than from pleasure. Many of our discussions do attempt, in the light of this sobering truth about the imagination, to lay bare the psychic distresses underlying the creations. The imagination is, among other things, the mind's way of taking charge of unsatisfactory reality, of dominating it, and forcing it to yield the meanings that the heart requires but the world does not provide. One of the marks of greatness in the classic stories and poems for children, therefore, is that the more they try to change and improve upon reality, the more light they throw upon its actual heights and depths.

We have designed our discussions to be helpful to general readers—perhaps even some youthful ones—as well as to teachers, students, librar-ians, and others interested in children's books. For further study, we provide a brief list of secondary readings in the field, which are referred to and sometimes quoted in the individual chapters. The original editions and a recent anthology (from which quotations of children's classics are taken) are listed in a primary bibliography along with certain essays by the same authors that shed additional light on their fiction.

We have taught Children's Literature courses for many years in the Eng-lish Department of the University of Washington, and we welcome questions and suggestions about this book. In the past twenty years, the study of children and literature has grown like Topsy, and all interested parties still have a great deal to learn from the subject and from one another.

1

CHARLES PERRAULT

Stories from Times Past, with Morals—Tales of My Mother Goose

Suppose that a parent or teacher offers to read to a child or children some "stories from times past," and suppose that a child asks, "What are 'times past'?" What might the parent or teacher say? Perhaps, "Oh, you know, the olden days, uh, before any of us were born." What must such a thought or image mean to a child? A time before anyone alive was born? That's magic. Such a time and such a world could only be imagined—faintly or vividly or dreamily—by a child without much "realistic" knowledge of history, of earlier eras. If the grown-up reader added that the stories would be "Mother Goose" stories, then the child listener might understand even better. For these are stories from a time past when the creatures could speak and when a Mother Goose was in some sense mother to human children as well as to her own. What I am getting at is that "Stories from Times Past" or "Mother Goose Tales" or "fairy tales" or stories beginning "Once upon a time . . ." all signal to any listener, child or grown-up, a special request for relaxation, enjoyment, dream, and separation from this everyday, workaday world. And, even if there may be morals attached to the tales, morals which suggest some sort of application of story to a child's behavior and deportment, still, such morals tend to be tagged on or attached as after-lessons. For the stories themselves are working at far deeper levels of wonder than tend to be addressed by conventional rules of morality.

Where do tales from "times past" originate? If we answer, "They are folktales," then what do we mean by that? Who are the "folk"? In order to enjoy the tales, a child need not ponder such a question, of course, but even a child listener, not to mention a child reader, may operate upon some sort of assumption, no matter how rudimentary, as to where the stories are coming from. The child probably knows that the parent or teacher or other person reading or telling the story did not personally make it up. Is there a basic category of "storymaker" in a child's mind? Who are the storymakers that children imagine? People just like their parents and teachers? Probably not, because parents and teachers don't go around generally talking about animals who can speak; parents and teachers mention such creatures only when they read books or sit down to "tell stories." And if modern storytellers were not living, as pretty obviously they weren't, in the time of "once upon a time," then the fairy stories and Mother Goose tales of modern storytellers must have come to those storytellers from "outside."

Very small children, who could think of the tales as if they might really have originated with the fairies or with Mother Goose, might be thought of as grasping the essentially dreamlike quality of the tales. As soon as children become aware of their own dreams they can imagine stories emerging from realms uncontrolled by parents and others. To the extent that children recognize or sense that daydreams, fantasies, strong wishes, and desires also create dreamlike stories in us, then such recognition or sensing also provides an intuitive grasp of origins for the tales, so many of which are themselves filled with precisely such wishes and fantasies. That is, the tales are, in part, the collective dreams of millions of people, "the folk."

Any child, but particularly an older child, might have heard that the tales of a teller such as Perrault are actually folktales. And such a child may have a conception of the "folk" as "peasants" or "country people" or "poor people" or "common people" who lived in bygone eras. But even a child who senses that the stories are like old and often-felt dreams and desires, such a child could well ask: If these are stories that peasants made up long ago, then why do we still tell them? One answer to this question is that the proof of the pudding is in the eating: We still tell the old stories because they still interest us. To the next question—Why do they still interest us?—there are many, many answers, but to make any one answer or combination of answers persuasive it would be best to work with specific tales. Still, before doing so, we should glance for a moment at some implications of the point that we can never work truly with a tale "itself" but only with some particular rendering or version of the tale. Perrault's is one of the first collections specifically connected with children and one of the earliest collections still popular today. What does it mean to say that the Mother Goose stories one is reading to a child are Perrault's versions?

Perrault's tellings are products of a certain time and place. Perrault was born in Paris in 1628. His father was a lawyer, and he became one, too, before taking the position of Controller of Royal Buildings. Later he became a member of the French Academy. In 1687 he published a long poem attacking classical writers in comparison to moderns. This piece angered several of Perrault's contemporaries, who engaged him in a furious and extended literary debate. In the year that his debate ended, 1694, Perrault published three verse tales, which were well received. In 1696 Perrault published eight more tales, this time in prose, in a French periodical and again in a separate volume, entitled *Stories from Times Past, with Morals— Tales of My Mother Goose.* They were first translated into English about thirty years later and grew steadily in popularity. Perrault appended rhymed "morals" which have often been omitted in later editions.

Tradition has it that Perrault intended to write the tales in verse (in the fashion of La Fontaine) but that, having told the stories to his son, who wrote them down, he became entranced with the innocent, bluff, hearty style of his son's prose renditions and decided to use his son's versions. It seems more probable, though, that Perrault himself wrote the tales.

It is often said that the Perrault versions of these tales have become the standard versions in the mind of the general populace, but many American parents may be surprised at the "continuation" of "Sleeping Beauty," the Hansel-and-Gretel–like opening to "Hop o' My Thumb," the double ending of that same tale, and the unsoftened ending to "Little Red Riding-Hood." To compare Perrault's versions of the tales, furthermore, to the versions of the Grimms, Joseph Jacobs, or other writers helps to identify the distinctive traits of Perrault's view. Certainly the world of the Perrault tales appears a trifle elevated or urbanized beyond the peasant folk milieu found in the tales of the Brothers Grimm or of Jacobs. In Perrault we find considerable attention paid to furnishings and fabrics, rooms with inlaid floors, full-length looking-glasses, ruffles and red velvet, gold cases for table settings, and mirrored halls, as if we were to look at the tales from a securely middle-class perspective. But the solidity of settings only makes more eerie the paradoxical world in which fairy godmothers appear like wishes, a "good old woman" lives in a castle fifteen years without human contact, a queen betrays cannibal longings, animals talk and mingle with humans, and a key takes on a mysterious and ineradicable stain. It is as if the bright and comfortable space of our ordinary domestic existence opens out toward a darker, ghostly penumbra. In the same vein, Perrault gives us, on the one hand, repetitions of the rages-to-riches formula in "Cinderella," "Hop o' My Thumb," and "Puss in Boots," but, on the other hand, he casually destroys our anticipation of success in "Red Riding-Hood." And even when some stories nominally end well, we remember best the moments of horror, as when the cannibal night-prowling Queen would eat Dawn and Day, or when Bluebeard's wife, facing instant death, hears not of rescue but only of nature's disinterested cycles of decay and growth: "the sun, which makes a dust, and the grass, which looks green." To read or hear Perrault's tales, then, is to experience a curious contrast between the solid, real, ordinary, safe domain of domestic existence, on the one hand, and the dangerous, wish-granting, metamorphic, dreamlike realm ever ready to impinge upon the first.

"The Sleeping Beauty in the Woods" is a "fairy story" in that it involves the world of fey or fairy forces, but Perrault's stories rarely display an attitude of awe toward such forces. In the tale of Sleeping Beauty, we are first told only that fairy godmothers are desirable for the "gifts" they may confer, and the creatures seem humanly recognizable in their delighting in gifts of tableware. Then it turns out that the gifts of the fairies are such items as beauty and wit, but again not much is made of that. Thus magic in Perrault's tales assumes a modest proportion and even pales perhaps beside the energies of will, greed, and love presented in the non-fairy protagonists. Perrault throws in, moreover, a rationalist's jab at fairy powers when he says that the Princess happens to prick her hand with the spindle "either because she was too quick and heedless, or because the decree of the fairy had so ordained."

Perrault's casual tone in treating fairy magic is reduplicated in his "asides" commenting wryly upon the young lovers. Despite the still-closing hedge, the prince "did not cease from continuing his way; a young prince in search of glory is ever valiant." Here is Perrault's comic equivalent for the tragic formula: character is fate. Then Perrault lets us know that the Princess, upon awaking and looking upon the Prince, beholds "him with eyes more tender than could have been expected at first sight." To catch the sly and wry tone of Perrault as he deals with the courtship ("their discourse was not very connected"; "They had but very little sleep—the Princess scarcely needed any") or as he mocks the courtiers ("as they were not in love, they were ready to die of hunger") is to open the way for apprehension of the surprising power of the story as it harps away on the central matter of family and appetite. Indeed a key tension experienced in reading Perrault is that between the urbane surface and the often horrific substrata.

Probably the majority of folktales involve protecting, renewing, and fostering the family. In this sense they are "about" love and regeneration. "Sleeping Beauty" is no exception, for the two halves of the story both portray efforts to cherish and protect infants, the younger generation, against malign rapacities of age. Appetite appears to be the crucial element in the tale. The Queen's cannibalism in the second half of the tale at first seems to have no counterpart in the first half, but the actions of the wicked fairy in the first half may constitute a kind of transmuted analogue of the cannibal Queen's. The wicked fairy comes to the christening feast and is given spoon, knife, and fork but is not given any case for the implements; possibly the suggestion is that the wicked fairy's instruments of appetite are incompletely subdued or encased. She mutters "threats between her teeth," and her decree is that the Princess shall have her hand pierced, as if the punishment of the child's invaded body suits the crime of leaving knife, fork, teeth, and so forth, bare at the christening feast. Whether or not the references to the fairy's eating utensils and teeth constitute a suggestion of incompletely subdued instincts toward child cannibalism (with which the parents may have a guilty connection), it is certain that the rest of the story continues to refer to appetite.

When the Princess falls into her sleep of one hundred years, her perhaps threatening parents are sequestered from her, and kitchen appetites are put to sleep as well: The cooks, undercooks, and kitchen maids all fall asleep; the turn-spits at the fire fall asleep; the porters stop drinking their wine and fall asleep. It is significant, surely, that whereas in fact the sleeping palace is imaged in terms of appetites laid to rest, the "common opinion" of those who live around the enchanted place is "that it was an ogre's dwelling, and that he carried to it all the little children he could catch, so as to eat them up." "Common opinion" is both wrong (ogre-ish appetite has been put to penitential rest in the palace) and right (the child cannibalism will appear or re-appear with the Prince's mother).

The Prince who finds Sleeping Beauty is out "a-hunting"; he reawakens appetite throughout the palace. Everyone who is not in love is ready to die of hunger. The opposite of love in the story is hunger; the original king and queen wanted a child, to create new life, more than anything else. But then the reflux of giving is taking. As if in answer to the primitive question— Why do we create tender babies if not to eat them?—Perrault's source story shows the Princess's baby sucking the poison splinter from her finger: As we nourish our infants, so they awaken us to life. They grow, we also. Perrault omits this incident which was connected to indelicate behavior of the Prince, but Perrault does immediately reinvolve the Prince and Princess in the world of appetite. A "sharp set" lady of honor tells the newly-waked Princess "that the meal was served," and so they enter the mirrored hall where they sup and are served. This conflation of appetites toward sex and food is continued as the Prince tries to deceive his ogre-ish mother with the tale that he has been only to the cottage of a charcoal-burner and has eaten only "cheese and brown bread," as if she should not connect her son to anything suitable for her perverted appetite.

When the Ogress-Queen's agent, the "head cook," comes to kill little Dawn for food, Dawn expresses her own appetite asking "for some sugar-candy," whereupon the cook relents, weeps, and lets the knife fall from his hand. Perrault's story, like the source story, "teaches" that children are not food (our knives are inappropriate to them and should remain encased like the table settings, or dropped out of sight) but are creatures of appetite like us. It is fitting that the cannibal Queen should accept the cook's tale of the intended victims being "devoured by mad wolves," and it is doubly fitting that she herself should be devoured in the end by her own agents of appetite. Her rage of greed intensifies to a species of self-consumption, and the story illustrates that the hunting, consuming, destructive aspects of desire must give way to or recognize as paramount the loving, seminal, creative aspects of desire. We are told in the last sentence of the story that the King was "sorry" for his mother but comforted himself with his children, and this is a turn full circle from the opening sentence which said that the king and queen were "sorry" that they had no children, "so sorry that it cannot be told." Sorrow for lost or consumed life here is silent, inexpressible; what can be told is the story of new life, the generation of families, and the comfort of children.

Perrault's "Sleeping Beauty" may be usefully compared to the Grimms' "Sleeping Beauty." Consider the effects of eliminating the second half of the story, the change to the traditionally unlucky number of thirteen (fairies), the intensified psycho-sexual overtones in the Grimms' tale (the stair, the key, the flax, the brisk spindle, the young men caught on the thorns around Rosamond, and so forth), and the loss of Perrault's wry, overseeing intelligence. The story may be further connected to other stories such as "Snow-White" or "Aschenputtel" in which preadolescence is similarly imaged in terms of sleep or a magic spell. In an earlier version of the tale, in Basile's *Pentamerone* (Day 5, tale 5), 1636, the Prince is seen as a rapist, the cannibal queen is his wife (not mother), and the two children are named Sun and Moon. Such comparison leads toward the study of folktales generally. Those interested in such further exploration might begin with works such as those listed in the Bibliography to *The Classic Fairy Tales*, edited by Iona and Peter Opie (see our Bibliography).

"Little Red Riding-Hood" is another story, like "Sleeping Beauty," in which the child heroine is threatened by male appetites that appear to conflate hunger and sex. Here the child is eaten, and one may wish to question the justice or injustice of Red Riding-Hood's fate. If, as seems likely, Red Riding-Hood's naivete in not knowing that the wolf was dangerous will be judged excusable or at least no grounds for her death, then probably one will find her fate undeserved. It is true that she directs the wolf very specifically to her grandmother's house, but if she did not know that the wolf was a threat, then she can hardly be blamed. The question then may arise whether the finale is made "immoral" only for the purpose of warning children against some kinds of innocence.

Certainly the whole philosophy of the cautionary tale deserves to be examined. Ordinarily such tales counsel children not to do willful, appetitive things such as enter a forbidden garden (Peter Rabbit), play with matches (Struwwelpeter), or run away from home (Pinocchio). In many cautionary tales, however, the crime is made perversely exciting enough to overpower the punishment in interest if not "value." "Red Riding-Hood" is different in that the caution is against the "crime" of unsuspecting innocence and the crime is not as interesting as the punishment. At this point, one may be tempted to look more closely for some evidence of fault in Red Riding-Hood. One possibility is supplied by the psycho-sexual reading of Bruno Bettelheim in *The Uses of Enchantment* who argues that the "little" girl in her red hood with her static or ailing mother and grandmother represents a premature assumption of mature sexuality, that she competitively betrays her grandmother, and that the wolf's advances represent a deserved seduction. It would not be difficult to reach even beyond Bettelheim to describe Red

Riding-Hood in terms of her exclusively feminine domicile; no father or grandfather is in evidence, only the adoring mother and grandmother; the foods are the soft custard and feminine butter pot. Riding-Hood brings the soft feminine up against the male phallic world of the forest, the faggot-makers, and the gaffer wolf with his penetrating "teeth." And so on. But the story in Perrault's hands seems much less serious and psycho-semantic in its import. It is organized linguistically more in terms of a joke. Red Riding-Hood becomes identified by her clothes and talk as objectionably cute and tedious. She is all nature and no art, a "country" girl who is pretty but not beautiful, who is above all "little." Having been given the name of her clothes, like Little Goody Two-Shoes, she is all role and no person.

After her mother tells Red Riding-Hood to go to her grandmother and to "carry her a custard and this little pot of butter," Red Riding-Hood informs the Wolf (who asked only where she was going) that she is going to see her grandmother "and carry her a custard and a little pot of butter." The Wolf picks up the mimic intelligence of the phrase and uses it in telling the grandmother she has been "brought a custard and a little pot of butter sent to you by mamma." Sure enough, the Wolf forecasts the phrasing of Red Riding-Hood who then uses those very words at her grandmother's door. In the same way the Wolf mimics the grandmother in repeating the gnomic phrase "Pull the bobbin, and the latch will go up." Then Red Riding-Hood uses the formula "Grandmamma, what great ——— you have got" five times just as the custard and butter pot were mentioned five times. Pretty plainly, in Perrault's view the Wolf is not only eating Red Riding-Hood up but also shutting her up. Perrault tells us that it is "dangerous to stay and hear a wolf talk," but then Red Riding-Hood and her grandmother do not really listen to the wolf's voice since they live by rituals of dress and speech, the forms and not the content. In their world the girl is known by her hood, and so the grandmother is known by her "night-clothes" and not her wolfish arms, legs, ears, eyes, and teeth. Perrault rubs it in very nicely.

"Blue Beard" contains the same preoccupation of Perrault with relations between outer appearances and inner character. Here the women judge the man by externals of his furnishings (positive) and beard (negative) and give too little credence to the information that his previous wives have disap-peared. Blue Beard's wife and friends are initially too much taken up, more-over, with the richness of the material world that he provides. Ignored is the point that the tiniest breach of faith is still a breach; the lavish abundance and comfort of material pleasures do not at all signal a laissez faire, forgiving, easygoing disposition in the owner who may have "a heart harder than any stone."

The talismanic words in the tale are polar opposites: "great"/"little"; "riches"/"dust." In Blue Beard's house of surpassing magnificence, reality and meaning are shown to lie in little things, on the ever-repeated "ground floor." The forbidden "little closet" lies at the end of a "great gallery" and is approached by a "little back staircase." The door is opened with a "little key." The attention of Blue Beard's wife has been turned away from the rich trappings of thoughtless existence to the little room of mortality. Once accused by Blue Beard, she finds herself pleading for "one little moment." Perrault sets this precious instant of life against the seemingly impervious fact of the uncomprehending world where the sun or a flock of sheep stirs up "a great dust" and fails to betoken rescue which lies "yet a great way off." Beyond any erotic interpretation of the tale such as seeing the key and stain in terms of marital infidelity (see Bettelheim) lies the reading, more responsive to the whole text, that Blue Beard's wife is made to see sharply the value of sheer life at the ground level. As for Blue Beard's wealth, once he dies and his wife inherits it, it is unwarehoused and put to use.

No doubt there is an important dimension to the tale of Blue Beard, as in "Sleeping Beauty" and "Red Riding-Hood," of woman confronted and tested by the masculine (the pricking spindle or the hunting prince or the wolf in bed or the husband's "key") and asked to feel thereby the tremendous power and seriousness of her sexual nature. In all three tales, furthermore, the heroine appears mistreated, too rudely shocked (after "temptation") into her self-discovery. Why did Blue Beard tempt his wives (particularly the first when, presumably, no secret lay in the closet)? And who could think that their indiscretion merited death? But moral equations rarely seem the chief concern of the fairy tales. Rather the view of life presented therein emphasizes the strange, awesome, "unfair" mutability that threatens fabulous danger and suffering but also offers fabulous insight or reward.

"The Master Cat, or Puss in Boots" is too light a tale to be loaded with analysis and ruined like a joke explained. No doubt most children do appreciate at some level many of Perrault's humorous touches such as "The youngest, as we can understand, was quite unhappy" or "he booted himself very gallantly" or "Monsieur Puss" or the way the youth's two or three respectful glances cause the princess to love him "to distraction" or the difficulties of Puss in walking on the tiles. The questionable morality of the successful con man failed perhaps sufficiently to trouble earlier, less enlightened ages than ours, but no doubt our youth and our children will recognize the purely playful intent of the story.

One linguistic pattern in the story may help to illustrate how Perrault tends both to mock and to celebrate middle-class materialism. The miller is said to leave "*no more* riches . . . *than* his mill, his ass, and his cat." Later in the first paragraph we are told that the youngest had "*nothing but* the cat." This pattern recurs through the story and appears in various translations. Thus Puss tells his master: "You have *nothing* else to do *but* to give me a bag." And later: "You have *not so poor* a portion *as* you think." As in "Blue Beard," the "nothing" or the "little" proves to be the key to everything. Puss tells his master: "You have *nothing* else to do *but* go and bathe in the river." The Princess "*no sooner* sees the youth *than* she falls in love." And so on. This is of course the formula of magic, a kind of creation *ex nihilo*, which intensifies the humorous dynamic of the tale. Such a linguistic feature, once noted, may encourage us to read carefully and to respect the surface of the text, albeit a translation, rather than reduce it too quickly to allegory or moral or universalistic meaning.

"Cinderella, or The Little Glass Slipper" betrays the insistence of Perrault, if not folk consciousness, that little things may lead to great consequence, that often the lowly deserve to be raised high, and that moral worth should engender the greatest reward. As usual, Perrault refuses to take the story too seriously and enjoys the fanciful exaggeration of the low-raised-high as the coach is made from a pumpkin, the horses from mice, the footmen from lizards, and the coachman from a rat. He gives Cinderella a sense of humor as she toys with her stepsisters (after they return from the ball) and later laughingly asks to try on the glass slipper. In other versions of this story, and there are a great many, Cinderella is aided by a bird or other creature who appears to be the reincarnation of her mother's spirit (see "Aschen-puttel"), and it is often stressed in the other tales that the prince must see Cinderella in her rags and recognize that she is both beautiful and poor, both high and low. Thus the tale seems designed to advance a reverence for the metamorphic nature of life in which great service and beauty may be found in or won out of apparently unpromising forms.

Part of the fascination of the story comes from Perrault's deft and detailed handling of both the mean and the magnificent environments. Cinderella's wretched work, clothing, and place are keenly contrasted to the fineries of her stepsisters. Though he says that "Cinderella, in spite of her mean apparel, was a hundred times more handsome than her sisters," Perrault never takes the radical step of proclaiming that Cinderella is more to be admired in her lowly state than in a higher one. Any ambivalence about the desirability of wealth is finally resolved in favor Cinderella becoming a princess. The tale deeply gratifies children's and our longings for familial support, food, finery, social status, maturity, revenge, magical power, and so on. No wonder that it is one of a handful of the world's best-loved stories.

Against the heavy-handed psycho-moralizing of Bettelheim who lauds the tale in terms of Oedipal conflicts, sibling rivalry, and a vaginal slipper, might be placed the more skeptical questioning of Jack Zipes who asks (in *Breaking the Magic Spell*, p. 173):

> Why is the stepmother shown to be wicked and not the father? Why is Cinderella essentially passive? . . . Why do girls have to quarrel over a man? How do children react to a Cinderella who is industrious, dutiful, virginal and passive? Are all men handsome? Is marriage the end goal of life? Is it important to marry rich men? This small list of questions suggests that the ideological and psychological pattern and message of *Cinderella* do nothing more than

reinforce sexist values and a Puritan ethos that serves a society which fosters competition and achievement for survival.

Despite the captious tone of such questions, they point to the possibility of looking at Perrault's tales from feminist or socio-economic or other perspectives in addition to the psychological one.

We can learn a lot, too, from a detailed comparison of Perrault's "Cinderella" with the Grimms' "Aschenputtel." Is the heroine more active in the Grimms' version, and, if so, to what effect? Is the quality of magic in the Grimms' tale more poetic and profound than in Perrault's version? How does this affect the overall impact? What are the differences in our responses to a golden versus a glass slipper? Perrault invented the glass slipper. Why? Is it more "pure" and more purely non-utilitarian than a gold one? Does it thus emphasize the extent of Cinderella's journey? Is it secretly appropriate to her origin amid the hearth and ashes in which, Perrault alone insists, Cinderella willingly sits? Is it because ashes and glass both come from the fire? But then the glass slipper would reveal any toe or heel-cutting on the part of the stepsisters and so Perrault, perhaps gratefully, omits this part of the story? Is the glass slipper, as Bettelheim suggests, also symbolic of virginity—being fragile and, once shattered, irretrievable?

Perrault seems fond of tales that get the heroine in a tight place, encasing or covering her: Sleeping Beauty in the little tower room or surrounded by the hedge through which the prince comes, Red Riding-Hood in her cloak or in bed with the wolf, Blue Beard's wife entering the "little closet," the princess in her coach into which the Marquis of Carabas enters, Cinderella in her ashes or coach or having the slipper put on. Why are there so many such stories that present women in terms of enclosures that males penetrate? Is it just genital symbolism? Or also societal emblematics for the constricted, repressed, and vulnerable state of women? And why might Perrault and his society have been specially interested in or attuned to the meanings of such tales? To reconsider children's literature in the light of such questions is inevitably to enhance it and to encourage our interest in an ever deeper study of literature and culture.

"Hop o' My Thumb" takes us back to the themes of infanticide and cannibalism first encountered in "Sleeping Beauty." The faggot-maker's sons move out of the frying pan into the fire: Their parents would abandon them so that the parents may have enough to eat, but then they come to the house of an Ogre who would eat them directly. That the Ogre only mistakenly slays his own daughters provides little matter for reassuring the young of parental love, and Perrault's wry comment that "this Ogre was a very good husband, though he ate up little children" only intensifies the sense of generational conflict running through the tale. What can reassure the child or any reader is the sprightly manner in which the diminutive but resourceful hero overcomes all obstacles. Children's literature, if not most folk romance, tends toward suspicion of the parental generation and celebration of the comic drive for freedom displayed by the younger generation. Often the hero is, moreover, the youngest child as in "Hop o' My Thumb." In a patrilineal system, the youngest child would be unlikely to take the father's given name or inherit his property and so may be more fully identified with a spirit of independence and individuation which denies the parents' power or right to dominate—kill or eat—the children.

Perrault gives less middle-class ambiance to "Hop o' My Thumb" than to the other tales. It remains more folkish. Perrault may be conceding this as he toys with the ending, making perhaps concessions to genteel morality by suggesting that Little Thumb may not have robbed the Ogre but instead entered the system and made money from the "business of a messenger" equipped with seven-league boots. That the hero or heroine in many of the tales is careful to share the wealth and provide for the rest of the family suggests again that intense generational conflict and sibling rivalry need only be temporary, again a happy if fanciful note of reassurance for youthful readers or listeners.

To come back to the question of why parents, teachers, and children still listen to and read Perrault's tales, perhaps the safest answer connects to their indisputable value as sheer entertainment. Beyond that, the tales obviously can be interpreted as addressing a huge number of moral, social, and psychological issues; and books, both helpful and muddled, are still pouring from the presses purporting to tell "the meaning and importance" of such fairy stories. This is not the place to assess the relative merits of interpretive theories; suffice it to say that children of all ages have found the tales fascinating, not only because they have artistic merit but also because they make vivid our crises of existence—the regulation of appetite, humankind's relations to animals and to the rest of nature, the dangers of curiosity, the imminence of death, our drives for affection and acceptance, our responses to injustice, generational conflicts, the loss of innocence, the saving powers of hope and humor—all the concerns that beckon maturing beings deeper into life. Perrault's avoidance of condescension and his variegated tones of Gallic delight in the tales assure that they will be read and listened to happily ever after.

2

MARIE LE PRINCE DE BEAUMONT

Beauty and the Beast

Like the tales of Charles Perrault, "Beauty and the Beast" is a folk tale given artful form by a cultured eighteenth-century French author. The author in this case was Marie Le Prince de Beaumont (1711–1780), who at the time she wrote the story was an expatriate living in London, in flight from an unhappy marriage. In 1756 she published *Le Magasin des enfans*, a collection of tales and essays supposed to be delivered by a "wise governess" to "several of her students." "Beauty and Beast" was among them. The *Magasin* was soon translated into English and several other languages, and "Beauty and the Beast" quickly emerged as the most popular story in it.

Mme. de Beaumont probably got the tale from a much longer version published in 1740 by Mme. Gabrielle de Gallon de Villeneuve. Mme. de Villeneuve's version was over three hundred pages long. Mme. de Beaumont retold the story at more reasonable length, omitting thousands of words of elaborate description, conversation, and repetitive episodes and giving the story the form in which it has become best known in the Western world.

In their anthology *The Classic Fairy Tales*, Iona and Peter Opie call this story "the most symbolic of the fairy tales after Cinderella, and the most intellectually satisfying." Certainly it shows Mme. de Beaumont's concern for genteel virtues like honesty and tenderness and loyalty, a concern somewhat more explicitly moral and philosophical than one is likely to find in the oral folk tale. The kernel of "Beauty and the Beast" is the same as that of the Grimms' "The Frog Prince" and Asbjörnsen and Moe's "East o' the Sun, West o' the Moon": A young woman is required by circumstances especially involving her father to live intimately with a beast. When she can accept him, an enchantment is broken, and he ceases to be bestial, changing to a handsome young prince whom she can happily marry. "Beauty and the Beast" develops this kernel in its own particular way, ultimately giving a literary effect rather different from those of the other two stories.

Mme. de Beaumont sees her story as the story of a triangle—the girl, her father, and the beast. Beauty's feelings for her father are crucial throughout the narrative: She at first rejects her suitors because "she would rather live some years longer with her father"; when his business collapses, "she could not think of leaving her poor father in this trouble." Life without her father is, to her, simply unthinkable. "I would much rather be eaten up by the monster, than die of grief for your loss," she tells him. When her father leaves her with the beast, her first wish is for a sight of her father, "and to know what he is doing at this moment."

Beauty's learning to love the beast is a process of allowing him to take the place her father has occupied in her affections. The father has been a provider of home, food, gifts; the beast becomes the same. Beauty's relationship with her father has been one of mutual courtesy and consideration and generosity; her relationship with the beast becomes the same. Separated from her father, in a mirror Beauty sees him dying of grief for her and hurries to his side to save him; separated from the beast, in a dream she sees him dying of grief for her and hurries to his side to save him. In these definite, structural ways, "Beauty and the Beast" confirms the notion that a girl's love for her father is the forerunner of her love for her husband.

The fairy-tale logic of the story requires that we accept a couple of unrealistic premises. First, we must accept that a father who loved his daughter as much as Beauty's father loves her would consent, under any conditions, to permit her to take his place in the clutches of a mysterious beast. Second, we must accept that the same beast who so angrily demanded the life of a wayfarer as punishment for picking a rose from the garden should be honored as a paragon of kindness and generosity by the end of the story. These premises make sense only if one dismisses the expectation of surface realism and acknowledges that the story's coherence resides in a deeper level of mind and spirit. There is a sense, a principle, according to which stealing the rose from the garden is a terrible crime, a capital offense. Beauty has asked her father to bring her a rose. Beaumont tells us she makes this request only so that her sisters' greedier demands won't look so blatant. Yet in asking her father for a rose, she has in effect suggested that she sees him as a potential suitor—it is suitors who bring roses to young girls. The father must not do this, it is a heinous offense; the beast is "right" to be enraged. Further, he is "right" to spare the father's life only on the condition that the daughter give herself up to him—move from the father's house to the forbidding suitor's house.

In short, Beauty's request that her father bring her a rose is a taboo action which precipitates the romantic crisis in her life. It shows that the time has come for her to turn her love to another male, outside her family. (The beast again shows admirable wisdom in perceiving that his best bet for finding a beautiful lady who would marry him would be one so capable of love for her father that she would give her life for him.)

Mme. de Beaumont, of course, has a moral thesis as well as a psychological one in "Beauty and the Beast." Decency is the basis for true and fulfilling love in this story; kindness is more important than "superficial" qualities like wit, money, and good looks. Beaumont suggests that Beauty has learned decency from her father; she has learned to be decent herself, and she has learned to appreciate decency in others. She assures us repeatedly that the beast's good heart is what truly wins Beauty's affection. But the honest kernel of her story will forever insist that this in itself is not enough to bring romantic fulfillment. As we watch the narrative developing, we see for ourselves that the beast really, in effect, wears down Beauty's resistance to him by a combination of courtly, restrained behavior, a growing familiarity between them, and just the deftest evocation of guilt-feelings on Beauty's part. Beauty, being a well-taught girl with a powerful conscience, knows she shouldn't be so put off by the beast's rough and ugly appearance; she believes she ought to be able to love him for his goodness alone. "Am not I wicked to behave so ill to a beast who has shown me so much kindness? . . . He shall not be wretched any longer on my account; for I should do nothing but blame myself all the rest of my life." She returns to the beast at least partly out of duty, conscience-stricken, resolved that she will swallow her natural disgust for his ugliness and marry him anyway. This is the point, of course, at which his ugliness disappears, and Beauty is blessed with romantic reward in all its aspects: physical, moral, and emotional.

3

JOHN NEWBERY

Mother Goose's Melody

For several reasons, the Mother Goose tales of Perrault and the Mother Goose rhymes of John Newbery provide a specially fine introduction to children's literature. The fact that the tales and rhymes are very old and were not, for the most part, created for an audience of children reminds us that children's literature need not be written for children but may be freshly published with them in mind.

John Newbery (1713–1767), son of a Berkshire farmer, who became a printer's assistant and then, when his employer died, married his widow and moved the business to London, had read and admired John Locke's *Thoughts Concerning Education* (1693). Locke argued that considerable play and high spirits could take their place in an education that properly emphasized character training. Newbery loved children and began in 1744 to prepare a series of handsomely bound "pocket-books" for the combined amusement and edification of youth. In the stories that Newbery and those who worked for him (including Oliver Goldsmith) wrote, the values of learning (ABCs were often tucked in), industry, and commercial success were much stressed. But the tone of Newbery's production is far from solemn didacticism. He did, as did Perrault, append morals to the rhymes he published for children (c. 1765), as in *Mother Goose's Melody*, but the morals more often mock moralizing than they exemplify it. Both Perrault and Newbery create children's literature out of folk culture by adopting a complex, ironic perspective that both celebrates and winks at the innocence and simplicity of the material they present.

Over half of the rhymes in Newbery's collection had already appeared in print. Some may have been created or amended by Oliver Goldsmith, apparently the author of the pseudo-learned introduction and morals in *Mother Goose's Melody*. Newbery also included a second section, devoted to songs from Shakespeare's plays, but the rhymes were the heart of the matter.

The rhymes themselves, of course, are notable for both their content and form. They have less to do with religion, science, politics, and art than with more everyday concerns: appetite, folly, sport, naughtiness, haughtiness, romance, danger, nonsense, laziness, accidents, sleep, gossip, and time. The collective image of humankind suggests that we are self-interested, adventuresome, prone to misfortune and error, but generally able to survive. The central fantasy is of achieved well-being: to find security, food, warmth, love, understanding. At the same time, the drive to celebrate imagination, fantasy, nonsense, and freedom is respected. The forms of the rhymes suit the content in that the short lines provide driving, bouncy rhythms that match the energy of the actors described in the poems. The stress-count meters (counting numbers of accented syllables per line rather than total numbers of syllables) provide both regularity of pulse and freedom from academic formalities. When the lines are very short, the rhymes come into greater prominence, with their witty relations of sound and sense: a little more / a little ore; eat no lean / platter clean. Sometimes there is a surprising aptness beneath the nonsense: The *cow* jumped over the *moo*n. All in all, the colloquial phrasings, the neat and quick verse stanzas, and the wordplay contribute to a sense of the rhyme world made specially vital, verbally dynamic, and joyfully spirited. Those generations of children who have encountered the rhymes and found how skillfully and powerfully the language can be wielded are indeed uniquely fortunate.

Though the nursery rhymes are in one sense the most familiar text in "children's literature," many of them having been memorized by parents, teachers, everyone when very young, still the collection as presented by Newbery is rather a jumble, and it may therefore be useful to consider a variety of methods for sorting them out and pondering them. Many of the best known rhymes are obviously for young children ("Patty cake, patty cake," "Hush-a-by baby," "One, two, three," "Here's A, B, C," and so on). Others are traditionally told to children ("Ding dong bell," "See saw, Margery Daw," "High diddle, diddle," "Ride a cock horse," "Jack and Gill," "Little Jack Horner," "Jack Sprat," "Bah, bah, black sheep," "Dickery, dickery, dock") or traditionally accompanied by hand movements ("Pease-porridge hot," "This pig went to market," "There were two blackbirds"). Other rhymes seem designed for older children ("Boys and girls come out to play," "Trip upon trenchers," "Little Tom Tucker," "Round about") or for youth ("What care I how black I be," "We're three brethren out of Spain"). Some of the rhymes are relatively sophisticated ("There was a little man," "Shoe the colt," "There was an old man," "When I was a little boy," "There was a man of Thessaly"). Thus one can obtain a rough sorting by grouping the ages of appropriate audiences. There are of course many cross-overs, and a good many of the rhymes have universal appeal.

The rhymes may also be sorted in terms of their functions. Some are teaching rhymes ("One, two, three," "Here's A, B, and C"). Others are admonitory ("Cross patch, draw the latch," "Ding dong bell," "Tell tale tit," "Three children sliding on the ice"). Others capture proverb lore ("She could have but the cat and her skin," "The longer I live, / The more fool am I"). There is the tongue twister ("I would, if I cou'd") and the lullaby ("Hush-a-by baby"), the complaint ("I won't be my father's Jack"), and the satire ("Three wise men of Gotham," "There was a man of Thessaly," "There was an old woman"). But many of the rhymes cannot be pinned down to a single or specific function, and that raises the question of the many functions that are served by such poetry.

If one answer to the issue of functions is that some of the poems express the freedom or apparent functionlessness of nonsense, then we may still ask whether nonsense functions in some sense, nonetheless, as sheer emotional release? delight in verbal play for its own sake? a kind of esthetic exercise? relapse into the fanciful play of childhood? attack on the primacy of "sense"? desire for laughter? If another answer is that many of the poems reward our interest in sonic and rhythmic effects, then this should lead to some consideration of just how the poems make use of meter, rhyme, assonance, and the like. To take "High diddle, diddle" as an example, one may begin by noting the stressed beats. The poem seems generally organized toward a pattern of beats—2, 2, 3, 2, 2, 3—in successive lines, but lines one and four verge on having three beats each. No line, furthermore, contains only two-beat feet or only three-beat feet until we reach the last two lines when the poem smooths out and speeds up (in accordance with the running action at the end). Older children (and their elders?) may be surprised to note such metrical artistry and may be encouraged to approach the poems with renewed respect and interest. Many of them may know slightly differing versions of this rhyme, and reasons, if any, for various word choices might be considered. Does "High diddle diddle" refer proleptically to jumping over the moon, and is it therefore preferable to "Hey diddle diddle"? Is the pun on "cow" and "moon" intentional, or only an interpreter's perverse ingenuity? "Laugh'd" and "craft" obviously rhyme; why then has the word "craft" been changed to "sport" in other versions of the rhyme? Such questions can help anyone to see the rhymes as created and crafted things and not just static artifacts handed down ex cathedra.

To see the rhymes as created works of art may invoke questions about their origins and modes of transmission. Dedicated inquirers might delve into the historical contexts and the occasional nature of some of the rhymes. Why, for instance, do the wise men come from "Gotham"? Is the name "Jack Horner" completely fortuitous? Why "Banbury cross"? And so on. Such details, beyond the scope of our discussion, may be pursued through

The Annotated Mother Goose, edited by W. S. and Ceil Baring-Gould, to *The Oxford Dictionary of Nursery Rhymes*, edited by Iona and Peter Opie, and, less confidently, to *The Real Personages of Mother Goose*, by Katherine Elwes Thomas. A cautionary note deserves to be sounded, however, that study of the rhymes in their historical context does not always add a great deal to an understanding of their meaning or impact. But certainly a recognition of the great antiquity of many nursery rhymes may provoke wonder as to why and how such quirky, non-contemporary bits of language should have been so long preserved in both printed and oral traditions.

When very young children first hear the rhymes, they have little defense against their oddness, because such listeners are too inexperienced to oppose their own sense of linguistic rightness or modernity. Furthermore, the referential nature of the words is probably much less important to the very young than is the sheer sonic play involved. An infant may have no knowledge of "pease-porridge" or even porridge at all, but the sounds of the words and the clapping accompaniment may be imprinted in the mind from age one to life's end all the same. It is notable, too, that many of the rhymes are probably learned from mother, aunt, grandmother, or sisters whose claims to attention are great. The rhymes, indeed, have probably been orally transmitted over the centuries primarily through women, and anyone interested in this probability might wish to ponder its implications for the form and content and impact of the verse.

The collected rhymes make up a world of attitudes and desires that deserve attention. What, for example, are typical classes of hopes and fears in the poems? of imagined rewards and blessings? of punishments and accidents? Are there typical attitudes expressed in the poems toward work, marriage, old people, promises, eating, trade, journeys, language? Is there an identifiable brand of wisdom or characteristic advice in the poems? In what sense do the rhymes collectively portray the sheer vitality and resilience of our human substance? Are women and men separated by role and nature in the rhymes? What do the rhymes collectively say about children? about nature? about animals? And so on. Such questions bring to the fore the observation that experience of the rhymes may differ greatly between children and adults. Each person may view such differences in a unique way, but it is rewarding to ponder such questions when reconsidering children's literature from an adult perspective. Certainly Newbery's collection, like the many other excellent collections of nursery rhymes that have followed it, constitutes a quintessential form of children's art, one that deserves not only continuing transmission to new generations but also caring consideration of form and meaning.

4

THE BROTHERS GRIMM

Fairy Tales

The most famous and enduring of the stories of Jacob (1785–1863) and Wilhelm Grimm (1786–1859) are interesting for a number of reasons and to a number of different audiences, but one key to their immortality is the power they have to touch the reader's or hearer's feelings on quite basic, even intimate levels, dealing as they do with primary matters of ego and belief, family solidarity and hostility, and fears and desires about survival, sex, status, and power. Whether one approaches them as a psychologist, a sociologist, a moralist, or just an uncritical consumer, they yield revealing perceptions of human life in which millions of people have seen themselves.

Among the simplest to appreciate are stories like "The Brave Little Tailor," a cheerful, amoral fantasy of the self bringing the world to its knees. This story is the essence of what might be called the David-and-Goliath theme in the fairy tale, the story of a small, weak, and unprepossessing hero who wins out over a whole series of large, powerful, and heartless adversaries with a nice mixture of immoderate self-confidence, a little luck, and a lot of ingenuity. Whatever its origins in the mists of pre-literate folk composition, it is a story which adapts readily to children, since it frankly heroizes a child-type: the little person surrounded by big people who often seem to want to harm him. In a fantasy of brain against brawn, cleverness against brute force, and mental and physical agility against thick-headed, short-sighted bullying, "The Brave Little Tailor" roundly confirms that the bigger they are, the harder they fall.

What makes the little tailor's story so directly appealing is that he is so free of encumbrances: No family depends on him, he is trying to please no father or overcome no older brothers, he is not grappling with any curse or enchantment. His motives are simple and psychologically comfortable: Discovering that he can kill seven flies with a single blow, he becomes impressed with himself, assumes that the rest of the world will be equally impressed, and sets out to claim the fortune which he supposes is due any hero so impressive as he.

His deceptions have enough flair and color to them to give a sort of magical aura: the cheese he squeezes the whey out of and the bird he throws into the sky (convincing a giant that each of these objects is a stone), his tricking two sleeping giants into fighting each other by dropping stones on them, his trapping a unicorn by getting it to run its horn into a tree and a wild boar by getting it to follow him into a "chapel which chanced to be near." Colorful as these gimmicks are, some readers will still wonder at the remarkable stupidity of the giants, kings, and beasts who fall for them. It would be nice if all big bullies were really as gullible and unthinking as these are. Yet, unrealistic as they may be, the story does have a cogent idea about them: The motives on which these bullies operate (pride, greed, ungoverned appetite) do work against clear-sightedness and level-headedness of the sort the tailor possesses. It is important to the dynamics of such stories as these that the little hero doesn't start the conflicts he gets into; it is always somebody else, somebody who wants something too much to permit him to see clearly what's before him.

"The Golden Bird" is a related tale; here again a "little hero" makes his way through a series of adventures to triumph in the end. But the stakes of the game and the rules by which it is played are more intriguing and suggestive here, and the whole story is more complicated, morally and artistically. It begins with a vaguely Biblical situation, a royal garden faintly reminiscent of Eden in that its owner is concerned with the theft of his apples. The story quickly establishes that it is to be concerned at least partly with a son's proving himself worthy in his father's eyes, as it tells of two undutiful sons who fall asleep at their posts and forget their assigned quests, and one dutiful son who persists.

The hero's quest, then, begins as an errand for his father and his king, a duty rather than a personal desire. That pattern is repeated as the story develops. The youth sets out after other prizes not because he wants them, but because a king wants them: He is to fetch the horse for the king who has the bird, and the princess for the king who has the horse. At a certain point, a fluid fairy-tale shift takes place, and the fox who has become the hero's helper announces, "We will have all three, the princess, the horse, and the bird." By the end of the story, the idea that the bird, horse, and princess are rightfully the kings' has been tacitly dropped, and these prizes belong to the hero. The bird will not sing, the horse will not eat, and the princess will not stop weeping until he comes. All this is engineered through the aid of a talking fox.

"The Golden Bird" is a notable example of a helper story, in which the hero acquires an assistant with miraculous powers. ("Cinderella," "Aschenputtel," "The Elves and the Shoemaker," and Hans Christian Andersen's "The Tinder Box" are various others.) The fox, crucial to what makes "The Golden Bird" meaningful and memorable, is a complicated figure. At the very end we learn that he is the princess's enchanted brother, which suggests that he has a kind of deep, clairvoyant purpose in treating the hero as he does. Moment to moment in the story, though, he is a giver of good advice which is constantly being disregarded: He advises the hero not to put the golden bird in the golden cage, not to put the golden saddle on the horse, not to let the princess speak to her parents before leaving, not to ransom his brothers from the gallows, not to sit on the bank of a river. All these pieces of advice the boy ignores. Yet the fox stays with him anyway, and one marvels, at first, at what a patient and tolerant assistant he is.

It turns out, though, that the salient issue is not whether the boy obeys or disobeys the fox's advice (it is advice, not commandments), but the spirit in which he acts. He has the kind of innocence and good-hearted impulse for life and the fine gesture which is at the heart of many fairy tales' philosophies. He takes the fox's advice about staying at the humble inn because to go and carouse with the brothers would be lazy and mean-minded. He heeds the advice about stealing princess and horse and bird because these are fine prizes, more glorious by far than drinking at a nice inn, and he wants them. He puts the bird in the golden cage and the golden saddle on the horse, and permits the princess to say good-bye to her father, because he appreciates the fineness of bird, horse, and princess, and desires to treat them well. In a similar, though not identical, sense, he helps the brothers and trusts them not to betray him because of his high-minded and optimistic attitude. He can learn a lesson, of course—when he comes back home at the end of the story, he disguises himself, to guard against his brothers' treachery. Likewise, the second time the fox asks him to kill him, he accedes to the request, having learned that appearances and reality are not always the same.

Ultimately we can see that the apparently stupid things the hero does throughout the story are actually the right things. On the one level, they are right because they proceed from the hopeful and affirmative spirit which fairy tales generally endorse and celebrate. On another level, they are right because they make events open out to take in the whole set of prizes—bird, horse, princess, and the suitable punishment of the bad brothers. Presumably the fox, as the princess's enchanted brother, is somehow aware of that. One might compare his function here with that of the birds who lead Hansel and Gretel through some harrowing steps to an ultimately rewarding culmination.

Another of the Grimms' stories, "The Water of Life," can profitably be compared with "The Golden Bird." The stories have several elements in common, so much so that they might be called two tellings of the same story: a king who asks for a fabulous object; three brothers who set out one by one to fetch it; a mysterious helper who presents himself, is rebuffed by the first two and appreciated by the third, and gives crucial advice; a quest for the original object which opens out to include other prizes as well, these of value to the young hero himself rather than to the old king; the young hero's generosity to the evil brothers, and their treachery in return; the king's temporary delusion that the older brothers have fulfilled the quest; and the final revelation that the youngest is the deserving one.

But for all the conventional elements these two stories share, they are quite distinctive tales, each with its own aesthetic, emotional, and even philosophical implications. Almost point for point, corresponding elements in the two stories can be seen to have a whole different feel. One king says, "One feather is no use to me; I must have the whole bird"; the other muses that the Water of Life would save his life, "but it is very hard to get," and "I would rather die than place you in such great danger." The first pair of older brothers shoot arrows at the talking fox; the second pair only call the dwarf "an old busy body." The fox carries his young hero on his tail, pities and scolds him, and works miracles for him; the dwarf sits in one place and sedately gives two pieces of advice as his hero passes by. The first hero kisses his princess and gets her to elope with him; the second finds his princess sitting on a couch, she does all the talking, and he leaves her sitting there to go on about his errand. Consistently "The Water of Life" is less vigorous, violent, and bizarre than "The Golden Bird," its symbols and emotions more sedate and dignified. It begins not with a greedy king's desire to hold onto his golden apples and to possess a gorgeous bird, but with a truly somber situation: A king will die unless someone brings him a magic restorative, the Water of Life. That phrase, of course, has a rich Biblical background, the "water of life" or "living waters" symbolizing spiritual renewal in both the Old and the New Testaments (see Isaiah 12:3, Jeremiah 2:13 and 17:13, and the Gospel of John 4:7–15 and 7:37–39). The iron wand which the dwarf gives the hero bears some resemblance to the rod of Moses (Moses' rod figures in several miracles, and is associated with the Water of Life in Exodus 7:1–17 and Numbers 20:2–13). The magic bread the hero finds in the enchanted castle, bread which will feed people inexhaustibly, recalls similar miracles in Matthew 14:13–21, Mark 6:32–44, Luke 9:10–17, and John 6:1–15. The sword which can slay whole armies recalls God's intervention in the wars of Israel in the Old Testament (see, for example, II Kings 7:1–20), and Jesus' saying "I come bringing not peace but a sword" in the New.

This is not to say that "The Water of Life" should be read as a systematic religious allegory like Edmund Spenser's *The Faerie Queene*. But the Biblical images do contribute to the sober, serious mood of the tale, and suggest that the good characters' gracious behavior has moral and spiritual weight.

The hero's acquisition of water, bread, and sword does not have the strong, aggressive edge that the hero's acquisition in "The Golden Bird" has. He moves almost as if through a pageant of muted splendor and courtly virtue, collecting his prizes without violence or chicanery, rescuing the princess without exertion, helping the besieged kingdoms through which he travels, stirring the executioner-huntsman to pity, and hiding meekly from his brothers' treachery and his father's anger. In his world, the best wisdom is to passively allow necessary events to run their course.

The thesis of "The Golden Bird" was something like, "Life will give its richest prizes to him who knows how to want and take them with a hearty, high-minded grasp." "The Water of Life" projects a soberer and more austere view of how the best rewards come, and to whom. The evil brothers are wrong to think of getting the kingdom for themselves as they set out; their greed disqualifies them, all through "The Water of Life." The hero thinks of others—of the old king, of the imprisoned brothers, of the princess at the end of the golden road—and all things fall to him as if of their own gravity,. The psychology (never mind the theology) here is not far from the admonition "Seek first His kingdom and His righteousness, and all these things shall be yours as well" (Matthew 6:33).

If stories like "The Brave Little Tailor," "The Golden Bird," and "The Water of Life" dramatize the imagination's wish for conquest and triumph, others in the Grimms' collection focus on darker things, the mind's deep fears. "The Wolf and the Seven Little Kids," for example, is about a situation frequently encountered in real life: a mother's concern, when she goes away and leaves her children alone, that predatory strangers will hurt them. Baby birds lie quiet in their nests, fawns sit still in the underbrush, and human children watch public-service announcements on television about not opening the door to strangers: The fear on which this story is based is as real as sleep or hunger.

The premise here, as in other fairy tales, is that the predatory stranger is dangerous partly because he can resemble the people whom one trusts and even depends upon. In "Little Red Riding-Hood," the wolf dresses in the grandmother's nightclothes; in "Snow White," the queen disguises herself as a helpful old woman with wares to enhance Snow White's beauty; here, the wolf transforms himself into a semblance of the kids' mother.

Notice how the story's denouement carries this idea of the wolf as the false mother to a surprising and grimly just conclusion. The wolf makes parts of himself (his voice, his paws) resemble the mother's to fool the kids. After he has eaten them, though, he becomes an "imitation mother" in another way, with the kids living inside his body. Then, in the murky, unexplained moral psychology that applies here, he is given instead the "children" his greed and treachery deserve: a bellyful of stones that carry him down to his death.

Often in fairy tales about those who want to eat the protagonists, the would-be eater is eaten (e.g., the wolf in "The Three Little Pigs" or the ogre–mother-in-law in "Sleeping Beauty in the Woods"), or at least cooked (the witch in "Hansel and Gretel"). Here the concept is intriguingly different: A voracious male pretends to be a mother, and the pretense goes much farther than he ever intended.

"Rumpelstiltskin" may be about fear, too; it may even be about the fear of someone who illicitly wants to take one's mother's place. Clearly, though, in "Rumpelstiltskin," this is something other than a moral issue. Viewed morally, this story makes no sense. Rumpelstiltskin is the least offensive of the male characters. The miller wants to "give himself consequence" and boasts of his daughter until the king seizes her. The king is cruel and greedy, threatening to kill the girl unless she spins him gold. Only Rumpelstiltskin helps the girl out of her plight; in fact, up to the point where he asks for her child in payment, he is a "helper" in the fashion of Puss in Boots or the godmother in "Cinderella." The storyteller doesn't even bother to vilify him by saying that he wants the queen's child for some sinister purpose, to kill it or eat it. Yet it is he who must be thwarted, his humiliation providing the "happily ever after" payoff at the story's close. It seems that the only way to properly experience the effect the storyteller has in mind is to accept the coldly economic dealings of the miller and the king as normal, and to focus one's attention on the little man who tries to insinuate himself where he mustn't go, into the network of human marriage and parenthood. The fun of seeing him so enraged that he dashes his foot through the floor (the Grimms' original actually takes the violence a step farther and says he rips or splits himself in two) has to proceed from a deep feeling that, no matter what service he may have performed, he cannot deserve the reward he wants. Being who he is—a droll-looking little man with an inhuman name and aspect—he is beneath the benefits of fairness.

Perhaps the reason for this story's ages-old popularity, despite its bluntly unfair distribution of rewards and punishments, is the memorable use it makes of an ancient folk-magic motif, the idea that to possess the name of a fairy-creature is to possess power over him. (Other familiar instances of this belief are in the Biblical stories of Adam, whose dominion over the animals is manifest in his being empowered to give them their names, and Jacob, who wrestles with a mysterious creature at the Jabbok River and tries unsuccessfully to extort the creature's name. The Hebraic tradition of forbidding the pious to speak the name of God comes from this same sense that to know and use a spirit's name is to set oneself over him.) There is considerable suggestive power in the idea of a little man of unknown name, dwelling on "a high hill among the trees of the forest where the fox and the hare bid each other good night." Perhaps there is a modicum of justice in the story after all: Such a creature may deserve defeat if, in his unseemly gloating, he lets slip the secret of his identity, much as Samson deserves to be defeated when he lets slip the secret of his strength.

Other Grimms' stories focus more directly on recognizable problems in family dynamics. Such famous tales as "Hansel and Gretel," "Rapunzel," and "Snow White" make unforgettable narrative comments on primal conflicts among parents and children, and offer, symbolically, hope for the resolution or transcendence of these conflicts.

"Hansel and Gretel" is a drama of parent-child antagonism, specifically the child's wish for food from his mother and his sense that he is vulnerable to her, and in her power, which can turn hostile. This basic wish-fear receives extraordinarily artful expression in "Hansel and Gretel," a story admirable for its deftly appropriate symbolism.

As in "Snow White," the mother is the villain, but here we have no muted sexual rivalry between mother and daughter. Male and female alike are the victim-heroes of this conflict. The issue is who will feed whom, who will do the eating and who will be eaten. The contest for food is established as crucial at the outset. The stepmother is concerned that she will not have enough for herself if she shares with her children. She gives them bread, but only as a ruse, to lull them into feeling secure so that she can abandon them.

What the witch in the gingerbread house threatens to do to the children is really the same thing that the stepmother has attempted, only more hideously and murderously aggressive. She, too, tempts them with food; but whereas the stepmother wanted to be rid of them, the witch coaxes them into her clutches. The stepmother wanted Hansel and Gretel's food for herself; the witch wants the children to be her food. Her treatment of both children on the first day, and of Hansel after she has put him in the cage, shows that under the apparent benevolence of food-giving can lie a murderous appetite: "The old woman, although her behavior was so kind, was a wicked witch, who lay in wait for children, and had built the little house on purpose to entice them." The interlude during which Hansel fools her by giving a bone instead of his finger is no real victory for the children. It just delays the showdown for a little, and underlines the witch's lust for the children's flesh: "Be Hansel fat or be he lean, tomorrow I must kill and cook him." As is so often the case in fairy tales, evil must be fought with its own weapons, and the children's victory will come not through some pretense that Hansel is unsuitable food (in a rational world he would be unsuitable food, but this is the world of irrational fear and desire), but through the children's turning vicious themselves: The old woman must be baked in the fire she had prepared for them. Obviously this is poetic justice, as is the queen's having to wear red-hot shoes in "Snow White." But here the witch doesn't just fall into the oven of her own necessity; Gretel pushes her in. Hostility here is mutual, not one-sided as was the envy in "Snow White."

After all the many references in "Hansel and Gretel" to food and the fear of starving or being eaten, what the children take after they kill the witch is not food, but jewels and gold. The stakes obviously have changed. With the killing of the witch, the old fight about eating is over—the witch is dead, and so is the stepmother, her death simultaneous with the witch's. The children's journey back home is completely different from the journey away. Coming away, they wandered for days and almost starved; going back, they cover the distance in a few hours, need no food, and face only "a great piece of water" as an obstacle. Crossing water in fairy tales is often an expression of making a bold and definite step, putting one's past behind, like crossing the Rubicon or the River Jordan. Here the particular issue is that Hansel and Gretel must make the trip one by one. In overcoming the hungry mother they have entered a new phase in which their independence—of their parents and of each other—is important. They come home not as dependents on their father, but as providers of wealth.

The role birds play in this story is worth noticing. Birds assume a kind of fateful agency, prodding events along the course they must take if Hansel and Gretel are to engage in and finally win the conflict with the hungry mother. First setting out from home, Hansel pretends to be looking back at his little pigeon on the roof. But this is a lie; the birds don't want Hansel and Gretel to go back there: They eat the trail of bread crumbs to keep them from doing it. In the woods a white bird attracts the children's attention and leads them to the gingerbread house—not as the witch's accomplice, but as a providential signpost, leading them into the necessary showdown. Finally, once the children have won the conflict, the white duck appears to carry them back to their father.

"The Seven Ravens" is another Grimms tale on the importance of solidarity among siblings when parents' emotions go awry. In this haunting and evocative story, an overfond father, doting on his baby girl (not the first father ever to have done this), impetuously renounces his sons, whose only "sin" is their excessive eagerness to please him and their fear of his wrath. He rashly damns them and thereby robs them of their humanity. Outbursts of hate, especially from parents, have persistent consequences, the story shows; the king recognizes that he has gone too far in cursing his sons, and wishes he hadn't done it, but is powerless to undo the results of his anger.

The storyteller reasons or intuits that it is up to the beloved child, not the volatile parent, to remove the fatherly curse from her brothers and give them back their humanity. It makes psychological if not logical sense. The girl has done nothing intentionally to hurt her brothers. Indeed, for years she does not even know that she has ever had brothers. When she learns of them, she feels responsible for what has happened to them and guilty about it, and obliged to release them from their spell, even though her parents rightly insist that "her birth was only the innocent cause of it." Fanciful as the details may be, the outlines of a real-life situation are discernible here. The favored child may not have intended to stunt her siblings' lives by making them feel deprived of their parents' best love, but still the burden rests on her, as the possessor of that love, to help them salvage their happiness. In the story, the emblem of her parents' love is the ring they give her. They give it to her, not to the brothers; but by loving them she can in some sense transmit its good effects to them.

The form the girl's quest takes confirms the idea that family constellation is the story's primary subject. Her journey among the heavenly bodies loosely reflects the family problem. It recalls the dream Joseph has in the book of Genesis (another story about a favorite son having to intercede for siblings who have angered their father), in which the sun and the moon symbolize his father and mother and the stars symbolize the brothers. Here the sun is too hot and fiery (apt enough, considering what we have seen of the father's temper), and the moon cold and chilly and carnivorous (we know nothing of the girl's mother with which to compare this). The parents, that is, are no help. The stars have the friendly and appreciative attitude her brothers will have when she finds them; they tell her how to complete her quest, and even try to give her the means by which to complete it, the piece of wood to unlock the mountain. But the story shows that she must give of herself, by sacrificing her finger, to redeem them. Some religious overtones can be heard in this sense of the power of sacrificial blood, but the main feeling is that the daughter must show that she herself, not as someone's errand girl, wishes the brothers to be blessed. The story ends with a scene of reunion not between parents and children but among sister and brothers. The anger of fathers can do great damage, the story indicates, but the love of brothers and sisters has great restorative powers.

Often enough, however, the love of brothers and sisters is precisely what is lacking in the fairy tales. "Cinderella" is one of the best-known examples of a fairy-tale heroine at war with her sisters; but the Grimms' "Aschenputtel" (which means "cinder girl") is another version of the same story which dramatizes most pointedly some of the stakes and resources involved in such a conflict.

The basic plot-outline of "Aschenputtel" is the same as "Cinderella": Two ugly stepsisters, abetted by their mother, oppress and abuse the young heroine. A king holds a magnificent three-day ball in order to find a bride for his son; the stepsisters attend the ball in their finery, and the cinder-maid goes secretly, dressed in beautiful clothes gotten by magic. The prince falls in love with her, but she leaves the ball hurriedly each night, the third time losing her shoe. She is identified as the rightful bride when hers is the foot that will fit the slipper.

Despite the similarity of their destinies, Aschenputtel is really a very different person from Cinderella. Aschenputtel is much more active, assertive, and human. She hates having to do all the dirty work and does not voluntarily spend time sitting among the ashes. She helps the stepsisters prepare for the dance only under duress, and she insists that she be allowed to attend it as well as they. She meets the dishonest stepmother's challenges head-on; and, when the stepmother reneges, she invokes the power of the hazel tree and the white bird to override the stepmother's orders. To demand gold and silver finery is all her idea, as is her behavior at the dance. She leaves because she wants to, she hides in the pigeon house because she wants to, she makes the prince come looking for her because she wants to. There is little doubt that Aschenputtel is intentionally playing hard to get.

This tale applies fully the stern fairy-tale justice to the evil the stepsisters have committed against the heroine. Here is no turning the other cheek, no improbable forgiveness. The stepsisters must mutilate their feet in futile attempts to deceive the prince. Further, according to the Brothers Grimm, they suffer even worse punishment.

> So as the bridal procession went to the church, the eldest walked on the right side and the younger on the left, and the pigeons picked out an eye of each of them. And as they returned, the elder was on the left side and the younger was on the right, and the pigeons picked out the other eye of each of them. And so they were condemned to go blind for the rest of their days because of their wickedness and falsehood.

The passage artfully, if gruesomely, draws together motifs from the story: the birds that do Aschenputtel's bidding or defend her rights, and the loss of sight for the losers in a story where "looking good" has been the focus of competition.

One final major difference from the Perrault version is in the nature of Aschenputtel's magic helpers. For Aschenputtel, strength and help come unambiguously from the early love she has had from her good mother and her father and from her present adversity: a hazel tree brought by the father, growing out of the mother's grave, watered with her own tears. The symbolism of the tree and the white bird that comes to sit in it suggests that nature, the organic principle of life, conspires on the side of strength growing out of parental love. It is Aschenputtel's power to command: Tree and birds unfailingly do her will.

In sum, "Aschenputtel" may be described in terms which do not apply perfectly to "Cinderella": it is a sharp and intense fantasy of an embattled girl in conflict with a cruel family. Its assumption is that such cruelty can be overcome with the resources one draws from parental love going back to one's earliest years, and with the incentive which adversity gives to fight back. The ultimate victory is to find a lover outside the family, whose authority transcends that of the home.

Generally speaking, that is the solution to the problem of "Snow White" as well, although the problem is substantially different. It is customary for fairy-tale heroines to be beautiful; but in "Snow White" beauty is the central subject, not just an adornment—physical female beauty, the kind that makes men turn to jelly and inspires murderous jealousy in other women. In this story the teller hardly bothers with making Snow White "as good as she was beautiful"; nothing is said about her being especially generous or loving or virtuous. All the males in the story are moved by her beauty. When the queen first sends her out to be killed, "she was so lovely the huntsman had pity on her." The dwarfs' reaction on finding her sleeping in their bed is "O Goodness? O gracious? what a beautiful child is this?" And the only basis for the prince's love for her is her beauty, since all he knows of her is how she looks lying in her glass coffin.

More important than the males' feelings for Snow White, though, is the feeling that the envious stepmother has for her; that is the emotional core of the story. The queen hates Snow White for being more beautiful than she is. Hers is a kind of exaggerated fairy-tale dramatization of a real-life tension between older and younger women (found most often, one supposes, in the more submerged hostile feelings a mother might have for her daughter), deriving from the knowledge that the younger woman is destined to supplant the older in physical attractiveness. In the expression this feeling receives in "Snow White" it has become a madness or an obsession; the practical value of being beautiful (e.g., as a means for attracting a desirable husband or making one socially successful) has been forgotten. The queen's only audience is her mirror.

The story-teller quite frankly assumes that the queen's attachment to her mirror is a natural part of being beautiful, even though she has carried it to an insane extreme. Snow White, too, has a vein of narcissism, in perfect keeping with her identity as the most beautiful of girls. When the wicked stepmother seeks to kill her, she rightly judges that her vulnerable point is her concern for beauty, and so offers her embellishments for her appearance: a lace bodice and a comb for her hair. The third of the stepmother's weapons is also appropriate to the theme of the story: a poisoned apple "beautiful to look upon, being white with red cheeks, so that any one who should see it must long for it." In short, the apple resembles Snow White herself, and Snow White cannot resist such a bait.

Many readers wonder about the red-hot shoes that appear, unexplained, at Snow White's wedding: Who are the "they" who prepared them, and why does the queen have to put them on? Probably the truest answer is that the shoes are the natural emblem of the queen's self-consuming envy, suitably embodied in a last bit of beauty-enhancing finery for her feet. On that level, she herself has prepared the shoes, and it is her own compulsion that obliges her to put them on and dance until she falls down dead.

"Rapunzel" is another well-known Grimms tale on mother-daughter conflict. Here, the conflict is between an overly possessive parental love such as the witch has for Rapunzel, and the normal, healthy romantic love Rapunzel and the prince have for each other.

Fairy tales which take up the darker or more threatening aspects of parental feelings often replace a natural parent in the story with someone who stands in the same authoritative or emotional position as a parent, but without the biological ties. That is what happens in "Rapunzel": By the symbolism of fairy tales, the witch "is" Rapunzel's mother. (Notice the odd role the witch is given in Rapunzel's birth: a childless couple is yearning for a child, but until the husband steals food from the witch's garden, they cannot conceive. The child's conception and the fact that she belongs to the witch are both introduced at exactly the same time. Notice, too, the similarity between the way this witch gains possession of Rapunzel and the way the beast gains possession of Beauty in "Beauty and the Beast": A father caught stealing something for someone he loves has to give up his offspring as a result. Not coincidentally, both these stories are about the conflict between a girl's love for her parent and her love for a suitor.)

This grotesque mother, the witch, simply wants to keep Rapunzel all to herself—an extreme projection of a natural parental impulse. She is not like the queen in "Snow White," jealous of the girl's beauty; she is not like the stepmothers in "Cinderella" or "Mother Hulda," unappreciative and discriminatory among siblings; she doesn't want to eat Rapunzel, or abandon her, or sell her to strangers. She just wants to keep her. But that means preventing her from growing up and becoming a wife and mother on her own, and this is therefore wrong.

In *The Uses of Enchantment* Bruno Bettelheim points out a number of oddities in the story which indicate that this particular conflict has some ambivalent and mixed feelings in it, and is not the naked conflict between good and evil which many fairy tales project (148–50). For one thing, the story has Rapunzel accidentally reveal the secret plans to elope, as if she herself had some lurking desire for the witch to keep her there (where she has, after all, been secure and cared for). And when the prince climbs the tower and discovers Rapunzel gone, he himself jumps from the tower (the witch doesn't curse or injure him), as if he at least partly recognizes that he has done something wrong in invading the sanctuary.

Ultimately, of course, it is right in the story for Rapunzel to leave the witch, bear the children she has conceived, and re-unite with the prince "happily ever after." The trauma of battling their way from the mother's over-possessive love is alleviated by the passage of years and the tears the heroine sheds.

A story offering its own unique perspective on the drama of family conflict is "The Almond Tree" (titled "The Juniper Tree" in many translations), one of the strangest, most suggestive, and most powerful of the Grimms' tales. Like "The Water of Life," it has a religious and Biblical resonance, but it resounds with a very different style of spirituality. Whereas "The Water of Life" was tranquil and quietistic, "The Almond Tree" is weird and surreal and visionary. Here we are dealing with a storyteller of unusually bold originality and an apocalyptic literary imagination.

The human situation which "The Almond Tree" deals with is fairly familiar to readers of fairy tales: A beautiful child is born to a beautiful mother, whose influence survives in a tree growing over her grave. A stepmother, jealous of him and afraid that he will have preference over her own child, murderously hates him. His stepsister has a Gretel-like loyalty to him. His father loves him but is helpless before the machinations of the new wife.

But these familiar fairy-tale elements are oddly skewed in "The Almond Tree": The beautiful child whom the wicked woman hates is a boy, not a girl; her own daughter is not mean like her mother, but sympathetic and sensitive; the murderess does not seize the victim's flesh for herself, but feeds it to the deceived father; the rewards and punishment at the end of the story are dealt by the victim himself in the transfigured form of a bird.

What is perhaps most memorable about the story is the stress it lays on the dramatic, suprarational power enveloping these human lives. Its characters are subject to deep, overwhelming passions that form a kind of overt fatefulness in their lives. Passion is motivated by factors beyond the characters' knowledge or control. The good mother wishes the normal good wish for a child; when her wish is granted, "her joy was so great that she died." The bad mother has the normal fairy-tale hatred for a stepchild, but after she has killed him she feels an extraordinary "great terror" that grows to madness as her doom approaches: "I feel very low, just as if a great storm were coming." "I am terrified, my teeth chatter, and there is fire in my veins." "I feel as if the house were on fire." Finally, prostrate with terror, she cries, "Even if the world is coming to an end, I must go out for a little relief," and runs to her death under the millstone.

Everyone in the story is susceptible to rapturous states. Marjory is grief-stricken at her brother's death and turns inexplicably "glad and light-hearted" when the bird appears from the almond tree. The father goes wild with hunger as he devours his son; later, hearing the bird's haunting song, he feels an oceanic elation. The goldsmith, the shoemaker, and the miller's men are all similarly entranced by the transcendent beauty of bird and song.

At the heart of "The Almond Tree" is a conventional fairy-tale premise, the idea that love's power to restore is greater than hate's power to destroy. This common bit of optimistic philosophy gains new force in a story that conveys the sense that human wills are somehow caught up in a divinity that shapes all fate. The description of the boy's resurrection and transfiguration stands comparison with the visions of Isaiah or Ezekiel:

> Then Marjory went to her chest of drawers, and took one of her best handkerchiefs from the bottom drawer, and picked up all the bones from under the table and tied them up in her handkerchief, and went out at the door crying bitterly. She laid them in the green grass under the almond tree, and immediately her heart grew light again, and she wept no more. Then the almond tree began to wave to and fro, and the boughs drew together and then parted, just like a clapping of hands for joy; then a cloud rose from the tree, and in the midst of the cloud there burned a fire, and out of the fire a beautiful bird arose, and, singing most sweetly, soared high into the air; and when he

had flown away, the almond tree remained as it was before, but the handkerchief full of bones was gone.

It would be misleading to say that tales such as "The Almond Tree," "Rapunzel," or "Snow White" are designed to teach moral lessons about how
parents and children ought to treat one another. Rather they are imaginative
scenarios, projecting real-life family tensions in fairy-tale terms, and finding
their happy endings in the artistic and psychological materials available to
them.

There is one fairly well-known Grimms' tale which does take a sort of
moral view of the situation, however: "Mother Hulda," a taut, efficient,
symmetrical fable on the subject of good and bad daughterhood and good
and bad motherhood. Not all folk fairy tales teach a lesson, moral or ethical
or even pragmatic, but this one clearly does. The daughter who minds her
mother and does her chores should be (and so, in fairy-tale logic, will be)
covered with gold, celebrated, and rewarded; the spoiled daughter who sits
around idly should be covered with pitch, degraded, and punished.

As is the case in many fairy stories, the good daughter is oppressed and
discriminated against at home, and so turns to the outside world, to strangers,
for approval and vindication. "Mother Hulda" is unusual among fairy tales,
however, in that the person she encounters in the world beyond is, quite
explicitly, a mother (not a husband or a helpful animal or a dwarf). And she
is not an ogreish mother, raising the very cruelty or hunger of the original
mother to a monstrous form which must be defeated, as in "Hansel and
Gretel" or "Rapunzel." Mother Hulda's house represents not a new home
of the girl's own, or any other form of permanent independence from her
original home, but rather the girl's home as it should be with the rules
administered fairly and rewards going to the daughter who deserves them.
The idea that Mother Hulda's house is a perfected version or extension of
the girl's original home is patent when Mother Hulda says to her, "It pleases
me well that you should wish to go home, and, as you have served me
faithfully, I will undertake to send you there!" As the just and fair mother,
Mother Hulda can bestow on the girl indisputable proof of her merit: gold.
"Then she went in to her mother, and as she had returned covered with
gold, she was well received."

What of the magical apparatus in the story, the talking apples and bread-
loaves and the cock that announces the identities of the "golden" and "dirty"
girls when they return? What do these details contribute to the story? Well,
of course, they make the story a fairy tale. Without them, we would have
a naturalistic parable in which a girl works hard but receives no respect at
home, and goes out and gets a job working for someone else who gives her
credit for what she does. When she returns home with the wages she has
earned, her mother is impressed. Add the magical details, and the process
smacks of magic, not just common sense.

But there may be more to it than that. The good girl shakes the apple tree and takes the burning bread out of the oven not because some authority-figure tells her to do it, but because the apples and the bread themselves, personified, need taking care of. Her behavior is right not just because mother said she should do it; it is right because the things themselves, the objects of work, require it. Having a bird rather than a human being recognize the smirched and gilded girls as they return reinforces the same notion: that the difference between the two girls is not just one reflecting arbitrary parental preference, but is real and objective and testified to by the natural world.

And then there are the love stories. Of course one could call any fairy tale that concludes with a marriage and a "happily ever after" a love story, and then the category would be very full and miscellaneous. But there are tales which focus centrally on the challenges and problems of erotic or romantic love, and this category is smaller, and more interesting.

"The Frog Prince" is about love; first, though, it is about revulsion. If "Snow White" was about beauty and the drama that can cause, "The Frog Prince" is about ugliness. If the real-life inspiration for "Snow White" is the envy older women (such as mothers) feel for younger women (such as daughters), probably the real-life inspiration for "The Frog Prince" is the abhorrence a young girl might feel at being obliged to live intimately with someone who seems to her ugly and repulsive (such as an undesired husband). Perhaps the underlying feeling that produced this story is the natural anxiety about one's first sexual encounter; perhaps it is about repulsiveness of a more general kind.

At any rate, and whatever its sources in the materials of ordinary life, by the time it reaches the form in which the Brothers Grimm found it, the story has become a compact little drama of a very particular kind. A transcendently beautiful princess, the youngest of a lot of sisters and perhaps a bit spoiled, loses her favorite toy in a well and makes a thoughtless bargain with a "thick, ugly" frog to get it back. Her "sin" here is mere carelessness; she just doesn't take the frog's demands seriously. Only when the frog has made elaborate efforts to press his claims, and only when her father angrily insists "that which thou hast promised in thy time of necessity, must thou now perform," will she in any sense make good on her promise. And even then she does it grudgingly and against her will. Many readers, having heard prettified modern re-tellings of this story, are surprised to read that the well-known transformation from frog to handsome prince takes place not when the princess kisses him but when she finally loses her temper entirely and throws him against the wall.

What difference does this climactic difference make? In versions where the princess kisses the frog (a pattern parallel to the conclusion of "Beauty and the Beast"), the underlying logic seems to be that if one offers love and tenderness to the repulsive suitor, he magically becomes handsome—which means, roughly, that seen through the eyes of love he is not ugly but quite the contrary. Obviously the wall-smashing episode doesn't proceed by that sort of reasoning. Here, the idea seems to be that the girl, backed literally into a corner by her own careless bargain, the stern admonition of her father, and the terrible ugliness of the frog, acts angrily and desperately and passionately, and that brings about the transformation. She doesn't become "nice" in this scene; if anything, she gets meaner; she drops the hollow motions of feigned hospitality which she's been going through at her father's moralistic insistence. She wishes awfully that the ugly frog would get away from her and suits her actions to her wish. The story-teller has said that this story takes place "in the old times, when it was still of some use to wish for the thing one wanted." The feeling here would not so much be "beauty is in the eye of the beholder" as "desperate straits require desperate measures."

The final paragraphs of the story, concerning Henry the faithful servant, substantiate this suspicion that the story-teller is not basically saying that just anybody looks good if you consent to love him. This final section, which actually makes up almost a third of the story, establishes that "The Frog Prince" is the prince's story as well as the princess's. The prince has an identity; he is not just any old prince, but a prince with a servant named Henry who could die of grief for him. The symbolism of the iron bands around Henry's heart evokes the sense of a deep and important trouble prior to the frog's appearance in the well (without having to spell that trouble out in distracting detail). We know only that this one particular princess must save him. Just what she must do is not specified—only that *she* must do it. This princess has to react passionately to this prince in order for the magic to work.

"The Frog Prince" does suggest, then, that we require that our mates not be repulsive; and that the passion of our wish is what makes it come true. To express this idea in the image of a frightened girl smashing her repulsive suitor against the wall is to cast it in quite unsentimental, perhaps even primal terms.

But not all fairy tales envision such a happy ending to love. "The Robber Bridegroom," for example, also takes up the matter of the repulsive suitor. Here, though, no magic transforms him; indeed, his ultimate reality is horrible, and the only resolution is to escape his clutches.

"The Robber Bridegroom" is a very grim story, most harshly naturalistic for a fairy tale (the only bits of magic in it are the talking bird that futilely warns the girl of what she is getting into, and the peas and lentils that spring up unnaturally soon). In effect, it is a rebuttal to "Beauty and the Beast": Whereas that story shows that beneath the ugly, ferocious exterior of the man one's father gives her to lies a gentle and lovable soul, "The Robber Bridegroom" proposes that a suitor may look all right and yet harbor in his bosom a gang of fiends who seize young girls and do horrible things to their bodies. Here we find no magic to make the repulsive bridegroom beautiful; here the story-teller settles for unmasking his bestiality and destroying him, leaving the girl at home safe with her father. "The Robber Bridegroom" has its deepest roots in anxiety about the harshness and violence of sex; its solution is not redemption but escape.

Proceeding upon this fundamental image of a girl's marriage as delivery into the hands of masculine depravity, the story-teller's artistry is devoted primarily to the machinery by which that depravity is brought to light. The evil into which the girl goes is affectingly symbolized as a lonely house, "dismal and unhomelike," in the middle of a wood "where it was darkest." She reaches it by following a trail of ashes. The house itself stands empty; the girl must go into the cellar to encounter its truth. There she finds another woman, a valuable ally. Being a woman, she sympathizes with the girl; being old, she understands what men are up to although she herself is not an object of their lust. The horrified girl there watches a gruesome parody of a wedding—the "bride," a version of herself, is given the ceremonial wine to drink, and then brutalized to death. The essence of this scene is given into the heroine's keeping in the form of a mutilated finger wearing a ring, emblem of marriage.

The teller gives one rather deft expression to the idea that life can overcome death, with the detail that the ashes blow away but the peas and lentils spring up and lead the girl back home. He or she takes more interest, though, in the device of having the girl report her entire experience as if she had dreamed it and then reveal at the crucial moment that the dream was the truth. This technique has nice dramatic value within the story. It may also legitimately call attention to a truth about the story as a whole: that what we are being given here is a nightmare about the horrors of sexuality, a nightmare which in the tale comes true.

"Repulsive spouse" stories, seen from the female perspective, tend toward the grim or horrible, until or unless love's magic transforms beast or frog into prince. "Repulsive spouse" stories told from the male perspective tend toward comedy, as if the unhappiness of a henpecked husband or other mismatched male were somehow less serious than a woman's. Surely the most famous story of this kind in the Grimms' collection is "The Fisherman and His Wife."

"The Fisherman and His Wife" is a one-idea story and, in that respect, simple. But it is a matter of some delicacy to focus on exactly what that one idea is. Probably it works best to start with the obvious thematic questions: What sin does the wife commit, and what is her punishment? There are some easy, obvious answers: Her sin is that she wants more than she may have, and her punishment is that she gets nothing.

But what does she want, exactly? Her first request (for a nice little cottage) and maybe her second (for a big stone castle) makes it appear that she just wants material well-being and its comforts. But then her requests become more blatant, and we see that what she wants is eminence, status, power. By the end of the story, she has gotten to be Pope, and has gone beyond that, demanding to be the equal of God Himself. She has passed over from ordinary greed into blasphemy.

What is her punishment? Prometheus, who defied the gods and stole fire, was tied to a rock and condemned to have his liver eaten out by an eagle forever. Adam and Eve, who defied God and tried to make themselves wise like Him, were evicted from Paradise and condemned to eventual death. The fisherman's wife, on the other hand, gets nothing; she is right back where she started from. Does this mean she has gotten off lightly, her "sin" implicitly forgiven? Or has her brief taste of glory made her original poverty a kind of hell on earth for her? The story doesn't say.

That's because, in the final analysis, the story is not primarily concerned with how the wife feels. It sees from the husband's point of view, and that is crucial. The imaginative heart of the story, and the life-situation which inspired it, is the marriage in which a man feels that his wife demands more of him or of life than he can give her, or perhaps more than he wants to give her. (In this, it belongs with Washington Irving's "Rip Van Winkle" and James Thurber's "The Secret Life of Walter Mitty" as fantasies of the hen-pecked husband.) The premise that this situation produces for the story-teller is "Once upon a time there was a man who was content, but his wife was not." He doesn't try to explain how or why a man would be content to live in a hovel, so content that when his wife tells him he should have wished for more, he can't think of anything to wish for. It is just the given of the story: The man is content, the woman is not.

Her sin, then, in terms of the implicit value-system of this story and others like it, is not just that she wants more than she may have; it's that she wants something other than her husband wants. Notice the refrain the fisherman chants to the fish: "Such a tiresome wife I've got / For she wants what I do not." Viewed in this light, the ending of the story, with the wife back where she started, is not intended to emphasize the punitive aspect. It is intended as a happy ending: The husband gets his way after all. And the solution is *final*: "There they are sitting to this very day."

"The Twelve Dancing Princesses" is a love story, of sorts—love viewed here not as the harrowing prospect of physical intimacy, as in "The Frog Prince" or "The Robber Bridegroom," nor as the adjustment of demands and concessions between a man and a woman over a lifetime together, as in "The Fisherman and His Wife," but love as dancing, music, wine, pleasure, and romance. And "The Twelve Dancing Princesses" takes a particular slant on the subject: It is about the generation gap, the conflict between high-spirited daughters, "dancing princesses," who want to go out at night and have a good time, and their father, who wants to foreclose their night-wanderings and marry them off. Age differentiation matters in this story. When the king proclaims his wish for spies to discover his daughters' night-life, the kings' sons who volunteer are inappropriate to the task, being of the daughters' generation. The job requires an old soldier, conscious enough of his age that in the end he makes a point of asking for the eldest daughter for his wife. The soldier himself receives help from an old woman. It is age versus youth in "The Twelve Dancing Princesses."

The story-teller takes a remarkably balanced and uncommitted view of this conflict, revealing none of the persistent bias in youth's favor that many fairy tales have. There is much to be enjoyed in the idea of twelve beautiful girls who slip down a trap-door into a sparkling romantic netherworld where handsome princes await amid groves of silver, gold, and diamond trees, a beautiful castle by a lake, music, and wine in gold cups. It is a milieu worthy of F. Scott Fitzgerald's beautiful people. The young couples are not trolls or cannibals or in any respect depraved. They may show a somewhat callous disregard for the way the young men set to spy on them are summarily beheaded, but it is the father who sets the terms and does the beheading.

The older men's interest in the princesses' subterranean goings-on is ambivalent. That his daughters' dancing slippers are constantly being worn out gives the king quite pointed evidence of how they are spending their evenings and makes him nervous. Yet what he says is not that he wants the dancing stopped, only that he wants to know where it is happening. Presumably the dancing is to be discontinued at the end of the story, but nothing is said about the princesses' being punished.

The old soldier takes an even more obvious pleasure in the princesses' night life. He finds precious trophies when he follows them, and returns willingly and unnecessarily after learning their secret. He plays little cat-and-mouse games with them, particularly the youngest, stepping on her gown, drawing her attention with the breaking branches, riding in her boat. He dances with the princesses and drinks their wine. He obviously delights in sharing their pleasures, and teases them with hints of his presence in their otherwise exclusively youthful domain. As their father's agent, he is there to stop the unauthorized festivities, but he is also there to enjoy them. This same feeling of "I'm too old for this, but so what?" carries over into his choice of a bride: He disqualifies himself as a mate for the youngest, which suggests that each generation should keep to its own, but he accepts her older sister, which shows he does not disqualify himself completely.

Ultimately, "The Twelve Dancing Princesses" is a rather sophisticated grown-ups' fantasy. It acknowledges that wine and dancing and romance are mainly for the young, and that fathers work to dampen youthful spirits. Yet at the same time it is a tale in which a hero from the father's world, a hero no longer young, worn out with soldiering, can enter the glamorous domain of youth and claim its best prizes for himself.

Finally, there is "'The Sleeping Beauty," in some respects the quintessential fairy-tale love story, since it is about virtually nothing but a young woman's coming to maturity with the appearance of a young man meant just for her.

The story has a complicated background. Europe first read it in Basile's

Pentamerone in 1636, where it is called "Sun, Moon, and Talia." In that version, a king, already married, discovers the sleeping beauty Talia, rapes her in her sleep and impregnates her, and leaves. Two babies are born to her while she is yet asleep, and one of them awakens her by sucking out of her finger the splinter that has brought on her sleep. The king later returns to her and loves her and the two children, though he keeps them a secret from his wife. The wife finds out about the secret family, however, sends for them, and tries to have them killed and cooked and served to her husband. Her plans are foiled, she is killed, and the king marries Talia.

When Charles Perrault retold the story for children, he understandably omitted the rape. He substituted a jealous mother for the jealous wife, a mother who, for her own ogre-ish reasons, wants to eat her son's wife and children. She comes to a gruesome end similar to that of the wife in Basile's story.

The Grimms' version of "The Sleeping Beauty" is the one most modern readers know, the one that ends with the prince's making his way through a magic hedge, waking the sleeping girl with a kiss, and marrying her. It seems that in its brevity the Grimms' version has caught the heart of the matter: The Grimms' story is much the simpler and, lacking the whole section concerning the ogress–mother-in-law's desire to eat Sleeping Beauty and her children, the more idyllic and conflict-free. Evil is hardly an issue in this story. There is the uninvited fairy's anger, of course, but a sufficient answer to that, in the story-teller's opinion, is that the harshness of her curse should be nullified. It hardly turns out to be a curse at all, since Rosamond's whole world falls asleep with her, and is found intact when she wakes up. Many kings' sons are said to lose their lives trying to penetrate the thorn-hedge, but that amounts to little more than a dramatic way of showing that the girl's time of awakening has not yet come; when the right prince appears, the hedge turns to flowers before him and welcomes him in.

However one approaches the story, it seems likely that one will consider the implicit comments it contains on the sexual maturing and awakening of a young girl. Many details in the story suggest that the rigors of female maturation are, in some fundamental way, its inspiration: The fact that "the curse" comes upon the girl when she's fifteen, accompanied by the flow of blood; the fond father's wish to prevent it from happening; the imagery of the prince entering the girl's enclosure with ease when the time is right; and his bringing her to fulfillment with his love and a kiss.

5

HANS CHRISTIAN ANDERSEN

Fairy Tales

"We can begin by saying that happy people never make fantasies, only unsatisfied ones," Freud wrote in his essay on the relation between imaginative writing and day-dreaming.

> Unsatisfied wishes are the driving power behind fantasies; every separate fantasy contains the fulfillment of a wish, and improves on unsatisfactory reality. The impelling wishes may vary according to the sex, character and circumstances of the creator; they may be easily divided, however, into two principal groups. Either they are ambitious wishes, serving to exalt the person creating them, or they are erotic (47).

There is little doubt that unsatisfied wishes inspired Hans Christian Andersen (1805–1875) to write, and to write what he did. Neurotic, vain, skittish, inclined toward hysteria and melancholy, Andersen lived a life of yearning and self-denial, of awkward advances and embarrassed retreats. His fairy tales were an outlet for feelings of frustration that troubled him all his life.

His biographer Elias Bredsdorff summarizes the conditions of his earliest years this way:

> In a candid letter to a friend who knew him better than most, Andersen once described himself as "a swamp plant." It is a valid description. Andersen's background was, from a social point of view, the lowest of the low: grinding poverty, slums, immorality and promiscuity. His grandmother was a pathological liar, his grandfather insane, his mother ended by becoming an alcoholic,

his aunt ran a brothel in Copenhagen, and for years he was aware that somewhere a half-sister existed who might suddenly turn up and embarrass him in
his new milieu—a thought which haunted his life and dreams (16).

From the beginning, Andersen turned to fantasy and make-believe to
escape this reality. "I was a curiously dreamy child," he recalled. "As I
walked about, I kept my eyes closed as often as not, so that people finally
believed I had poor vision, despite the fact that this one of my senses was
and is especially keen." He remembered being permitted to lie in his parents'
bed for hours "in a waking dream, as if the actual world did not concern
me" (*Fairy Tale of My Life* 8). He liked to sit at home alone, playing with
the puppet-theater his father made him, sewing clothes for his dolls and
making up stories about his dolls and himself. "I told the boys curious stories
in which I was always the chief person," even though "I was sometimes
rallied for that" (*Fairy Tale of My Life* 21). In particular, he recalled telling
a little girl at school that he owned a castle, that he was a changeling child
"of high birth, and that the angels of God came down and spoke to me"
(*Fairy Tale of My Life* 9).

As a child, Andersen was squeamish about women, sex, and sensuality,
and he never really outgrew that feeling. "I felt a strange dislike for grown-
up girls, or for girls of more than twelve," he later wrote; "they really made
me shudder; in fact, I used the expression about anything which I did not
like touching that it was very 'girlish' " (Bredsdorff 20.) When he was twenty-
nine, and his more worldly friends encouraged him to frequent houses of
prostitution in Naples, Andersen wrote in his journal:

> It made me very sensual and passionate, but I resisted the temptation all the
> same. If I get home without having lost my innocence I shall never lose it. . . . I
> am still innocent, but my blood is burning, in my dreams everything inside
> me is boiling. . . . I'm sure experienced people will laugh at my innocence, but
> it isn't really innocence, it is an abhorrence of this thing for which I have such
> a dislike. (Bredsdorff 281)

As did his feeling about sex, Andersen's fiction grew directly out of his
childhood. Many of his stories are like free-form children's fantasies—improvised, unplanned, exaggerated, as free as dreams and as compulsive. And
they serve many of the same psychological purposes that the child's fantasies
serve, in that they talk of ambition and romance in narratives whose only
rules are the requirements of wishes and fears.

But the stories Anderson wrote as a man are not free-hearted celebrations
of ego and eros. They begin in normal desires for self-exaltation and love;
they address themselves to those subjects, and they expand with an energy,
a sheer force of invention that apparently comes from Andersen's deep
feelings. But the stories are shot through, too, with the fears and aversions
and inhibitions Andersen felt as a child. From the horror he first felt at the

world of his childhood, and at the poor figure he himself cut in it, Andersen created dreams not of unfettered pride and passion but of their opposites, humility and chastity. Ordinary instincts for self-aggrandizement are present in his tales, but the tales themselves are devoted to censoring those instincts rather than fulfilling them. The heroes and heroines of his imaginings are brave fugitives from carnality—meek and humble adventurers who win by renouncing victory, lovers whose sensibilities are so untuned to crudity that their failing to find happiness becomes a mark of their superiority. In his tales, Andersen declared himself the champion of innocence and the enemy of pride, desire, and ambition.

He wrote love-stories by the dozen; "The Little Mermaid," "Thumbelina," "The Steadfast Tin Soldier," "The Shepherdess and the Chimney Sweep," "The Sweethearts," and "The Bog King's Daughter" are perhaps the most famous. Through them all runs one story, the basic Andersen fantasy. The central character is small, frail, more likely to be female than male—above all, *delicate*, an embodiment of that innocence which is harmlessness, that purity which is incapacity for lust. He/she is usually incapable of ordinary motion, physically unsuited to pursuit or consummation: The tin soldier has only one leg, the mermaid has no legs at all, Thumbelina is carried from place to place as if she were crippled. Andersen's imagination is much taken with *statues* as the emblem of chaste erotic feeling: The tin soldier and his ballerina are inanimate figurines, the shepherdess and the chimney sweep are made of porcelain, the little mermaid falls in love with a marble statue before she ever sees the prince in the flesh. (It is fitting that Copenhagen has immortalized the little mermaid herself as a statue.) In another story, "Psyche," the hero creates a statue of the girl he loves, the pristine symbol of his devotion. The girl herself rejects him.

Andersen's ideal lovers are often rejected. A few of the folk-tales he retold, such as "The Tinderbox," end with the hero married and living happily ever after; but the stories he made up himself do not. Usually something prevents marriage—rejection, misunderstanding, snobbery, fate. At the end of "The Bog King's Daughter," the heroine steps out onto a balcony on her wedding night and simply disappears. Andersen does not care very much if love is satisfied in this world, since the conclusion his fantasy really works toward is splendid, mystical death: the launching of the soul out into the infinite, leaving troublesome flesh behind. "Glorious! from love to love—to fly from earth to heaven!" says Andersen, describing the death of the hero in "The Ice Maiden." "A chord broke, a sound of mourning was heard; the icy kiss of Death conquered that which was to pass away; the prologue ended that the true drama of life might begin, and discord was blended with harmony." Similarly, the little mermaid leaves her body behind and becomes a daughter of the air. The tin soldier and the ballerina die together in flames, he melting into a tin heart and she reduced to a bright spangle. The shepherdess and the chimney sweep "loved one another until they broke." Thumbelina dons white wings and flies away with her fairy lover, who is "as white and transparent as if he had been made of glass." The bog king's daughter becomes "a lovely beam of radiance, that flew upward to God."

Physical sensuality in these stories tends to be pictured as grasping, slimy, and disgusting. Thumbelina is coaxed, abducted, and clutched at by a toad and her son, by a fat black mole, and by an ugly insect before she flies away to the fairy king; the shepherdess is pursued by a satyr who had "a long beard, . . . horns sticking out of his head and the legs of a goat." The princess in "The Bog King's Daughter" is shudderingly embraced by "a decrepit old monarch; a mummy as black as pitch and shining gruesomely like the slugs that slither in the dark woods." Frequently the physical ordeal Andersen's lovers must go through in pursuit of transcendent love is a descent into dark, close, filthy places. The tin soldier floats down a gutter into a sewer and is swallowed by a fish; the shepherdess and the chimney sweep have to creep up and down a chimney flue; the ball and the top in "The Sweethearts" meet in a garbage bin where "all kinds of things were lying: cabbage stalks, sweepings, and dust that had fallen down from the roof."

Andersen's sharpest vision of sensual horror is in "The Little Mermaid." There the heroine, smitten with love for a human prince, sets out to find what she must do to make him love her in return. The grotesque ordeal Andersen contrives for her is a direct fantasy-enactment of the idea that, in order to be a wife, a girl must submit to rape. She must divide her tail, and the experience is an excruciating one. She has to travel down to a terrible forest in the deepest part of the ocean, through polyps "like hundred-headed snakes," with "long slimy arms, with fingers like supple worms" that reach out to grab her as she "puts her hands together on her breast" and hurries past.

> Now she came to a great marshy place in the wood, where fat water snakes rolled about, showing their ugly cream-colored bodies . . . there sat the sea witch feeding a toad out of her mouth, just as a person might feed a little canary-bird with sugar. She called the ugly fat water snakes her little chickens, and allowed them to crawl upwards and all about her.

The witch tells her that if the prince is to love her, she must lose her tail with a sensation of having her body pierced by a sword. "The little sea maid drank the burning sharp draught, and it seemed as if a two-edged sword went through her delicate body. She fainted in a swoon and lay as if she were dead."

Nowhere else in classic children's literature is there so terrified a vision of sex seen through the eyes of innocence. The scene in "The Ice Maiden" in which Rudy accepts death as his lover is calm by comparison:

> And he looked in her wonderfully clear eyes, only for a moment he looked into them, and—who shall describe it?—in that moment, whether it was the

life of the spirit or death that filled him, he was borne upward, or else he sank into the deep and deadly ice-cleft, lower and lower.

When she kisses him, "a chill that never ends ran all through his spine and touched his brow." Here, as elsewhere, Andersen compresses into one scene the contradictory ideas that death is erotic, and that one can escape eroticism by dying. Something of that same paradox is present in another Andersen story, "The Garden of Paradise," which posits sex as original sin. A young prince falls from innocence by kissing the lips of a beautiful naked woman, and death is both the reward and the punishment for his action.

> Then there resounded a clap of thunder so loud and dreadful that no one had ever heard the like, and everything fell down; and the beautiful Fairy and the charming Paradise sank down, deeper and deeper. The Prince saw it vanish into the black night; like a little bright star it gleamed out of the far distance. A deadly chill ran through his frame, and he closed his eyes and lay for a long time as one dead.

This troubled view of sex is important even in Andersen stories which are not explicitly about erotic subjects, for it explains his obsession with innocence in many forms. *Innocence* is the watchword in Andersen's fantasies. No virtue rates so high with him as childlike purity, by which he means freedom from adult desire, ambition, and thought. He found inspiration of a sort in folk-tales, because they often begin with heroes who are simple, humble, and child-like. But he had to change the folk-tale pattern in order to bring out his personal fantasies. The traditional folk-tale shows its protagonist's growth and happiness directly; he gets money, love, and power— as for instance in Andersen's own re-telling of "The Tinderbox," in which a soldier seizes a princess, kills her father, and ascends to the throne; or "Little Claus and Big Claus," in which an underdog-hero kills his rival and gets rich. The stories that Andersen made up himself turn this pattern inside out. Like folk-tale heroes, Andersen's start poor, but his stories demonstrate that the poor in spirit are blessed. Like them, Andersen's heroes hurl themselves into life, but discover that they would do better to die and be with God. In an Andersen story, it is better to be the peasant girl who can hear the nightingale than the chamberlain who cannot ("The Nightingale"); better to be little Gerda, who trusts and believes and wants to stay home, than Kay, who "gets a piece of the Devil's glass in his eye" and questions and criticizes and explores ("The Snow Queen").

In story after story, Andersen makes fun of and punishes people who care about money and power and artifice and prestige and critical judgment; he celebrates the humble and long-suffering and credulous and sentimental. His attitude belongs partly to Christian asceticism, and partly to nineteenth-century Romantic primitivism, sentimentalism, and anti-intellectualism, and no doubt takes many of its forms and phrases from those philosophies. But for Andersen personally the value of innocence is closely tied to his nightmarish view of sex, a fact which is easily discernible in several of his most famous stories. For him, to be innocent is, first and foremost, to expunge or repress one's sexual urges.

One especially graphic case in point here is his tale "The Red Shoes," a story Andersen found to be a particular favorite in the Puritan strongholds of Scotland, Holland, and the United States. Read in the loosest, most abstract terms, the story is a parable on the idea that pride goeth before a fall: a pretty girl, preoccupied with beauty and finery, shows her vanity, is punished for it, and learns her lesson. But given the concrete details of Andersen's personal fantasy, the story vibrates with sexual panic, celebrating innocence that is won through the repression of sexuality.

Andersen records that "The Red Shoes" was inspired by a memory from his youth:

> In *The Fairy Tale of My Life*, I have told how I received for my confirmation my first pair of boots; and how they squeaked as I walked up the aisle of the church; this pleased me no end, for I felt that now the whole congregation must know that my boots are new. But at the same time my conscience bothered me terribly, for I was aware that I was thinking as much about my new boots as I was about our Lord. (*Complete Fairy Tales* 1075)

Out of that bothersome conscience came Andersen's story, with the new boots transformed to red shoes, and Andersen, the boy wearing them, transformed to a pretty girl named Karen.

What Andersen consciously thinks of as an emblem of pride and vanity, he unconsciously imbues with sexual significance in a number of ways. First, he gives his heroine the name of his scandalous half-sister, the one who disappeared into the red-light districts of Copenhagen and later embarrassed her brother by turning up with a common-law husband. Shoe and foot symbolism tends to be sexual in many uses—the Old Testament and other folk-literatures often say "feet" as a euphemism for sexual organs, and foot-fetishism is a common neurotic device for expressing forbidden interest in the genitals. That "The Red Shoes" emanates from Andersen's memory of a ritual of puberty and of his flaunting the new boots he had for that occasion also helps to place it psychologically. Andersen emphasizes the sexual quality by making Karen's shoes red, the traditional color of unruly passion, and by making them dancing shoes, with a power to catch her up and carry her away against her conscious will: "When she once began, her legs went on dancing. It was just as though the shoes had obtained power over her." Giving herself over to their excitement, she faces the debility Andersen associated with sexual excess: "Thou shalt dance . . . dance on thy red shoes, till thou art pale and cold, and till thy body shrivels to a skeleton."

She must first acquire the red shoes against her mother's wishes; it is a man who sets them doing their fearful, orgiastic dancing, an old soldier with a beard "that was rather red than white, for it was red altogether." When he touches them, they begin dancing.

The shoes "grow fast" to Karen's feet and will not come off—they are part of her body. The only way she can purge their evil is to cut off the offending members. "Do not strike off my head," she begs the executioner, "for if you do, I cannot repent of my sin. Strike off my feet with the red shoes." He does as she asks, and she becomes like Andersen's other acceptable lovers: crippled. For a time, thoughts of the lost sexuality still linger; she sees the red shoes dancing before her when she tries to go to church. Finally, in an agony of contrition and self-reproach, she wins God's mercy, and He sends His sunshine: "and her heart became so filled with sunshine, peace, and joy, that it broke. Her soul flew on the sunbeams to heaven; and there was nobody who asked after the red shoes!"

"The Red Shoes" is a harrowing, gothic little tale to be sure, and that may help explain its popularity. Actually, it does not succeed very well in advancing the dry moral idea that we should be humble and love God better than ourselves. What the solid events of the story convey is rather the idea that there is something we are tempted to do with our feet, but old ladies and ministers and angels don't want us to do it. If we refuse to listen to their warnings, a leering old man will touch our feet and set them working and we won't be able to stop. Then we'll be glad to have the grown-ups chop them off, and to be allowed to die and go to God. I suppose there is more than one way to say what that fantasy means; but any description that fails to account for the evocative image of the red-bearded man touching the girl's feet and setting them dancing uncontrollably has hardly done it justice.

Andersen himself was aware—at least partly—of the psychological links between his inhibited sexuality and his artistic creativity, his wish for fame as an artist, and his longing for death. The story "Psyche" shows clearly that he believed that his pursuit of ideal beauty and immortality through art and religion sprang from sexual longings that he could not allow himself to fulfill.

"Psyche" is the story of a young artist, poor and unknown, who strives for perfection in his art but cannot produce anything that satisfies him. His worldly friends tell him that he is too much the dreamer, and that he has not really tasted life. They urge him to plunge into physical experience and enjoy it. They invite him to join in their orgies, and he is excited by their offer. "The currents of his blood flowed rapidly in his veins, and his imagination was on fire." But he cannot bring himself to go with them; he feels too great a sense of purity within himself, a pious restraint. Instead of joining in the fleshly delights, he turns toward working in clay and marble, as a superior alternative to physical lust. "He yearned to express in his sculpture what his spirit told him of infinity; but he found himself unable to do it."

The answer is that he sees a girl, just in passing, and falls in love. At first he makes no attempt to approach her; he turns his attention to a mental image he has of her as she becomes alive in his mind. He sets to work on a statue of her, made from marble dug from heaps of broken glass, rotten vegetables, and decaying garbage. With these materials—a fantasy image snatched from a passing glimpse of a beautiful girl, and white marble extracted from the filth of ordinary life—the artist constructs an image of perfect beauty.

He wants to believe that he now has what his friends have, only better. "Now I understand the meaning of life," he rejoices." "Love is the essence of it all. With love one can see beauty and delight in true loveliness. The riots and debaucheries of my friends are empty and vain, the bitter dregs of experience, rather than the pure sacramental wine with which the enlightened heart hallows this life." But despite this brave speech, he finds that his feelings for the statue are rooted in those dregs of erotic passion. "Soon his mood changed, and he forgot about God and his passionate tears. Now his mind was filled with the image of his Psyche; he imagined her before him, as pure as snow and as rosy red as the light of the dawn. He determined to find her, to meet and talk with this beautiful, living maiden, who walked as others might dance, and whose voice was glorious music."

His attempt to make love to the girl is a disaster. He manages to kiss her hand, and finds it so soft and lovely that it sets his nerves afire. "He was beside himself with desire, so excited that he talked without knowing what he said. Words rushed from his lips like lava rushing from the crater of a volcano, and he was as powerless to stop them as he would have been to stop the volcano. Deliriously, he proclaimed his undying love for her." Contemptuously, she spurns him.

His lust aroused, the young artist yields to his friends' coaxing and spends a riotous night with some beautiful peasant girls. Andersen's metaphors convey the sexual excitement, release, and disappointment the artist feels: "The blossom of life flourished briefly, flamed up, and then shrivelled away. A vile odor merged with the smell of the roses, and overcame his mind and soul. The fire of his excitement guttered out, and darkness came." Sickened with guilt, he buries the beautiful statue, enters a monastery, and begins a lifelong struggle to suppress the impure, sensual thoughts that spring up inside. "He imprisoned and tormented his body, but the evil came not from his body but from within, from his mind." He dies at last, his body and bones rot away, and the centuries pass over the unmarked grave of the statue which his love inspired him to make. At last, workmen digging a grave in a convent unearth the statue. No one knows the name of its creator.

But the prize, the reward for his struggle and his quest, the symbol that revealed the divinity within him, his Psyche, will not pass away. Even though his name is forgotten, the beauty of his vision abides. In the glory of the statue, the spark of the artist's greatness still shines; and people passing by can see, and admire, and adore it.

What Andersen says in this elaborate parable is that the erotic hunger which other men feed with a big healthy swallow of life ("not only the bread, but the baker woman") has for him been diverted to a hunger for ideal beauty and fame and spirituality. But he can find no satisfaction in these ideals; he goes to his grave cursing "the weird fire that seemed to consume his body." The statue he has made is beautiful, perfect, and his own, a product of his imagination inspired by passion. But there is no primary gratification to be had from it, only highly theoretical pleasure in the hope that this embodied fantasy would constitute a "prize, the reward for his struggle and his quest, the symbol that revealed the divinity within him."

Andersen's stories are like the artist's statue, mined from the "dregs" and "filth" of ordinary life with energy that might otherwise have been spent in sensual revels. Their substance is the stuff of desire, the drive for love and power; but the art that shapes them is self-doubt and anxiety and troubled conscience. So they become in the end monuments to chastity and innocence, a marble statue in a nun's grave: no abiding satisfaction to their creator, but still something to be admired by others; "the spark of his greatness still shines; and people passing by can see, and admire, and adore it." Thus, finally, and by a most circuitous route, is the desire for love and eminence to be fulfilled for Andersen.

6

HEINRICH HOFFMANN

Struwwelpeter

Heinrich Hoffmann (1809–1894) was a Frankfurt physician who in his medical practice developed the technique of making friends with young patients by improvising "humorous little stories" and illustrating them "with a scrap of paper and a few touches of the pencil," as he described it. So when, in 1844, he went Christmas shopping for a book suitable for his three-year-old son and found none to his liking ("What did I find? Long tales, stupid collections of pictures, moralizing stories, beginning and ending with admonitions like: 'the good child must be truthful,' or 'children must keep clean,' etc." [Hürlimann 57]), he wrote and illustrated his own. The result was *Der Struwwelpeter* (a name variously translated "Shock-Headed Peter" and "Slovenly Peter"). When personal acquaintances expressed an interest in Hoffmann's hand-made book, he printed a small private edition himself. This proved so popular that he contracted with a commercial publisher for larger printings. Within a very few years, *Struwwelpeter* was on its way to becoming one of the most popular children's books of all time. During Hoffmann's own lifetime it appeared in more than a hundred editions and has continued to be reprinted until the present day. One literary historian has called it "after Grimms' tales, surely Germany's greatest contribution to children's literature" (Hürlimann 62).

The nature of its greatness, or the reason for its astounding popularity, is not entirely obvious. The pictures are crudely drawn, the humor of the text is broad and rather conventional, and Hoffmann's attitude toward the moral lessons of his poems is difficult to locate. He intended the book as a desirable alternative to the bookshops' "moralizing stories, beginning and ending with admonitions," and to some extent he does ridicule such moralism. Yet his poems are not thorough mockeries of the cautionary tale, of the sort that Lewis Carroll incorporated in *Alice's Adventures in Wonderland*. In *Struwwelpeter*, Hoffmann's imagination plays over the basic substance of the cautionary tale and associates a number of oddly suggestive absurdities with various kinds of childish badness. Ultimately he finds comic satisfaction in the idea of naughty people nightmarishly punished.

The verses and pictures of *Struwwelpeter* have a compression of incident and staging, and a blunt, flamboyant high-spiritedness that makes reading them a quite different experience from reading straight didacticism. All the same, though, one can hardly escape noticing that Hoffmann's imagination never really gets outside the balanced, closed moral accounting system of rewards and punishments in which goodness mechanically brings benefits and wickedness automatically brings penalties. As is often true of parodies, Hoffmann's book plays freely with the surface details of the conventions that inspired it but retains their basic structure and much of their meaning. His opening or introductory poem establishes that explicitly enough: It divides into two stanzas, the first proclaiming that good children shall have pretty Christmas gifts, the second that bad children shall have none.

The opening poem establishes another, slightly more devious point: It says that bad children "shall never look / At this pretty Picture-book." That is to say, *Struwwelpeter* itself is a cog in the rewards-and-punishments machine. Logically, anyone who is reading it cannot be a bad child (i.e., he is not like Shock-Headed Peter or Cruel Frederick or Foolish Harriet of the story-poems to follow), or he wouldn't have the book. On that level, Hoffmann invites the reader to join him in a smug celebration; "we" well-behaved, obedient, and prudent people are entitled to laugh at the folly and pain of "them," the mean, silly, or naughty others. And yet Hoffmann is not really encouraging his child-reader to utter complacency. The closing lines of the introductory poem, and the whole tradition of the cautionary tale according to which the subsequent poems are framed, carry implicitly a warning as well: Don't be like those bad people, or what happened to them will happen to you. No child who reads or hears the lines "Naughty jumping girls and boys / Tear their clothes and make a noise . . . / And deserve no Christmas box" is apt to miss the point that he is being admonished and not just entertained.

It is well to notice the compulsive balance and symmetry of Hoffmann's illustrations. The opening picture is almost mathematically precise in the way it balances every detail on the right side with a corresponding detail on the left. Formality and rigidity pervade even the silliest of his pictures, aptly conveying the sense that their "merriment" and "funniness" are kept strictly within bounds of good child-rearing moral philosophy.

Hoffmann's rogues' gallery opens with "Shock-Headed Peter," a figure unique in the collection in that he presents an image, not a story. His slovenliness is a sight to see ("Just look at him! there he stands"), not a pattern of behavior which, in Hoffmann's mind, precipitates disastrous events. Actually, Hoffmann's picture shows him less a sloven (his clothes are neat and his hands and face are clean) than a resolute, defiant grower of hair and nails. He obviously didn't just forget to trim his nails or comb his hair. He is a picture of pride on his solid pedestal, his legs firmly braced, his hair and nails radiating splendidly like plumage or the sun's rays. And his defiance draws its appropriate response, the narrator's disapproval: "Anything to me is sweeter / Than to see Shock-Headed Peter." Somewhere behind Hoffmann's inspiration for these verses may be the sense that hair represents sexual virility and therefore has universally been a delicate issue between fathers and sons, since a boy's flaunting his hair is a tacit challenge to his father's dominance. Whatever the underlying explanation for why men sometimes hate it that boys let their hair grow long, the case of "Shock-Headed Peter" suggests clearly enough that it has to do with pride and defiance.

"Cruel Frederick" is, at the outset, in Shock-Headed Peter's proud and defiant position, legs spread, weapon raised on high. He can ride unobstructed over such helpless victims as flies, birds, kittens, and hired girls; but he meets his match when the masculine Tray appears. Tray is only partly dog; he is also partly man: He grows red with anger, and later he laughs and sits in a chair and eats the boy's dinner. Like all proper romance-heroes, Tray does not look for trouble. Frederick has to kick and whip him "more and more" before Tray finally settles his hash. The issue between Frederick and Tray is not who is kinder or less cruel; it is who can dominate the other. Tray wins out not by comforting Mary or reviving the kitten; he does it by taking Frederick's whip (he still has it in the final picture, hanging over the back of the chair), laying Frederick low, and usurping his seat at the table. Frederick's comeuppance is both that his intended victim inflicts greater pain on him, and that he has to go to bed and take medicine, evidence of his weakness. From the bold, upright position of the first picture, Frederick is reduced to being flat on his back in bed in the last picture, coddled like a child or an invalid by a smiling, solicitous doctor.

In this as in all the *Struwwelpeter* poems, one is left to speculate on its lasting appeal. It will not do just to say that Hoffmann is making irreverent fun of moralizing, secretly celebrating Frederick's wickedness. Frederick goes from pride and glory to pain and humiliation, and his fall is justified in the poem. Neither can it really be said that Hoffmann mocks the kind of people who think in such melodramatic terms of crime and punishment as shape Frederick's story. To do that, Hoffmann would exaggerate the details of Frederick's sin and just deserts; but he does no such thing. To exemplify a boy's cruelty by saying that he torments animals and servants is entirely orthodox (see, for example, the Mother Goose rhyme "Ding Dong Bell," or Ruskin's "The King of the Golden River"). And to envision him punished by being bitten on the leg and sent to bed to take "nasty physic" is no exaggeration over sober cautionary tales, either. Tray's sitting at the table and eating Frederick's dinner is a bit silly, but the effect of it is to add humiliation to Frederick's discomfort, or to show that he is not only bad, but ridiculous.

Ultimately, "Cruel Frederick" is not a parody of a cautionary tale; it is a compressed, energetic, comic rendering of one. Hoffmann's pictures and rhymed couplets, executed in a spirit of jocularity, inevitably suggest that Hoffmann feels some ironic detachment from the educational importance of his theme. But irony here is the mannerism of a man so comfortable with the conventional wisdom of his form that he is entirely easy in handling it sportively.

The governing idea in "The Dreadful Story of Harriet and the Matches," that a disobedient child who plays with matches will burn herself up, is most obvious. In Hoffmann's rendering, two chanting cats who look on, helplessly commenting on Harriet's tragedy like a dramatic chorus, shift the cliché toward a kind of stately ritual or dance, ending in the cats' exaggerated cathartic weeping.

Like most animals in *Struwwelpeter*, the cats are worthy and sensible creatures. Their entire function in this poem is to raise their paws increasingly high in gestures of warning and renunciation (they repeatedly "stretched their claws, / And raised their paws"), predicting disaster from the first time they speak. Beyond that, they can or will do nothing to save Harriet from her fate; they cry "make haste, make haste" at one point, but neither of them helps Harriet douse herself or goes for help.

The ambiguity of the story's setting further emphasizes that Harriet's infatuation with matches is entirely a personal affair, involving her alone. The table she takes the matches from looks like an indoor table, and indoors seems the appropriate place for a forbidden orgy with matches; but the floral border along the right side of the pictures, the channels the cats' tears cut in the ground, and the fact that no house burns down, suggests that the episode takes place outside. Hoffmann's sense seems to be that Harriet sets herself afire wherever she could destroy herself without setting anything else on fire with her.

Any modern reader of "The Story of the Inky Boys" will have to begin by sorting out the kind of racism Hoffmann is denouncing from the kind he uncritically accepts. Clearly Hoffmann believes it is naughty for Edward, William, and Arthur to hoot and laugh at the black boy. Just as clearly, though, Hoffmann supposes that the boy is a "woolly-headed Black-a-moor" who would turn himself white if he could and that to be turned black is a punishment. The basic, unspoken logic of the situation is that of course anyone would rather be white than a woolly-headed black, and it is not nice for the privileged ones to tease the unfortunate about his unhappy condition.

The God-like Agrippa who admonishes the boys and, when they ignore his admonitions, blackens them in his ink-well is (like the giant tailor in "The Story of Little Suck-a-Thumb") a particular kind of moral and psychological symbol, half bogeyman and half wise, impartial judge. One may in some respects associate Agrippa with Hoffmann himself: Agrippa is obviously some kind of a writer like Hoffmann, and, again like Hoffmann, he is responsible for turning the tables on the naughty boys. Perhaps some sense that the boys are Agrippa's puppets or characters over whom he has absolute control explains why Hoffmann draws the boys as fixed, unmoving figures. Except for switching their identifying toys from left to right hands, or vice versa, in the third picture, and moving Edward's free hand a bit, Hoffmann pictures them in exactly the same positions from first to last. In the final illustration, instead of taunting the black boy from below, they are following him, as in a parade, in exactly the same positions. Possibly Hoffmann handled their figures in this way so as to make it clear that the blackened silhouettes are the same three boys as he started out with. Whatever his reason, the ultimate effect is to suggest that the three brainless boys are essentially subhuman cutouts, set in their positions and their attitudes and incapable of learning or changing. They have moved into the Black-a-moor's own vaguely jungle-ish world in the last picture—the scaffolding and festoonery there and the tropical birds sitting on them are cartoon Africanisms. The boys' laughing mouths are still open, their index fingers still raised. Now, though, the boys are going with the Black-a-moor on his own path, rather than pointing at him in derision.

"The Man that went out Shooting" is really a rather different kind of story from the rest of the *Struwwelpeter* episodes. It almost sets aside the cautionary-tale pattern of blatant naughtiness blatantly punished and moves toward a broad slapstick comedy the subject of which is boorish ineptitude, not evil. Probably Hoffmann assumed that his readers would recognize the resemblance between the hunter and Cruel Frederick, and understand that his game-shooting is bad. We're told in the opening line that he does shoot hares. But everything we see of him in the story itself makes us doubt that such a buffoon as he is could ever shoot anything. He's near-sighted, lazy, cowardly, and clumsy. He so loves his hunting outfit that he wears it even when the weather is too warm for it. All in all it seems appropriate for the hare to sit and laugh when she sees him setting out.

But the hare is hardly less ridiculous than the hunter. In effect, she does what she can to transform herself into him, seizing not only his gun but his spectacles too, launching out on the same helter-skelter pursuit that he had intended. When she finally blazes away, she misses her mark.

Unique among the *Struwwelpeter* poems, "The Man that went out Shooting" is not about children; its chief fool is a grown man and his adversary is a mature hare, mother of a child. This is the only episode, too, in which Hoffmann makes a point of showing that innocent bystanders suffer consequences: The man's wife has her coffee shot out of her hand, and the hare's daughter gets her nose scalded. On some level, Hoffmann seems to feel that adult high jinks are a different matter from childish naughtiness. Energies are let loose that do not yield the nice, pat moral conclusions; bullets fly and onlookers had better watch out. Only in the children's world are moral lines kept clear and straight; when men and mothers let fly at each other, "Oh dear!" as the hare-child says, "Such fun I do not understand."

Of all the *Struwwelpeter* episodes, "Little Suck-a-Thumb" is perhaps the most sudden, brutal, and mysteriously inevitable. With the sins and follies Hoffmann addresses in most of his other chapters, punitive consequences suggest themselves more or less naturally: If you play with matches, you'll burn yourself up; if you torment a dog, he'll bite you. Even "The Story of the Inky Boys" has an aesthetic if not a realistic logic to it: If you make fun of blackness in another, you may turn black yourself. But the sin of thumb-sucking is different. It is intrinsically harmless, since it concerns only yourself in a sensual and pleasurable way. So Hoffmann, like many parents and parental types even unto the present generation, distills the question of why you mustn't do it down to a dramatic and terrible simplicity: The big people don't want you to do it, and they're capable of cutting off the offending member if you defy them.

Discussion of this episode can open out into a consideration of the general issue of why grown-ups are inclined to see thumb-sucking as shameful and intolerable. Hoffmann's text sheds little light on that question. Perhaps by its very silence, it testifies to the primary or axiomatic way in which the forces of the superego or conscience must mortally oppose the instinctive pleasure of oral gratification that thumb-sucking gives. That these prohibitive forces should be embodied in the form of a scolding Mama and a great, long, red-legged man with shears seems exactly right, true to the spirit of anxiety which "Little Suck-a-Thumb" expresses.

In "The Story of Augustus who would not have any Soup," Hoffmann addresses one of the really classic power-struggles parents have with children: the conflict over whether the child will eat what and when he is told to eat. The issue is a perfect one for even the most well-behaved of children to challenge his parents' authority over him. On the one hand, providing food for one's offspring is a most fundamental parental duty, culturally and, for all we know, instinctively engrained in a parent's intentions toward his child. On the other hand, in actual practice it is very difficult to force someone to eat something if he doesn't feel like it. "You can lead a horse to water but you can't make him drink" applies to more than the equine species. Furthermore, a child can resist the blandishment of food unconsciously and find himself not simply unwilling but unable to eat what's put before him. This constitutes the most insidious rebellion of all, since it occurs below the level where bribes, threats, and other coercions have effect.

"The Story of Augustus" only implicitly dramatizes the parent's part in this conflict, but the basic dynamic is clear enough. Up to the time of his crisis, Augustus has always eaten and drunk "as he was told." And it's plain that once he refuses his soup, he's not going to be given anything else until he capitulates and eats it. It is "a *sin* / To make himself so pale and thin," says Hoffmann [Emphasis added]. The graphic touch of the soup-bowl's following Augustus to his grave and sitting there like a watch-dog is right on target. The real point of Augustus' story is not, "You'll starve to death if you miss your soup for five days." It is, "Woe unto you if you defy your parents; you cannot win, for they will stand firm though it should mean standing on your grave."

As did "The Dreadful Story of Harriet and the Matches" and "The Story of Little Suck-a-Thumb," "The Story of Augustus" presents the recalcitrant child with thoughts of corporeal damage, the literal loss of his physical substance. Hoffmann's pictures employ a rather evocative shift in perspective compatible with such thoughts. As Augustus gets skinnier he also gets farther away from the viewer, until at last he is just gone.

"The Story of Fidgety Philip" is the mildest, least exaggerated, most realistically commonplace of the *Struwwelpeter* episodes. The concluding picture, in which Philip is entirely covered by food, dinnerware, and cloth, overstates the plausible reality, of course, offering a little low-key symbolism in the image of a sinner inundated by the consequences of his sin. But for the rest, the notion that a fidgety child might tip over his chair and pull the tablecloth with him is a tame fantasy, compared with Augustus' shriveling up to the dimensions of a pipe-cleaner, the giant tailor with the shears, or Cruel Frederick's Tray taking his master's place at the table.

Here, as in all the *Struwwelpeter* verses, the parents warn but do not punish the wayward child. The mother peering through her lorgnette and the father with his imposing dark coat may convey some sense of critical, judicial scrutiny and the possibility of recrimination (their disapproval is implied in Philip's being "in sad disgrace"); but within the tale itself, retribution happens without their direct participation. The fundamental myth of right and wrong that Hoffmann is endorsing in all these stories is that punishment proceeds not from a clash of arbitrary wills over who is to be boss, but from the very nature of things; good behavior works better than bad behavior, in the natural, physical realm. "Fidgety Philip" adds the piquant touch that the parents too suffer from the child's misbehavior, and "wonder how / They shall have their dinner now." Only in "The Story of Little Suck-a-Thumb" and "The Story of the Inky Boys" do some holes appear in that rationale, revealing that certain "oughts" are enforced by large, imposing men who don't have to explain themselves.

The foible Hoffmann mocks in "The Story of Johnny Head-in-Air" may strike the modern reader as a rather odd one to devote a sermon to: the habit of failing to look where one is walking. Probably Hoffmann was thinking of absent-mindedness generally here, with Johnny's love of looking up at swallows, sun, and clouds a kind of synecdoche for all wool-gathering and lack of concentration. Still, it is suitable to notice how very prescriptive and coercive an idea of child-raising Hoffmann assumes: Even daydreaming is at least faintly forbidden.

Following a pattern also found in "Cruel Frederick" and "The Man that went out Shooting," "The Story of Johnny Head-in-Air" invokes the animal world in demonstrating Johnny's folly. The dog in the first episode is apparently as guilty of inattention as Johnny is, given the fact that its imminent collision with Johnny is obvious enough that "every one" has time to cry, "Johnny, mind the dog is nigh!" before it happens. The "every one" of that episode comes into focus in the second episode as three fishes see exactly what is about to happen to Johnny, and come back after he's fallen in to "enjoy the fun and laughter" of teasing him.

The chorus-effect of the fish is rather different from that of the two cats in "The Dreadful Story of Harriet,"mainly because, even though Johnny looks somewhat dead floating face down in the next-to-last picture, he's not dead; he's just doused and silly. His only material loss is the writing book which shoots purposefully away on the line Hoffmann sharply etches in the water. Here Hoffmann projects the sense that the daydreamer walks through a world otherwise peopled with alert, attentive observers who see him coming, warn him, pull him out once he's fallen in, and laugh at his vagueness.

In some contexts common in other children's literature but far removed from Hoffmann's, the youthful tendency to dream is treated as one of the blessings or magic privileges of childhood. "A boy's will is the wind's will," says Longfellow admiringly, "And the thoughts of youth are long, long thoughts"; and Lewis Carroll's Alice dreams her way into Wonderland. But in the brisk Teutonic world of Hoffmann's verses, daydreaming is just the suitable occasion for a cold wake-up bath.

If Hoffman meant for Robert's being carried off by the wind in "The Story of Flying Robert" to be a threatening or fearsome image, like Harriet's incineration or Suck-a-Thumb's mutilation, one must suspect that he misjudged his material rather badly. One could take "The Story of Flying Robert" out of its position in the *Struwwelpeter* collection, perhaps remove Hoffmann's labeling Robert "a silly fellow" and saying he screamed and cried when the wind got him, and show it to an assortment of readers; and chances are, most of them would take it as a wishful fantasy rather than a threat. Usually in children's literature, flying away is a distinct privilege. MacDonald's Light Princess squeals with delight at being tossed through the air; Craik's Little Lame Prince finds both solace and adventure on his flying carpet; Andersen's Little Mermaid leaves her problems behind by becoming a daughter of the air. Says Robert Louis Stevenson:

> How do you like to go up in a swing,
>   Up in the air so blue?

Oh, I do think it the pleasantest thing
   Ever a child can do!

There are probably some situations in which Hoffmann's thesis "Don't go out in the bad weather or the wind will carry you away" would work as a cautionary admonition. In the fanciful context of children's literature, though, it is a hard point to drive home. In fact, Hoffmann himself may have recognized the positive appeal of escaping the world where "all good little girls and boys / Stay at home and mind their toys." His pictures clearly show that the rain falls only on the place Robert takes off from. Once he gets up into the sky, he's out of the rainfall that made it "wise" to stay indoors in the first place.

All throughout his collection of tales, Hoffmann contrived a lot of ways to frame his pictures; stairways, trees, sticks, giant quills, arches, vines enclose his scenes. Here, with "The Story of Flying Robert," he drops all pretense, and just frankly draws picture-frames around each sketch. Why? The frames can be seen in more than one light. Perhaps Hoffmann sensed that the spirit of this poem was too wild and free and libertine, so he instinctively decided he'd better get it under control by putting a container around it. On the other hand, the frames might be a sign of Hoffmann's lurking approval of Flying Robert; even though to the people in Robert's home he is gone and "never seen again," Hoffmann's frames show that he is still in "the big picture," which, as we can see, can be expanded to include a lot more than the toys on the nice safe living room floor.

PETER ASBJÖRNSEN and JÖRGEN MOE

East o' the Sun and West o' the Moon and The Three Billy Goats Gruff

Peter Asbjörnsen (1812–1885) and Jörgen Moe (1813–1882) did for Norway what Jacob and Wilhelm Grimm did for Germany: compiled and published its first and greatest collection of native folk tales. Born within a year of each other, Asbjörnsen and Moe became good friends as boys, when both boarded in the same house while preparing to enter college. Later, as men, inspired by the example of the Grimms, each of them began writing down tales they heard among the Norwegian people. They began their collecting independently of each other, but when they discovered their mutual interest, they began a collaboration that proved to be extremely harmonious and productive. (Asbjörnsen went on to a career as a naturalist and forestry administrator; Moe achieved separate fame as a poet and, eventually, as a clergyman, becoming in the last years of his life Bishop of Christiansand.)

They published the first of their *Norske folkeeventyr* in 1837 and continued issuing new, expanded collections throughout the 1840s. Their final collection came out in 1852 with notes and scholarly commentary. As collectors they proceeded after the manner of the Grimms: They set their stories down in simple, standard Norwegian, in the way that the stories were told to them, regularizing any oddities of dialect that might have been difficult for a general audience to understand.

Several of the stories Asbjörnsen and Moe first recorded achieved worldwide currency, such as "The Princess on the Glass Hill," "The Boy Who Went to the North Wind," "The Giant Who Had No Heart in His Body," and "The Husband Who Was to Mind the House." But "East o' the Sun and West o' the Moon" and "The Three Billy Goats Gruff" have proved to have perhaps the most universal appeal.

As in "The Frog Prince" and "Beauty and the Beast," the fundamental task in "East o' the Sun and West o' the Moon" is to work out the process for humanizing a bestial suitor. In the other two tales, physical intimacy came last; the bestiality had to be exorcised before it could occur. "East o' the Sun" has its own twist on the situation: Here, in a rather frank endorsement of sexual pleasure, the beast-suitor is a man, and a handsome one too, as long as he is in bed with the heroine, in the dark. It is only when she sees him—when her daytime, examining faculties are operating—that he is a beast.

"East o' the Sun" makes a strong and cautionary comment on the part parents play in the young couple's accommodation to each other. As in "The Frog Prince" and "Beauty and the Beast," the father has a definite hand in setting up the match. Here he virtually sells the daughter to the White Bear. He is not entirely high-handed about it, and he does what he can to convince the girl of the marriage's economic advantages, but the story does show that it is very likely a girl's father who gets her into this predicament, for reasons that do not have much to do with his looking out for her welfare.

But the mother plays the more crucial role in this little domestic drama. It is the girl's mother, the story says, who interferes with her daughter's yielding and trusting acceptance of her mate. It is the mother who plants suspicions in the daughter's mind, and warns her against accepting the man's peculiarities uncritically. "My!" she says, "it may well be a Troll you slept with!" It is she who provides the scrutinizing candle by which the bride will simultaneously discover her good fortune and lose it.

As if to underline the idea that mothers pose obstacles to young lovers' finding their own contentment with each other, the Prince explains that he has a stepmother who has bewitched him and who will now force him to marry her own long-nosed daughter instead of the beautiful girl he really desires. (Her influence here is a recognizable fairy-tale version of the possessive mother who wants to keep her son for herself rather than let a young girl have him.)

The movement of the story is generated, then, once the damage has been done, the mother's advice has been followed, the tallow has dropped, and the Prince and his castle are gone. By what means is the heroine to atone for her mistakes, and earn back the blessings that she has fumbled away?

First of all, the story insists, she has to travel. The whole long middle section of the tale, and the title itself, are evocations of the vast distance she must put between her past and her future. She leaves her meddling mother far, far behind her. Instead she meets "good mothers" along the way—the three old hags with the handy horses, who help her reach her lover, and freely give her the golden emblems of womanliness: the apple (an ancient symbol of sexuality), and the carding comb and the spinning wheel (representative of female domesticity). (These meanings are borne out later in the story when the Troll Princess, who wants to be the Prince's wife, demands them.) As if to emphasize the rightness and worthiness of her quest, the very winds themselves do all they can to help the girl achieve her goal.

Once she has reached her destination, the story establishes some odd new elements—the revelations that the Trolls have "some Christian folk" imprisoned next door to the Prince and that "only Christian folk" can wash out the tallow stains. All this talk of "Christian folk" introduces a general theological concept, suggesting that the spots on the shirt symbolize the girl's "sin" and that only Christianity provides the means whereby the sins of a repentant sinner (and the girl has certainly proven herself that) can be forgiven, her cloth made "as white as driven snow." But the teller has in mind other patterns as well, not so theological in implication. In several respects, the process by which the lassie got into trouble at the beginning of the story is reversed in this concluding episode. Before, it was the man who came to fetch the girl; now she comes to fetch him. Before, she was in a kind of prison; now he is. Before, she woke him all too easily, without even wanting to; now, she cannot wake him though she tries her hardest. Before, she stained the shirt; now, she cleanses it.

There is no avoiding the sexist implications of this story. Its ground-assumption is that a girl's best fulfillment comes in marriage, and that the proper attitude for her to have toward her husband is unquestioning trust. Her efforts (on her mother's advice) to pry into the secrets of masculine nature bring misery on her, to be undone only by a most elaborate and devout demonstration of her penitence and her desire to be taken back.

But it is appropriate to recognize, too, that the sexual dynamic in this story is not entirely one-sided. The man needs the woman, too, for his fulfillment; he depends on her to end the curse under which he has been placed by a possessive mother, a curse fully as baleful as the plight the bride's mother gets her into.

With "The Three Billy Goats Gruff," in just over four hundred words Asbjörnsen and Moe gave the world one of its most compelling and memorable tales, a kind of exquisite miniature romance perfect in economy and unified effect. Within its scale, "The Three Billy Goats Gruff" is a masterpiece of suspense, artfully created and satisfyingly resolved. Virtually everything about it seems inevitable, once the conception is grasped.

Exactly who or what are the three billy-goats? Are they brothers? Grandfather, father, and son? Just three goats with the same name? All we know is that they live together, agree on what is desirable (eating grass on the hillside), and rely on each other. But that is enough to tell us that they are a complete, harmonious and wholesome group, a family/society worth preserving.

The nature or identity of the Troll is just as mysterious, and just as obvious.

Simply by reporting that he has "eyes as big as saucers and a nose as long as a poker," lives under a bridge, and wants to eat everything that passes over it, the teller establishes exactly what he is: another version of the giant Cormoran who plagues Cornwall in "Jack the Giant-Killer," or the sea-monster that threatens Andromeda in the Perseus myth, or Grendel in *Beowulf*. He's ugly, he comes from down below, he's carnivorous and anti-social, and he needs killing. Further, he sets himself up for his own downfall. The greed that makes him dangerous, makes him conquerable. He waits for prey too powerful for him to handle.

The "symbolism" of the story, if one chooses to call it that, is so concrete and unelaborated on, that any labels one applies seem to reveal more about the particular interests of the reader than of the teller. Finally perhaps the most and least we can say is that "The Three Billy Goats Gruff" means what all stories mean that tell of baleful menaces confronted and overcome. Here that meaning is given with a kind of distilled purity that would be hard to improve upon.

8

EDWARD LEAR

Nonsense Poems and *Laughable Lyrics*

No circumstances of time or place fully account for the phenomenon of Edward Lear (1812–1888). No matter how many facts are gleaned for a portrait of his quirky genius—and there are many facts available for a detailed portrait—the essence of the man slips away. He remains as enigmatic as the nonsense for which he is famous.

Born in London, Lear was the youngest of twenty-one children. His sister Ann looked after him during his infancy and, as it happened, long after. He considered himself hopelessly ill-suited to marriage, which he never attempted. Bald, fat, short, big-nosed, bearded, bespectacled, and generally rumpled, he made the most in several ways of his physical and mental oddness. Portraying himself in grotesque poems and sketches and portraying countless other creatures in the same forms, Lear appeals insistently to our comic love of the odd and surreal. Though "his visage is more or less hideous," as he says, "how pleasant to know Mr. Lear!" "Pleasant" because Lear, like the people in his limericks, animals in his nonsense songs, and creatures in his illustrated alphabets and stories, revels in the many abnormalities, perversions, and anomalies that preponderate in life against the rare golden mean. Lear, in other words, votes for energy against order, for the strange against the norm, for travel and escape against rest and acceptance, and for the self-reflexive dream against mimetic "reality."

Lear made his living mainly by illustrating books on birds, travel, and landscape, by selling his topographical drawings and paintings, by accepting small sums from patrons, and by writing nonsense. Though he often complained of poor health, penury, and overwork, Lear labored and traveled with a restless, indefatigable energy, forever playing off against each other ideals of striving and escape. A bundle of contradictions, he seemed old in his youth yet incredibly "frisky" in his old age. The characters in his famous limericks are similarly ageless. Though the Old Men outnumber the Young Ladies (there are tactfully few Old Ladies), age or youth matters little to their behavior. All are mortal in folly. They live in a world of dreamlike coincidence, whimsicality, and inconsequential violence. The Old Man of the Dee is invited to scratch his fleas with a hatchet; the Old Person of Philoe rushes through the calm. Others are "horribly bored" (with a lurking pun on bored / jaded versus bored / punctured) or think to "flee" by "sitting" and "smiling."

The structure of Lear's limericks puts enormous stress on the beginning of the final line. Because he always ends the limerick with a word repeated from the end of the first or second line, the poems are geared, as it were, for anticlimax, and so the first stressed syllables of the fourth (last) lines generally contain the climactic emphasis: often violent—"So they *smashed* that old Man with a gong," "That it *killed* that Old Man of Madras"; often the key point of nonsense—"That *intrinsic* Old Man of Peru," "That *ombliferous* person of Crete," "That *borascible* person of Bangor." Lear's addiction to such linguistic anticlimax and false climax parallels his interest in neologisms and portmanteau phrases, an interest displayed, for example, in his nonsense botany or zoology ("Nasticreechia Krorluppia"), and in chiming poems ("Baky Maky Caky"; "Wary! Hairy! Beary!"). Lear is a protomodernist as he questions in a thousand ways our easy assumptions that words have stable references and fixed meanings. Lear anticipates the work of later authors who also drive language toward self-reflexiveness and free play.

Children, no doubt, take to Lear less because of his linguistic modernity and more because of his incessant verve, his mocking of adults, his gay rule-breaking, his intriguing drawings, and the fine sonorities of his longer poems. Who can forget that first rapt traveling to the Hills of the Chankly Bore and the Coast of Coromandel, where the Jumblies play and the Yonghy-Bonghy-Bò sings his song? To Lear and the many children's authors who have so conspicuously adorned the romantic imagination, no finer tribute could be given than to join them in company with the Owl and the Pussycat; of all it should be said:

> They danced by the light of the moon,
>   The moon,
>   The moon,
> They danced by the light of the moon.

Insofar as it contains "nonsense," the poetry of Edward Lear raises some of the questions already adverted to in our section on Newbery's *Mother Goose's Melody*. There is a special relevance of nonsense to literature for children, and several questions are involved. Does nonsense appeal to children partly because they can believe in it with a faith and vividness denied adults who have long ago narrowed down the parameters of reality and truth? Is it fundamentally nostalgic, reversing the direction of youthful growth, moving back from socialized to unsocialized behavior? Or does it perhaps forecast youth's access to rebellion and violence to be intensified with adolescence?

Some varieties of nonsense—such as the poetic tongue twisters, tautologies, and sound play of certain nursery rhymes—appear relatively free from any obligation toward "meaning" or "teaching," and children may delight for many reasons in uses of language that demand no didactic reverence. Lear's limericks include such nonsense. Many of them are rooted in one sort of paradox or another that baffles our custom of making sense out of human conduct. Why is the Old Man in the tree? In what sense is he "bored"? Who would think of calling a bee a "brute," especially a "regular" brute? Our lack of ready answers to such questions suggests that the poems are celebrating in part the resistance of life to interpretation. Things just are. And they are fundamentally odd. Paradox is everywhere. The man in the boat thinks he's afloat, but may not be (the illustration hardly settles the question). Is the Man of Dee somehow obliged to use the hatchet to scratch the flea? Does it not sound as if the Old Man who "perceives" a "young" bird "in" a bush and asks for silence must be looking at a diminutive thing? Certainly the question of the mysterious friends who apparently cannot see it seems justified: "Is it small?" The answer shocks with the delight of paradox, and it reverberates back to the original "Hush," hinting that it might not have been a request to avoid alarming the bird but rather a plea that the bird not be aroused against the perceivers. The Old Person of Bangor, similarly, whose rage seems to follow linguistically from bang/anger/gore in "Bangor," *tears* off his boots and *subsists* on roots: The first act is violent and brief while the second is not, yet the linkage suggests continuity, just as boots and roots seem unrelated (unless we are meant to think of the old notion of our feet as our roots or perhaps his need for vegetative calm).

Lear tells us that the person of Ealing was "devoid of good feeling." In general, the grotesque characters who inhabit Lear's limericks are similarly afflicted. They lack love. They rarely help each other or even communicate in a supportive way. The "they" who appear in many of the limericks are usually detached, uncomprehending, or hostile. Or else they are rebuked by the limerick protagonist. We are nudged to laugh at the fears of silly people, as the illustrations attest. Whether the laughter occasioned by this sort of satire is good-hearted or perhaps deficient in good feeling, each may judge independently.

It is amusing and perhaps revealing to consider why a verse form which is more often than not used by those with a propensity for indecent quips should be enshrined so universally among the classics for children. Is there a subversiveness in the limerick tradition that resonates to a subversive tendency in children's literature? Do children (and adults) respond to an erotic component in Lear's poetry? Such questions point the way to Lear's longer narrative poems.

"The Owl and the Pussy-Cat," "The Jumblies," "The Dong with a Luminous Nose," and "The Courtship of the Yonghy-Bonghy-Bò" are four of Lear's most famous narrative poems, and they deserve comparison. All are romantic quest poems involving journeys and the sea. The first two, "The Owl and the Pussy-Cat" and "The Jumblies," end happily and depict a journey and return. The latter two, "The Dong with a Luminous Nose" and "The Courtship of the Yonghy-Bonghy-Bò," portray separation and loss. The Owl and the Pussy-Cat "went to sea," and the Jumblies "went to sea." Going to sea in Lear's hands becomes associated with romantic adventure; those who go to sea are those who succeed, grow, carry life with them. The Dong and Lady Jingly, on the other hand, are left behind on the land in desolate circumstances, deserted by those they loved who have put to sea. "The Owl and the Pussy-Cat" and "The Jumblies" share the vitality of "pea-green" boat and sail, and they close with feasting, whereas "The Dong" and "Yonghy" close with loneliness and desire in final images of the restlessly searching Dong and of the Lady Jingly weeping into the jug without a handle. The symbolism of the first two poems revolves around ring and sieve, whose roundness Lear may associate with journey away and return or with traditional images of closure, harmony, perfection. The symbolism in the second two poems is not of circles but rather of projective things: the artificial nose of the Dong, his plaintive pipe, the heap of stones, the missing handle. No doubt psychological criticism might make much of the phallic images of Dong's nose and missing "handle" and the terminology of "dong," "dorking" fowls, sent by "Handel" Jones, and so on. Lear tempts us to identify an erotic component in his poems where happiness is marrying Miss "Pussy" with a ring from a pig's nose, or sticking your "feet" in "pinky paper" and spending the night together in a jar while spinning round and round, or courting a "Jumbly" Girl or a Lady "Jingly." The ring that pulls the pig, the sieve that catches food, the Jumbly girl landing among oysters, the Lady Jingly with her dorking fowls, all may be connected in a realm of promised satisfaction of appetite that wavers between or conflates food and sex.

Whatever their "deeper" meanings, Lear's narrative poems display his mastery of poetic craft, and readers owe it to themselves to note the panoply of Lear's gifts. First is an unerring ear for rhythm. Lear's lines are organized, like most nursery rhymes and most nonclassical and Anglo-Saxon poetry, according to a count of accents rather than a count of syllables. Lear's lines, generally of three or four beats each, contain "feet" of two or three syllables that may variously be denominated iambs, anapests, dactyls, and so on. The effect of the mixed-feet, accentual lines is to give a sense of easy, rapidly moving speech and a light dance rhythm as opposed to the walk or march of steady iambs. Lear's sonorities depend primarily upon repetitions which produce a lulling, hypnotic effect:

> What a beautiful Pussy you are,
>> You are,
>> You are!
> What a beautiful Pussy you are!

Sometimes the repetitions are used for the sake of wit as in the fourth stanza of "The Courtship of the Yonghy-Bonghy-Bò" when the two references to fish being "plentiful and cheap" serve to undercut Yonghy's declarations of love, suggesting that they both know the Lady Jingly Jones will be more interested in fish than in romance. Finally, there are such devices to note as the sly sonic wit of the jug with a "handle" brought up against Mr. "Handel" Jones as if there has been a displacement of handles to the loss of the Yonghy-Bonghy-Bò. Lear also likes to yoke extremes: "Silence" reigns on the plain, but "angry breakers roar" nearby; the Dong provides a "lonely spark" in the "gloomy dark"; the Yonghy-Bonghy-Bò rides on the Turtle through the "silent-roaring" ocean; and so on. Lear's mysterious, romantic names ("Gromboolian," "Zemmery," "Coromandel"), his dreamlike and uncontingent adventures, his lilting verse and deft, often original images all propel readers into a surreal and disorienting, if also captivating, experience of very genuine poetry.

9

CHARLES DICKENS

A Christmas Carol

What is the "Idea" whose "Ghost" Dickens says he endeavors to raise in *A Christmas Carol*? Is it the idea of Christmas humor? of good will and good cheer to everyone? of charity and of love? In such abstract terms, the idea shows none of the particularizing force that drives Dickens' tale along, that fashions a redemptive carol from everything that can be seen or heard, tasted or touched, the force that would draw, finally, a warm blessing from a cold, cold, heart.

Nothing could be less ghostly dead than the pervasive animism of Dickens's world in which an old man's blood becomes conscious of faint sensations, in which a clock displays a "rapid little pulse," in which flames cry out, air laughs, onions wink, potatoes knock, puddings sing, and all the air is filled with sounds and forms of heart-softening influence. Dickens's ghosts are not only the spectres haunting his plot but also the lively spirits he makes immanent in all the scenes and happenings addressed by his verbally crammed, quick-phrased, vitalist prose. *A Christmas Carol*, then, peculiarly enacts, even as it describes, society's song designed to celebrate how fresh new life may be won out of old.

Charles Dickens (1812–1870) was born in Portsmouth, England, the second of eight children. His father was a naval clerk of precarious financial circumstance. When Dickens was twelve, he worked for about six months in a "blacking warehouse" covering and labelling pots of shoe polish, and during this period his father was confined for debt in Marshalsea Prison. Dickens said that he felt, and dreamed long after, a stunning shame and grief stemming from this period. Certainly his later career combined themes of wide social protest and a personal search for economic security.

After serving as an attorney's clerk, Dickens became a court and parliamentary reporter, journalist, amateur actor and director, and novelist. From the beginning, many of his novels were read by children. *Oliver Twist*, appearing in 1837, attracted a huge following. Dickens was disappointed in sales of the serially published *Martin Chuzzlewit* (1843–44) and so decided to write a Christmas story, largely to enhance his income. Drawing upon rudiments of a ghost story appearing in his *Pickwick Papers*, Dickens quickly penned *A Christmas Carol*, the sales of which encouraged him to write four more Christmas stories for recurring holiday seasons. In 1853, he finished *A Child's History of England*, and in 1868 he published *Holiday Romance*, containing three stories for children reprinted as *The Magic Wishbone*. Dickens, the father of ten children, employed throughout his prolific career a child's eye view of things. He often, and perhaps romantically, saw, as Robert Louis Stevenson, Mark Twain, and other contemporaries saw, the best grace of life in the child and in grown-ups willing to re-child themselves.

To note the vernacular, dialogic vigor, and the patent morality of all-saving good will in *A Christmas Carol* hardly suffices to answer more deeply rooted questions that may energize its endless popularity. Why does Scrooge, the toughest skeptic imaginable, see Marley's face in the door knocker? What in Scrooge's personal history helps account for his deepest mindset, his breaking, his conversion? Why are the images of childhood so forlorn yet so conversionary? Whose perceptions make the London world so vivid yet surreal, contradictory, and transitional? Scrooge's or the narrator's? Does the narrator's way of looking at things inevitably blend over into Scrooge's way or the reader's way? Is the narrator as interested in Scrooge's mind and heart as he is in the reader's? Is the transfiguration of Scrooge truly believable? What is the residual impact of the tale? In pondering such questions as these, readers may wonder anew at Scrooge's geriatric, cackling redemption floating lightly on a life-sea of darkness, and they may wonder how that redemption can hold a candle to the chill bleak world wherein Scrooge doubts "if night had beaten off bright day" and wherein the sound of human laughter just might rescue him, and all of us, from "the unknown abyss, whose depths were secrets as profound as Death." Against such palpable and frozen dark as inhabits much of the story, are the spirits of Christmas Present, of Fezziwig and Scrooge's nephew, of Cratchit and Tiny Tim, enough to warm us to unshaking hope? Like the Christmas story itself, *A Christmas Carol* both seeds and questions faith in that outcome, that delicate issue.

Readers often come to *A Christmas Carol* with preconceptions bred of prior readings, film or theatre viewings, or gossip. To focus possibly diverse views upon a common object, we will look carefully at the opening of the story. Dickens's title was "A Christmas Carol in Prose, Being a Ghost Story of Christmas," and there may be some tensions in the title that bear exploration because they resemble tensions in the story as a whole. A Christmas carol is a song of religious joy. The story promises something similar. But a carol could hardly be sung "in prose." Is the author suggesting that he offers the story in the spirit of or as attaining to the essential spirit of a Christmas carol? Is he making a subtle and surprising claim for the power of his prose? Ghost stories, furthermore, are usually intended to frighten. They are not primarily aimed at religious joy. Christ may have appeared as a kind of blessed and blessing ghost at Easter, but Christmas is not generally associated with spirits of those who died. Christmas is, rather, a time of birth. Is the connection of ghost story and Christmas like the connection of prose and carol, a connection of sobriety with song, of judgment with joy? The chiastic repetition in Dickens' title of "Christmas" bracketing "prose" and "ghost story" suggests that Dickens may have intended just such a sugar-coated narrative pill, and the patterns "Christmas–Ghost–Christmas" and "carol–prose–story" further intimate the progress of the tale from high spirits down to low and back up again.

In his Preface, Dickens says he wants to "raise" a Ghost that no one will wish to "lay." The Ghost is, obviously, the spirit of Christmas joy and benevolence. By associating his "Ghostly little book" with the "Ghost of an Idea," Dickens cleverly personifies the book as the spirit of joy, and he connects this, furthermore, with himself, the "me" whom readers are asked to stay in humour with. The Preface thus amounts to a pretty powerful advertisement for book and author, the faithful friend and servant who thinks to keep his readers happy not only internally but with others, with Christmas, and (also important?) with Dickens.

The Contents reveals a five-part structure, perhaps suggesting analogy to five theatrical acts. The "staves" or stanzas of the carol hold onto the idea of a song, and the chiastic or abba structure of the full title is reflected in the way the first and last staves have titles with the deeply traditional one-two-three of the various ghosts placed in the center. The Contents is then, one more psychological device to help readers anticipate a comic–tragic–comic movement to the piece.

Once the reader has noted the title of Stave One, the first sentence of the story becomes doubly ambiguous. Marley "was" dead, but some part of him will yet live. Marley was dead "to begin with" means to begin the story with but also Marley seemed dead at first. So, even though the ostensible purpose of the paragraph is to persuade readers of Marley's death, the whole drift is to question precisely that event. Even the assertion that Scrooge's name was good upon " 'Change" can be taken proleptically to signal incipient metamorphosis. Then the second paragraph jollies the reader along, with Dickens practically saying in so many words, "Since, dear reader, we are plainly having fun with the idea that Marley died and was never heard from again, why not throw in some other questions about conventional truths such as whether door-nails are really dead and whether the hallowed wisdom of our ancestors truly deserves to live on?" Does such skeptical fun-poking suggest a willingness in Dickens to unhallow received truth and particularly to mock myths from the past? If so, that may be the comic writer's right: to doubt the demands of the past and to ease its tragic burdens. Though his call for action foreshadows Marley's call upon Scrooge, Hamlet's Father as a "middle-aged gentleman" taking a "stroll" is here transmogrified into a comic and secularly substantial ghost, just as Saint Paul's Churchyard is converted to "a breezy spot."

That Scrooge answered either to his own name or to Marley's helps the reader think of Marley's ghost, when it comes, as part of Scrooge's personality, and it reveals, too, that Scrooge identifies his personality with the counting-house, a personality as cold as the unfired flint and bitter wind which become metaphors for the man.

Dickens can employ a single paragraph to repeat in miniature the argument of his story's full title: Christmas is a glowing border of joyful song or poetry around a more ghostly, gloomy center of prose. Consider, for example, the description of the weather on Christmas Eve as Scrooge sits "busy in his counting house." The paragraph begins with the old opening of romance and fairy tale: "Once upon a time." Mention of "the good old days" and "Christmas Eve" deepens the aura of benevolent providentiality circumscribing local accident and change. But then the bulk of the paragraph works out the consequences of or the synchronous accompaniment to old Scrooge's denial of Christmas Eve as he sits "busy" counting. Christmas joy is questioned and challenged by the foggy cold, by the palpable reality of people stamping on stone. The clocks had "gone" three, but the day had never been light, and even the light of candles was but a "smear." The paragraph comes out somewhat the way it went in with personified "Nature," a figure from myths of "once upon a time." But a strange and powerful metamorphosis has taken place during the paragraph. The palpable fog has managed to smear the light, pour in at every keyhole, and turn the houses of civilization into "mere phantoms." "Nature," then, may be a force opposed to "Christmas." Ghost against ghost: The inner, subtextual conflict pits two phantasmal, spiritual forces against each other. The outcome is in question. For now, "Nature" supplants the "good day" with its dingy, drooping, obscuring fog.

The whole story of A Christmas Carol repeats in larger scale the tension and struggle suggested in miniature by the paragraph analyzed above. Which is more impressive and memorable, finally: the merry cheer in the tale or its horrific vision of death-in-life in the person of Ebenezer Scrooge? Does "Scrooge" stand in our minds for the redemptive capacities of the human heart? Or for the skeptic night of the soul? To see the battle lines as evenly drawn and the issues in doubt is to avoid a too-rapid assimilation of the story along sappy and conventionally sentimental lines.

It's plain enough that Scrooge stands for a spirit of defense and self-authority, a wish to keep at bay all claims for love that might expose one to vulnerabilities and pain. He sees Christmas in terms only of its costs: "a time," as he tells his nephew, "for paying bills without money; a time for finding yourself a year older, and not an hour richer; a time for balancing your books and having every item in 'em . . . dead against you." When Scrooge says that he would bury Merry Christmasers with a stake of holly through their hearts, the kind of burial once given to alleged witches, he pits his cynical rationalism, his self-promotion and survivalism, against what he sees as the superstitious witchery of believers in Christmas. In expressing this thought that celebrating the birth of Christ is but superstition, Scrooge verges on what Christians would term Satanism. Scrooge's nephew gets at the specious self-sufficiency and pride in Scrooge's attitudes when the nephew alludes to us being "fellow-passengers to the grave" and not, as Scrooge would have it, separate races bound on other journeys.

Dickens carefully exposes in an ever widening circle the shocking extremism of Scrooge's selfishness, moving from the man to his clerk, his nephew, and the charitable solicitors to show how thoroughly Scrooge rejects all claims to human intimacy and reciprocity, even to the point of terming the poor a "surplus population" deserving of death. Dickens also introduces little touches of information that help to set up the eventual confrontation of Scrooge with the ghost of Marley. We learn that Marley died exactly seven years before that night and that Marley had once lived in the very quarters now occupied by Scrooge. But before letting Scrooge go his dark way home, Dickens inserts a long paragraph reminding readers of the intense search for light and life carried on by Londoners everywhere despite the thick fog and darkness. Such counter-theming is necessary to reactivate our sense of dismay at Scrooge's acts of inhumanity as when he terrorizes the boy who attempts to bless him with a carol. Dickens thus daringly suggests that the carol of his book's title can hardly yet be sung.

Why did Scrooge see Marley's face? Dickens invites the reader to speculate about the reasons: "Let any man explain to me, if he can, how it happened." One should try. To assume that the face is wholly a projection out of Scrooge's guilty conscience or his unconscious mind may be prematurely to oversophisticate the approach of Dickens. He has already mentioned Nature brewing the fog as well as St. Dunstan and the Evil Spirit. Are these but idle metaphors? No, in the animistic world of the tale, their force is real, is it not? The world of the story is peopled with spirit forces such as the gruff old bell peeping down at Scrooge or the misanthropic water plug. So pervasive is the life of things in this world, a life seemingly independent of what is often called the pathetic fallacy, that one might well think Dickens intended to portray a sentient universe which may respond to human fears and hopes but which also may enforce its own desires. The appearance of Marley's face is one with the appearance of the three spirits who come, surely, in answer to some long-denied call within Scrooge and yet come of their own accord to force humane vision in the most unlikely candidate, to prove once again the Christmas miracle which proclaims a light in the lowliest place.

The psychological dynamic of Scrooge implicitly blaspheming against Christianity may be repeated in the description of Biblical tiles around his fireplace. The tiles are quaint, and their artistry crudifies and mocks the scenes they portray: angels on feather-beds, apostles in butter-boats. Or is this Dickens' way of insisting that Scrooge now has his own, individuated spiritual crisis to contend with, a crisis that crushes the whole of external tradition into the transforming furnace of his imagery and the startling archetypes that will issue from it? Dickens has to think of some way to justify not only the appearance of the three spirits but Scrooge's power to invest them with such transformative import.

That Marley comes from Hell, we know (even before being told of his "infernal atmosphere") from the hot wind blowing his hair and reddening his face and from his chain like a devil's tail. The jokes about Marley's transparent bowels, his possible difficulties in sitting, his being perhaps but an undigested remnant, gravy more than grave, are all explicitly said to be distractive, defensive measures on the part of Scrooge, but the wit suits as well one's sense of Dickens writing his own animistic comedy, only lightly Christianized, celebrating his own ghost story in prose just as much as (if not more than) the traditional carol of religious joy at the margins. Though Scrooge's horror is said to take on a deeper reality when Marley's jaw flops down upon his breast (the corporeal disfigurement more impressive than all the hokey paraphernalia of chains and boxes), still, Scrooge is soon back to his jokes and Dickens to his (indicting the ghost for a nuisance). Conventional threats of brimstone, Dickens suggests, are now somewhat inauthentic, "hard" upon one, likely to seem too "flowery." Marley's ghost remains the comic prologue to a play of deeper sentiment brought in the second Stave out of Scrooge's imagined childhood. There, a truer, if more romantic, emotion flows.

What day is it when Scrooge confronts the Ghost of Christmas Past? By the count of the clock, it should be one in the morning of the day after Christmas, and this makes sense of the idea of "Christmas Past," but, at the end of the tale, of course, Scrooge still has his Christmas day. Shall we call it all a dream? That will far from accurately reflect our responses to the narrator's assurances that "Scrooge awoke," "touched the spring of his repeater," and so forth. Persistent Sherlocks may opine that the spirits monkeyed with the heavy bell and with Scrooge's clocks, but the reader's confusion will arise only after the fact or upon re-reading and should serve mainly, I think, to invigorate an appreciation of Dickens' unconcern for ratiocinative certainties. The main drive in the story is toward the lost carol in Scrooge's heart and its rediscovery, toward feeling and not fact.

"The curtains of his bed were drawn aside; and Scrooge, starting up into a half-recumbent attitude, found himself face to face with the unearthly visitor who drew them: as close to it as I am now to you, and I am standing in the spirit at your elbow." Is this sheer tomfoolery on Dickens' part? Or does it serve any purpose? If Scrooge is as close to the spirit as Dickens is to the reader, then Scrooge is analogized to Dickens and the spirit is analogized to the reader? We are to look at Scrooge from the spirit's point of view. The concluding portion of Dickens' sentence, however, suggests an analogy between Dickens and the spirit. The reader may be encouraged to identify with both parties. Beyond that possibility lies the daring equivalence between the author and "the spirit at your elbow," as if Dickens openly took credit for truly conjuring up the spirits and saw himself creating an alternative pantheon of sub-deities. Dickens asserts, moreover, that he is actually present to the reader in the act of reading, an assertion that will be taken more literally or less literally depending upon how one views some rather complex questions of "presence," "absence," and the power of the "word."

The order of scenes in Scrooge's travels with the Ghost of Christmas Past deserves attention. The first views are largely happy and contrast strongly with the images of the boy-Scrooge as poor forgotten waif in a shabby, deserted schoolroom. A good deal is made of the power and detail and the emotive force of Scrooge's memories for scenes and events of long ago, suggesting that our childhoods are the repositories of our strongest and most precious feelings. Through little Fan's words "Father is so much kinder than he used to be," Dickens brings his reader to primal feelings of rejection and to an archetypal motivation sufficient to account for Scrooge's later behavior. As a boy, Scrooge had been kicked out of the family by his father and sent to a decrepit boarding school. His "rescue" by his little sister and his later befriendment by the avuncular Fezziwig proved insufficient to allay the earlier trauma of parental rejection that left Scrooge gasping and grasping for an impossible security. As his fiancée says to him, "You fear the world too much." This is one way, at least, to read the old miser's psychohistory.

As the "relentless Ghost" forces Scrooge to witness his past, the jokes and banter of the opening all die away. The "torture" of Scrooge becomes more and more genuine, and Dickens even adds salt to the wound by confessing how personally infatuated he himself is with his vision of Belle, the woman Scrooge failed to marry. Scrooge "cannot bear it." He extinguishes the spirit with no trace of humor in the description. When he rises next, some of the tough jauntiness is back, but he is "not the dogged Scrooge he had been" and even looks upon the Ghost of Christmas Present "reverently."

Dickens' grand panorama of the sights and sounds of Christmas cheer passes in pageantial review complete with authorial advices on what a shame it would be to quarrel on Christmas day and how only bigots would close bake shops to the poor on Sundays. This is no idle, commercially popular theme for Dickens. His works consistently argue concern for the poor, and the 1840s, in which the *Carol* was written, were a particularly hungry time in England. A few readers may find the Cratchits impossibly blessed with warm fuzziness, Tiny Tim too gooed to be true, and Scrooge's gushing plea ("Oh, no, kind Spirit! say he will be spared") unlikely in its suddenness. Remind them it's a ghost story. It's Dickens. It's Christmas: to be celebrated in every heart, celebrated, as Dickens daringly imagines, not only in the streets of London but among miners on the desolate moor, in the lighthouse on the reef, and far at sea upon the ship. Dickens deftly shuttles back and forth between scenes of lonely cheer in which embattled spirits still raise up eyes of hope and scenes of cornucopian gaiety, as at the home of Scrooge's nephew, where generous-minded folk comment directly, as did the Cratchits, upon the meaning of the miser's mean-heartedness.

"Bless those women; they never do anything by halves. They are always in earnest." If these sentences are "excused" as belonging to another era, though still read in this, one may still press on to ask whether there is not indeed a rather condescending and proprietary tone on the author's part toward each "exceedingly pretty" woman, each "little creature" with a "ripe little mouth, that seemed made to be kissed," so "provoking, you know; but satisfactory, too"? What is the place of women in the book? And what are their relations to men, the author, families, themselves?

Perhaps some readers find it shocking that the jovial Spirit of Christmas Present should have held beneath its robe all during the festive scenes the squalid girl and boy. Standing for Want and Ignorance, they cling "appealing from their fathers," and again the theme of the harsh progenitor tolls out. Caught in a spasm of authorial preachment, Dickens forecasts dire, devastating revenges from such deprived offspring. Again, skepticism and scorn view with celebration for dominance in the book. Do the glowing borders of the Christmas carol surround icy ghosts within? What is the balance in the book? Certainly, the Santa-like second Ghost vanishes amid its own imprecations and so provides an unbrightened transition to the spectral Phantom, the death forethought-on of Scrooge, and the macabre conversation in the charnel atmosphere of Joe's parlor.

As Scrooge confronts the possible consequence of his dying, the story enters its most protracted darkness. That the parade of miserables and the author's exclamations over the departed spirit of Tiny Tim seem much more sentimental than nowadays is fashionable might provoke us to ask if we agree with the fashion. Do we really or rightly despise Victorian or other sentimentality? If so, why? When? Can we be clear as to distinctions between quantity and quality of feeling? Might not one allegedly attack the quality of pity over Tiny Tim's demise (stock response, unearned, exceeding its object) when really one wished protection simply against the quantity or intensity of feeling? Robert Louis Stevenson reported that he cried his eyes out over the *Carol*. What kinds of arguments might be constructed in defense of "tear-jerking"? What defense of less sentimental displays of emotion needs to accompany the full and flowing response to strong literature? The dreamlike scene of Scrooge on his knees gazing upon his own grave draws surely upon archetypal resources in all of us. At some point, perhaps here, we need to confront the issue of why the story of Scrooge, an ugly old man with few claims to our empathy, should make such powerful impress. What shadow or spirit potential in each human soul does he represent? Why do we care what becomes of him?

The reformation of Scrooge is marvelous: innocent, energetic, comic, outrageous, sublime. It is deeply desired by every fiber of one's being that knows forgiveness, and especially self-forgiveness. One satisfying way to experience and feel this with more intensity than that usually provided by silent reading would be simply to read aloud: "I am as light as a feather, I am as happy as an angel. I am as merry as a school-boy. I am as giddy as a drunken man. A Merry Christmas to everybody! A happy New Year to all the world. Hallo here! Whoop! Hallo!" In this promise of frisking, laughing, age-wise frolic, this birth-in-death ("I'm quite a baby"), we experience some of our keenest longings. Scrooge's change of heart may seem comically grotesque, a fantastic miracle, but the many touches of madness, the surrealism of his dealings with the world on waking, really testify more to the unfathomable mystery of our own being and its profoundest aspirations. We may know something of the holiness of fools, but we stand outside of Scrooge redeemed, and we must treasure him from there, as if wishing on a star. The book's a blessing for everyone, but perhaps only child readers and listeners can be Scrooge the whole way, identifying intimately with his father-caused pains and with his second childhood. Truly, the tale feeds our youth beyond all.

10

JOHN RUSKIN

The King of the Golden River; or, The Black Brothers

Born in the Bloomsbury district of London, the only child in a wealthy family, John Ruskin (1819–1900) was educated at home until he went to Oxford. His parents wanted him to be a minister, and according to Ruskin, treated him severely, providing few diversions and much punishment. Ruskin did accompany his father, a wine merchant, on trips through England and the Continent, and on those trips he conceived both his lifelong reverence for nature and a keen sympathy for the plight of the poor. While still of student age, Ruskin suffered a disappointment in love, and in 1841, when he was staying with his parents in Surrey, he was visited by Euphemia ("Effie") Gray, who asked him to write a fairy story. *The King of the Golden River* was the result. In 1848 Ruskin married Effie Gray, as his parents' choice, and in 1851 he published the tale. About three years later his wife caused their marriage to be annulled on grounds that it was never consummated. Ruskin did not remarry.

As a youth Ruskin saw and admired the artwork of John Turner. Out of this experience grew Ruskin's famous defense of modern art, *Modern Painters* (1843), which helped change the taste of an era. Ruskin continued as art critic with *The Seven Lamps of Architecture* (1848) and *The Stones of Venice* (1853). After meeting Carlyle in 1846, he became increasingly concerned with socioeconomic issues; he led an antirailroad group, tried to help the working class, and charitably dispensed his very substantial inheritance.

Many of Ruskin's interests appear seminally in *The King of the Golden River*, which combines timeless artistry and everlasting modernity of theme. Ruskin's Biblical prose rhythms and parable style suit perfectly the story of black-hearted savagery and greed foiling themselves and giving way to the indomitable spirit of charity. Yet here the rewards of charity are not otherwordly, but are poured into the fertility of earth.

For Ruskin, nature is man's moral testing place. Those who, like the wicked brothers Schwartz and Hans, exploit nature for their own gain are condemned ultimately to fail. The solid wealth they would extract from the land is swept away in a flood of waters. Their gold melts into a river spirit, and they end as symbols, two black stones stuck in a stream bed, around which the waters merrily flow. That we should see and seek in nature a process, not a product, and that nature beckons us forward to foster life is suggested both by the adventures with the holy water and by the appearance of those two happy half-gods, the King of the Golden River and Southwest Wind, Esquire. By withholding their harvest and their "holy" water from those who need it desperately, the wicked brothers forfeit their claim to success. The water that is diverted from the needs of life can hardly be holy, and Ruskin makes palpable the crime:

> He opened the flask, and was raising it to his lips, when his eye fell on an object lying on the rock beside him; he thought it moved. It was a small dog, apparently in the last agony of death from thirst. Its tongue was out, its jaw was dry, its limbs extended lifelessly, and a swarm of black ants were crawling about its lips and throat. Its eye moved to the bottle which Hans held in his hand. He raised it, drank, spurned the animal with his foot and passed on.

Against Ruskin's moral fervor, with its dark realism, we find balanced his bracing humor and light fancy. The guardians of nature, it turns out, are roguish pixies, little old men who twinkle in their pride and prowess like the very epitome of Jung's archetypal helpers. They are, essentially, wind and water, the keepers of life in Treasure Valley. Gluck, the boy hero, in his innocent luck and happiness, deserves the company of the two powers, extends his hand to them, and earns their aid. Like the carefree youngest brothers in the Grimms' tales that Ruskin admired, Gluck does all "merrily." His unthinking, instinctive charity is of the best kind, proceeding from a pure heart, a natural grace. While his brothers are all calculation and greed, drinking to excess, Gluck welcomes the watery wind to his home, melts out the King of the Golden River, slakes the thirst of the dying, and makes the waters of the Golden River flow down to his valley. In its harmony of images, together with its plain humanity of spirit, Ruskin's prose poem works supremely well.

The King of the Golden River is only about fifteen pages long and does not bear a great deal of analytical weight. One way of approaching it is by noting the transition in children's literature around 1840 (and represented by Ruskin's tale) from the primary medium of folk tales and anonymous verses (in which only a translator or collector's sensibility intervenes between the "original" text and audience) to a primary medium of works written by specific authors specifically for children. Ruskin was steeped, obviously, in tales of the Grimms' mode replete with sibling rivalry, mysterious helpers, and happiness ever after. But his own personal sensibility stamps the character of his tale. The Grimms' tales reveal little of the reverence for nature that abounds in Ruskin's story, and Ruskin omits the customary bride-winning drive of the youngest brother. These two matters are not unrelated, for Ruskin's story has more to do with our human relations to the natural world of flora and fauna than to our aims for familial and social success so predominant in the Grimms' tales.

Ruskin says in his "advertisement," by way of excuse for the roughness or naivete of his story, that it was written in 1841 (when he was but twenty-two), apparently at the request of a child (Effie Gray was not really "very young" at the time), and with no thought of public scrutiny. Even in releasing the tale for publication, Ruskin asserts that he is yielding only "passive assent." It should be noted that the majority of children's classics by known authors are not the work of youth. The prevailing note in such works of generational conflict and of skepticism toward the superiority assumed by adults over children may follow from a characteristic psychology of older writers writing for children partly out of dissatisfaction with such assumed superiority and "maturity." Such giants of children's literature as Hans Christian Andersen, Lewis Carroll, Mark Twain, Robert Louis Stevenson, Kenneth Grahame, and Sir James Barrie were often inclined toward satire in treating grown-ups and toward nostalgia and sentimentalism in treating children. Ruskin does not wholly share this mind-set. Writing when he had barely achieved his own majority and at a time when he was recovering from a disappointment in love, he seems disinclined to romanticize the glories of youth. Gluck and his brothers, moreover, fill out a two-sided portrait that offers contrasting views of a complex issue: whether nature is primarily a means or primarily an end and whether life, accordingly, should be seen primarily in economic terms or primarily in religious terms.

Ruskin titles his tale around but not on the main characters, which are Treasure Valley itself and Gluck; the King of the Golden River and the Black Brothers are actually adjuncts to the more central forces of nature and happiness. Ruskin begins by devoting a paragraph to a "valley of the most surprising and luxuriant fertility," and the rest of his tale is spent, really, defining this fertility as it combines natural fecundity and a demand for spiritual largesse or charity. The key point about the wicked brothers, Schwartz and Hans, is that they "killed everything that did not pay": they shot, poisoned, and smothered wholesale, whereas Gluck was "kind in temper to every living thing."

As Ruskin draws the rather conventional plot of a Grimms-like tale out into a contemplation of nature, moving us from a social perspective to a natural one, so, predictably, he makes the weather provide the catalyst to get the story going. A too-rainy summer elsewhere accentuates the value of sunny Treasure Valley, but some of the people who come there for succor eventually starve at the door of the Black Brothers. At this point, as if some kinds of killing by the two brothers will not be countenanced, the wind and water intervene (in the personified form of Southwest Wind, Esquire). Nature enters the house as the socialized figure of a little gentleman capable of comic conversation. Then the house and valley are devastated and Gluck must enter nature as if in return to make amends for the exploitation by his family.

The elder brothers think to retreat to the city and goldsmithing, appropriate place and activity for the commercial instinct which lies at the base of their relations with nature. Gluck reverses the process of retreat when he melts out of the golden mug the King of the Golden River. Henceforth the tale is one of advance out into nature for purposes, albeit hidden, of penitence and replenishment. At the heart of Ruskin's story lies the metamorphic and metaphoric ambiguity of "gold" as it connotes first solid commercial wealth, riches, and second the fertility that accompanies shining waters. The melting of the mug (that would hold, fittingly, golden ale) into liquid form is the central image for the transformation in idea of a river of melted mineral gold into a truer, more natural golden river of fertility. The person who can cast holy water into the source of the river "for him only, the river shall turn to gold," because such a person will of necessity have passed the tests which show what makes water holy, precious, and "golden." Gluck shares with water its power to foster and nurture life.

Interpreters of Ruskin's story would do well to examine the details of Hans's journey up into the mountains as the imagery there of kaleidoscopic and inhabited forms (especially in the glacier) creates a sense of a living, judgmental world confronting the quester. Ruskin's intensification of feelings in Hans and landscape that bind them together toward the terrible climax marks one of the high moments in literature for children and all others asked to become knowing and brave in a charged responsibility to the living, natural world.

Though it probably is not the very most enlightening sort of question to ask of children's literature, a question that many of us may nonetheless find ourselves prompted to ask at various times during a consideration of a particular story written for children is the question of what those children, as opposed to adults, may "get out" of the texts. Ruskin's text suggests a serious moralism that is harsher but no less poetic than Saint-Exupéry's in The Little Prince, and it teaches all who read or hear it the same lesson of reverence for life, of respect for nature, and of the purity in will that often accompanies innocence. To find ways for children, as well as ourselves, to articulate heartfelt versions of these or related understandings is an important challenge, a challenge perhaps best met by a careful and loving return to those passages in the text that provoke our most feelingful response. What are those passages? Just how do they affect us and why? Can we amplify our feelings in some way that will permit us to be a little more conscious and accepting of them? To look for ways of sharing such a process, finally, between children and grown-ups could be one of the finest rewards of delving into the treasure caves of children's literature.

11

GEORGE MACDONALD

The Light Princess

The Light Princess is a nineteenth-century philosophical fairy tale, related by genre to Hans Christian Andersen's *The Snow Queen* and *The Little Mermaid*, John Ruskin's *The King of the Golden River*, Oscar Wilde's *The Happy Prince* and *The Selfish Giant*, Dinah Maria Mulock Craik's *The Little Lame Prince*, and to such twentieth-century successors as James Thurber's *Many Moons* and *The White Deer*, Antoine de Saint-Exupéry's *The Little Prince*, and C. S. Lewis's *The Lion, the Witch and the Wardrobe*. What these works have in common is that they employ story-devices associated with traditional fairy tales, but employ them in working out or advancing philosophical theses of particular, untraditional kinds; sometimes, indeed, tales such as these are oblique or implicit comments on the fairy-tale genre itself, taking as they do a rather knowing and artistically self-conscious attitude toward the fictional conventions they employ. The philosophical fairy tale has a kind of double perspective on its material: Readers are asked to attend to the story's characters and situations as being interesting in themselves, but they are also to be aware that large, abstract concepts are being articulated through them. In *The Little Lame Prince* Craik puts the point more explicitly than most authors ever do:

> If any reader, big or little, should wonder whether there is a meaning in this story deeper than that of an ordinary fairy tale, I will own that there is. But I have hidden it so carefully that the smaller people, and many larger folk, will never find it out, and meantime the book may be read straight on, like

Cinderella, or *Bluebeard*, or *Hop-o'-My-Thumb*, for what interest it has or amusement it may bring.

George MacDonald (1824–1905) was a man apparently born to make philosophical fairy tales. He was a Scots minister who turned to writing only after his unorthodox religious ideas offended his Calvinist parishioners and cost him his pulpit. He made a ringing success as an author. He ultimately published some thirty novels, several of them best sellers, as well as poetry, plays, literary criticism, essays, and translations. At the height of his popularity he was admired and praised by Lewis Carroll, John Ruskin, Alfred, Lord Tennyson, Charles Kingsley, Henry Wadsworth Longfellow, Harriet Beecher Stowe, and Mark Twain. In the 1860s and 1870s he seemed to have as fair a claim to immortality as any of these. Now, though, he is remembered chiefly as the author of a handful of colorful fairy tales for children.

MacDonald's early life was full of adversity. Although he lived to the age of eighty, he suffered most of his life from tuberculosis, the disease that killed two of his brothers in childhood and four of MacDonald's own eleven children. The son of an Aberdeenshire farmer, MacDonald worked his way through school, acquiring first a degree in chemistry and physics and subsequently a degree in Congregationalist divinity. He held only one pastorate, at a church near London, and that for only two years. He objected to the Congregationalist idea that certain people are predestined to eternal damnation and can do nothing to escape it. His own theory was that sinners would remain in hell just until they became convinced of their own wickedness and repented and that ultimately everyone would be saved. His congregation, in effect, fired him.

Although he lost his pulpit, he never lost his calling to preach. His fiction is distinctly that of a preacher; all his stories have conspicuous didactic themes.

The Light Princess is not MacDonald at his most religious. Yet the story does contain a gentle sermon against "lightness" (frivolity or carelessness), which is recognizable Victorian moralism. The heart of MacDonald's ulterior or figurative meaning here is an idea, or a linked set of ideas, about what it means for a girl to grow up. It is partly a moral idea, partly a spiritual one, partly biological. It is somewhat mystical and somewhat common-sensical. Basically, MacDonald's thesis is that maturation consists of overcoming one's "lightness" or lack of gravity, which has several related meanings here. On the most playful, superficial level, of course, it means having no physical weight; in a few passages, MacDonald takes a kind of science-fiction writer's interest in what it would be like to have no gravitational attraction, and to exist in what a space-age reader would call a constant state of free fall. He indulges in some improvised notions about how inertia might or might not operate on a theoretically weightless body, and he observes how the princess's situation points up the arbitrariness of up and down.

Of more concern to MacDonald is the sense of lightness as frivolity, a hollow and specious gaiety, an inability or unwillingness to take things seriously—in short, silliness. This is a kind of moral failing in the princess, although to hold her responsible for her irresponsibility is a bit paradoxical. This, though, is the general idea underlying such a scene as the one in chapter seven where her parents try to get her to speak seriously about her life:

> "Is there nothing you wish for?" resumed the king, who had learned by this time that it was useless to be angry with her.
> "Oh, you dear papa!—yes," answered she.
> "What is it, my darling?"
> "I have been longing for it—oh, such a time!—ever since last night. . . . It is—to be tied to the end of a string—a very long string indeed, and be flown like a kite. Oh, such fun! I would rain rose-water, and hail sugar-plums, and snow whipped-cream,—and—and—and—and—"
> A fit of laughing checked her. . . .

Accompanying this silliness or moral vacuity is a spiritual lightness, a lack of true human identity. She is more of a thing than a person, in this regard—a ball to play catch with, a kite, a bit of lint to be blown around by the breeze, a dandelion seed. Until she acquires gravity, she cannot properly be said to have a soul. She can only laugh,

> like the very spirit of fun; only in her laugh there was something missing. What it was, I find myself unable to describe. I think it was a certain tone, depending upon the possibility of sorrow—morbidezza, perhaps.

Finally, MacDonald's symbolism suggests that her childish lightness is also a lack of physical life and substance. She is out of touch with life not only morally and spiritually, but physically. She has to grow up in her body as well as her mind and soul; she must become biologically a woman, in order to put the "lightness" of childhood behind her. She must learn responsibility, the possibility of sorrow, and physical passion.

These three strands in MacDonald's conception of the princess's lightness weave in and out of the story in a pattern which is not entirely tight and systematic, but which nonetheless ultimately conveys some visionary sense of how sobriety, spiritual grace, and sexuality all do go together in a young person's maturation.

The opening chapters of *The Light Princess* are predominantly cheerful and comic; MacDonald obviously expects his reader to find little serious cause for alarm in the thought of a baby or a little girl who floats like gossamer and giggles constantly; lightness seems rather appropriate to the infant state. The first significant change in her nature, and the story's first turn toward seriousness, takes place in Chapter Eight, when she falls into water and makes her first partial acquaintance with gravity.

Water is mysteriously important in *The Light Princess*. It was a fertile image for MacDonald, pregnant with meaning. "It comes bubbling fresh from the imagination of the living God," he wrote in *The Mirrors of the Lord,*

> rushing from under the great white throne of the glacier. The very thought of it makes one gasp with an elemental joy no metaphysician can analyze. The water itself, that dances and sings, and slakes the wonderful thirst—symbol and picture of that draught for which the woman of Samaria made her prayer to Jesus—this lovely thing itself, whose very wetness is a delight to every inch of the human body in its embrace—this live thing which, if I might, I would have running through my room, yea, babbling along my table—this water is its own self its own truth, and is therein a truth of God. Let him who would know the truth of the Maker, become sorely athirst, and drink of the brook by the way—then lift up his heart . . . to the Inventor and Mediator of thirst and water, that man might foresee a little of what his soul may find in God (Lewis 81).

Falling into water, the princess falls into Life and begins making her engagement with it. Immersion changes her, makes her know something of what it is to have a body, and to take pleasure in it.

> At the same time she seemed more sedate than usual. Perhaps that was because a great pleasure spoils laughing. At all events, after this, the passion of her life was to get into the water, and she was always the better behaved and the more beautiful the more she had of it.

MacDonald is alert to the sacramental and spiritual symbolism of water (the baptism and Christ as "the living water"); his princess finds the beginnings of spiritual grace in entering it. The Satanic old witch in the story, with her Leviathan-like "White Snakes of Darkness," attacks the princess and her whole kingdom by drying it up. Having felt the water of life, the princess "felt as if the lake were her soul, drying up within her, first to mud, than to madness and death." A Christ-like sacrifice of a man's life is needed to save this living water. Thoughts of the crucifixion are obviously close to the surface of MacDonald's thinking when he frames the poem on the cryptic gold plate:

> Death alone from death can save.
> Love is death, and so is brave.
> Love can fill the deepest grave.
> Love loves on beneath the wave.

Religious connotations of water are accompanied by erotic connotations which may seem somewhat surprising in a pious Victorian story for children. But MacDonald is hardly less insistent on the sexual than he is on the theological allusions. Entering the water is unmistakably tied to the princess's romance with the prince. Her immersion is not only in the waters of spirit, but in the waters of sensuality. The long, loving swims the two young people take together are idyls of barely diverted eroticism. MacDonald puns explicitly on *falling in*—love and water. "The princess's pleasure in the lake had grown to a passion, and she could scarcely bear to be out of it for an hour." The amorous prince dreams "all night long that he was swimming with the princess."

The princess's introduction to sensuality, MacDonald suggests, is a two-step process. She falls into it accidentally at first (it may be pertinent to notice that her father inadvertently pushes her in), and her initial experience is an entirely undiscriminating delight in her new feeling of physicality. It has nothing to do with love as a desire for companionship with another person. Even after the prince has been ardently wooing her for days, she still cares only for the water, nothing for the prince's personality. "She did not care who the man was; that was nothing to her. The hole wanted stopping; and if only a man would do, why, take one." The prince overtly thinks of his filling the hole in the princess's lake as an erotic experience.

> "How lovely the lake will be in the moonlight, with that glorious creature sporting in it like a wild goddess!—It is rather hard to be drowned by inches, though. Let me see—that will be seventy inches of me to drown." (Here he tried to laugh, but could not.) "The longer the better, however," he resumed; "for can I not bargain that the princess shall be beside me all the time? So I shall see her once more, kiss her perhaps,—who knows? and die looking into her eyes. It will be no death."

Finally she, too, realizes the connection between sensual pleasure and personal love. Just as the water rises above the prince's head, and he apparently drowns, "love and water brought back all her strength," as MacDonald says, and she rescues him.

It isn't easy to specify exactly the logical connections among moral gravity, spiritual grace, and sexual fulfillment in *The Light Princess*. MacDonald is no D. H. Lawrence or Wilhelm Reich for whom sex is spiritual grace. Yet he has his own rather mystical view of life; and in that view, mature morality, spirituality, and sexuality are the cross-threads from which the completed existence is woven. The water of weeping is linked in his mind with the water of life and fertility; and both are linked to the Living Water of God.

> The princess burst into a passion of tears and *fell* on the floor. There she lay for an hour, and her tears never ceased. All the pent-up crying of her life was spent now. And a rain came on, such as had never been seen in that country.

> The sun shone all the time, and the great drops, which fell straight to the earth, shone likewise. The palace was in the heart of a rainbow. It was a rain of rubies, and sapphires, and emeralds, and topazes. The torrents poured from the mountains like molten gold; and if it had not been for its subterraneous outlet, the lake would have overflowed and inundated the country. It was full from shore to shore.

MacDonald obviously means to suggest that in the princess's learning to feel, think, and embrace there are deep and rich rewards. But he concedes, too, that there is also a sense of loss. "Is this the gravity you used to make so much of?" she says to the prince. "For my part, I was a great deal more comfortable without it."

On balance, though, MacDonald is not a sentimentalizer of childhood lamenting the passing away of innocence and gaiety. For him, entering the adult world of weight, care, responsibility and reproduction is good. "So the prince and princess lived and were happy; and had crowns of gold, and clothes of cloth, and shoes of leather, and children of boys and girls."

A question may arise about whether MacDonald is entirely self-consistent in writing a light and humorous story the theme of which is that lightness is folly. Certainly one can point out a number of instances of silliness in the story itself, such as the queen's borrowed quip, "I never made a jest, but I broke it in the making," or the pseudo-learned discourses of the Chinese philosophers Hum-Drum and Kopy-Keck. Regarding this question a couple of observations may be in order. First, most of the humor has a kind of moral or philosophical edge to it (e.g., MacDonald's remark that the princess's father needed portable steps to reach his throne, "for he was a little king with a great throne, like many other kings'") that keeps the reader alert to the story's serious interests. The argument between Hum-Drum and Kopy-Keck, the materialist and the spiritualist, is not just double talk. Each in his effort to reduce life lop-sidedly to all-physicality or all-spirit is an example of how not to be; the rounded sense of life's totality which the prince and princess achieve at the end of the story is just what these false wise men lack.

Second, MacDonald's humor changes in accordance with the story's development and reinforces its meaning. Physical grotesquery and much of the punning are restricted to the first half of the tale. MacDonald's tone pretty consistently steadies and darkens as the princess moves toward her conversion to gravity. The banter between the prince and the princess has something of the arch and purposeful suggestiveness of Shakespeare's witty lovers. And once the evil old aunt reappears in Chapter Eleven (MacDonald never uses her comic name "Princess Makemnoit" in this latter part of the story), the tone settles into romantic high seriousness with nothing silly about it.

12

DINAH MARIA MULOCK CRAIK

The Little Lame Prince

In its blending of satiric and romantic fantasy and in its dual impulses toward escape from and acceptance of worldly responsibilities, *The Little Lame Prince* epitomizes much of the Victorian temper in children's literature. Echoes of Hans Christian Andersen, George MacDonald, and Lewis Carroll may be heard throughout, and, in the case of Carroll, there is evidence that Mrs. Craik was directly influenced (though perhaps not enough) by the satirical whimsies of the Oxford don.

Dinah Maria, born in 1826 near Stoke-upon-Trent, Staffordshire, was the only daughter and eldest of three children born to Thomas Mulock, a bad-tempered and irresponsible clergyman, and his frail, long-suffering wife. The family moved often. At the age of thirteen Dinah taught Latin in the school run by her mother, and at eighteen she broke with her father, shepherded her maltreated mother and her two younger brothers back to Staffordshire, and then experienced the deaths of her mother and one brother. In 1846 she moved to London, where she began publishing a steady stream of books to support herself and her remaining brother. She became a highly successful novelist. *John Halifax, Gentleman*, her most popular work, narrates the rise of a poor orphan to the ranks of the gentry. The book extols the values of honesty and hard work and gives a hopeful portrait of mobility and mores among the middle class in England.

At the age of thirty-nine, she married twenty-eight-year-old George Craik, a publisher, and about five years later the Craiks adopted a daughter, Dorothy, who may have inspired *The Little Lame Prince* (1875) and whom Lewis Carroll photographed. Carroll liked Mrs. Craik's novels, as did many of his contemporaries, though there were dissenting voices, such as that of William Morris, who found them boring. Certainly, if one wished to find fault with *The Little Lame Prince*, one might object to its didactic thrust; the coy hints about an allegorical message; the quietistic admiration for uncomplaining sufferers; the unexamined political conservatism; and the bland, unparticularizing style ("I can't be expected to explain things very exactly"), betokening a somewhat pedestrian imagination. Still, most of these objections can be qualified by pointing to the book's great intertwining strengths. Thus the didacticism cuts in several directions. We have the opening satire on the unfeeling rituals and pomp of the court, where the ill health of the Queen and misfortune of the Prince are calmly ignored. The author shows the court substituting a kind of impersonal, bureaucratic deference in place of any intimate, truly loving contact:

> He had a magnificent nursery and a regular suite of attendants, and was treated with the greatest respect and state. Nobody was allowed to talk to him in silly baby language, or dandle him, or above all to kiss him.

The Prince's father is "indifferent" to his lameness; "his Majesty never liked painful things." As Prince Dolor's isolation, his spiritual ostracism, becomes more and more complete—darkening to a deadly tower—the reader may be at least tempted to forgive Mrs. Craik's romantic finger-wagging at adult failures to treasure the innocence of childhood. It turns out, moreover, that her hints of "a meaning in this story deeper than that of an ordinary fairy tale" are far from an advocacy of easy sentimentalism, for she asks us to respect and admire, not feel sorry for, the lame Prince. His capacity to bear his sufferings, his moral valor as he wrestles with "thoughts of great bitterness," all his strengths of character are valued as they help him mature. The author is intent upon "making him see the plain, hard truth in all its hardness," so that he can arrive at informed resolves for action, to "go out in the world, no matter how it hurts me—the world of people, active people. . . . They might only laugh at me—poor helpless creature that I am. But still I might show them I could do something."

Over and over, the Lame Prince works back and forth between the twin desires for action and rest, company and solitude, independence and dependence. As he advances and retreats across the quivering margins of his own maturity, Prince Dolor reenacts in unusually complete and honest fashion each child's hesitant groping toward the Experience that is hoped to be worth the loss of Innocence and so to be worthy of the name *growth*. Mrs. Craik in her turn is said to have grown to high stature. Handsome and good-hearted, a fine singer and active friend to those less fortunate, she gave bread to the poor and pensions to needy authors. She and her father were reconciled before her death in 1887. Whether we judge her character by

The Little Lame Prince or judge it by her character, we may find that the same lively faith animates each.

One approach to further consideration of *The Little Lame Prince* is through comparison of it to "Sleeping Beauty" and to MacDonald's story, *The Light Princess*. Each tale begins with the royal couple longing for a child, the wish being at last fulfilled, the celebratory christening ceremony, the harm to the child, and the uninvited guest. Perhaps there is an attitude underlying such stories that the first weeks of infancy appear paradisal in comparison to the later period in which the child must be presented to society and thus incorporated into an imperfect world of mixed friendship and enmity. Or is there also involved in the sudden disabling of the child a traumatic recognition or projection on the parents' part that the child is neither so perfect nor so impervious to outside criticism as once believed? In "Sleeping Beauty" and *The Light Princess*, the harm to the child issues from the malevolence of the uninvited guest, as if the sin of the parents in omitting a social grace were visited in magnified form upon the child. In *The Little Lame Prince*, the injury issues from the inattention of the nursemaid holding him, but the context makes it quite clear that the entire court is at fault. Not only was the "elegant and fashionable" state nursemaid "so occupied in arranging her train" that she "let" the baby fall to the marble, but also all the other members of the court (save the Queen) are described in terms of pride, superficiality, and unfeelingness. The King's brother "tried to seem pleased at the arrival of the prince"; "nobody thought much" about the Queen; all the people in the palace "thought themselves" lovely; the King "had grown used" to the Queen's absence; the courtiers are quite "satisfied" with the ceremony though they have almost smothered the prince; the courtiers treat the accident as "slight" because they are determined not "to let anything trouble such a day of felicity." All is done, in other words, for the sake of form, not feeling. Against this background of official pride and falsity is placed the young prince's expression of "earnest" inquiry. He does not fit, obviously, into a world made for show. His friendly godmother is, in the same way, dressed in plain colors, speaks plain ("baby" instead of "Prince," "wife" instead of "Queen"), and opposes truth to power. (Yet her magic provides an allure momentarily denied the prince.) Seen metaphorically, the prince's lameness is the result of the court's pride and the failure of adults to recognize the treasure of the child.

Mrs. Craik describes the prince as "earnest" but also "sweet" (one of her favorite words), and she seems most impressed by a paradoxically sweet gravity in the prince, his mother, and godmother. But such "sweet gravity" is only one possible gleaning from the tale, and each reader might find individuated versions of just what moral, intellectual, emotional, and other human qualities the author is promoting as most desirable. How seriously, moreover, they are promoted might become the succeeding focus of inquiry. Why, furthermore, might the work properly be termed "didactic"? What seems to be its main point or reason for being? We need such questions, if only to help us observe the mixtures in the story of preachment and entertainment, of moralism and imaginative play.

Through its central curve of action, *The Little Lame Prince* resembles *The King of the Golden River* as a kind of pastoral romance in which the protagonist leaves the typically corrupt home, court, or art context, and goes out into the country, nature, where he learns truths and takes on strengths that allow him to return triumphantly and to rejuvenate a moribund society. Notice that the Prince's mother was born in the Beautiful Mountains; his "faithful country nurse" is banished there; and "Nature, the safest doctor of all" comes to his aid. The degree to which Mrs. Craik indulges in a nature worship and child worship that may be called variously Romantic or sentimental should perhaps be pondered. Certainly the merits of such passages as the following are highly debatable:

> They rather perplexed people, those childish eyes; they were so exceedingly innocent and yet so penetrating. If anybody did a wrong thing—told a lie, for instance—they would turn round with such a grave, silent surprise—the child never talked much—that every naughty person in the palace was rather afraid of Prince Dolor.

Is this at all realistic or convincing? Are "naughty people" really "afraid" of shocked innocence? Should children be encouraged, at least for a time, to think so? Should they be made to doubt whether "naughty" people, like the Prince's uncle, can "enjoy" their ill-gotten gains? What are the proper functions, if any, of children's literature with a didactic cast?

Mrs. Craik's view of life as propounded in *The Little Lame Prince* is rather grim and determined. Note that the little Prince not only comes out of a court background of sterile pride but also finds comfort solely with women. Men, as imaged in the book, have little tenderness or sensitivity to childhood, beauty, or friendship. Only the Prince's mother, godmother, and occasional nurses care for him. Perhaps the most distressing theme is that of loneliness. Mrs. Craik seems to suggest that the child's "first childhood" may contain a kind of unselfconscious happiness but that later access to books may make the child fill with longings for the "world." Preadolescence becomes imaged as a time of wishing for magical flight to and power over the mysterious outside world. No doubt it is that sort of time for many children, but the total absence of youthful companionship and fellowship from the Prince's world makes it undeniably depressing. Mrs. Craik teaches the hard lesson that we must bear our lot, no matter how sad, but the situation into which she places the boy may seem to some beyond the limits of a normal child's endurance.

"You must be content to stay just what you are," says the godmother to the lame Prince. Mrs. Craik alleges that this conservative, unhopeful advice is meliorated by the tone in which it is given: "very firmly, but gently, too"; "her sweet manner softened the hardness of the words." Earlier we were told that the godmother's voice was "shrill but soft"; she is old but her smile is "sweet and childlike" just as the Prince is said to be in his turn "innocent" but very "penetrating." Some readers may find that Mrs. Craik pushes her paradoxes rather hard and that her attempts to put an adult view of life in a childlike perspective may be less than wholly successful. The bitter pill of having "to stay just what you are" can hardly be sugar-coated enough to become truly palatable. Even if we take the tale as intended to cheer or support mainly children who are specifically handicapped as was the Prince, we still may doubt whether the faded wisdom of the godmother (or the author) prating on about "the inevitable" and "making the best" of a bad lot and so on can hope to rouse the spirits of youth.

Luckily, after four sometimes dreary chapters, the little lame Prince and the story get off the ground. It's not easy to say why incidents of flying are rife in children's literature. Do children experience their growth partly or sometimes as a rise toward weightlessness? Are their fancies more nearly liberated than ours from the inalterable rules of gravity? Do they dream or think of flying in memory of relative weightlessness in the womb or in some quasi-sexual way? Whatever the reason, one may easily note the importance of flying in works of MacDonald, Carroll, L. Frank Baum, Sir James Barrie, A. A. Milne, and others. Compared to the incidents of flying in much other children's literature, the lame Prince's adventures with the travelling cloak may not impart much kinesthetic feeling, however, for Mrs. Craik's mind-set seems to be inhabited more by morals than by muscular memory.

Mrs. Craik does give the cloak a pixie-servant personality, and the adventures with it pick up the pace and variety of the action considerably. Whether the meaning of the story clarifies or mystifies in the process is another question. The Prince was supposed to "try, and try hard, before he gained anything," yet when he gets cold and wet, the bearskin and food and water appear at his wish, so that wishing becomes sufficient trying in spite of Craik's incessant preaching that "we have to accept it all," we have to bear, and so on. To deliberate, then, on *The Little Lame Prince* requires us to come at some point to the nub of its contradictions among passive acquiescence, wishing, and active striving.

Through the device of the gold spectacles and silver ears, Mrs. Craik suggests the importance for children of really looking at and listening to the minutiae of experience about them, but, again, whether Craik's own lack of detail and lack of feeling for nature encourage such naturalist's loving attention may be questioned. Craik is really less concerned with disinterested aesthetic observation than with evaluation of human conduct and the workings of society. The later part of the book pushes hard at the need for each child who would have a "kingly nature" to recognize that in social and political life "wretchedness is close behind the grandeur" and for each child "to be able to stand such a sight without being utterly overcome."

By dissipating false notions of beauty and grandeur, by showing the King helpless in his bed, the wretchedness behind the grandeur, Craik points to the true sources of beauty and grandeur as she sees them in a kingly moral nature. Her recipe for such moral perfection turns out to include three parts sheer endurance and patience and one part active winning through. The details of Prince Dolor's governance do not interest her, only the fact of his surviving to be taken away by others who want him for their king. The final chapter indeed continues to dwell upon how Dolor, when bothered by state squabbles "would take refuge" in the upper room, how his godmother continued to help him out of any difficulty," how he was "guided" by the opinions of his counsellors, and so on. He does perform magnanimous acts such as forgiving his enemies. Quickly, however, we reach the end in which the lame King announces how tired he has become and then wings his way to eternal rest with his godmother.

What, finally, is the overall tone of the story? Is the steady earnestness, the repetitive insistence on virtues of sweet tenderness, too cloying? Or is there a residual honesty and strength in the very darkness of the book? Do we accept the author's assertion that Prince Dolor becomes happy and can make us happy to think on him? Or are varieties of "lameness" in him and his story forever pronounced and regrettable? Probably no firm consensus will ever by reached on such questions. Nor need a consensus be reached. Merely considering such questions, however, allows one better to appreciate the strain of moralism that threads itself through much children's literature and brings such cross-qualifying deficits and rewards.

13

CARLO COLLODI

The Adventures of Pinocchio

The most interesting question about *The Adventures of Pinocchio* by Carlo Collodi (1826–1890) is what keeps it alive. According to most of the principles of good children's literature that modern critics and readers swear by, *Pinocchio* is an abomination. It is didactic, moralistic, and repetitive. It's the story of a child-hero brought, by a long process of ordeal, shame, and sermonizing, to a thoroughly puritanical self-hatred and rejection of play and pleasure; all along the way he is constantly either riddled with neurotic guilt and anxiety or scared out of his wits.

Yet *Pinocchio* survives as an amusing story; it remains in print and in relatively good standing in the literary histories and anthologies. The mystery is why and how.

An easy answer would be that Pinocchio is a classic figure of mischief, and "everyone loves mischief." But the easy answer, in this case, is wrong. Pinocchio is not mischievous. After the opening few episodes, in which he teases Geppetto and Master Cherry—episodes in which Collodi is just breaking the ice, before plunging into the insistent theme of the story—Pinocchio doesn't commit an act of playful naughtiness anywhere in the story. Mischief is causing trouble for trouble's sake. But Pinocchio doesn't want to trouble anybody. He just wants to enjoy himself and to be approved of by those who say they love him. As early as the ninth chapter, when he succumbs to the temptation to sell the schoolbook Geppetto has bought for him, he is "on thorns" as he does it, "irresolute and remorseful." Immediately after the encounter with Fireater and the puppet troupe, Pinocchio is already fully convinced of his immorality, and contrite about it:

> I have indeed been a bad son, and the Talking Cricket was right when he said: "Disobedient boys never come to any good in the world." I have found it to my cost, for many misfortunes have happened to me.

He falls in with the Fox and the Cat because they convince him that he can magically turn his five gold coins into twenty-five hundred, and "by tomorrow my papa will be a gentleman."

Throughout the story, that is the pattern: Pinocchio tries to enjoy himself or to make Geppetto or the Blue-Haired Fairy proud of him, but the means he uses are unwise; as a result, he suffers a devil's catalogue of physical ordeals (he is hanged into insensibility, caught in a metal trap and used as a watch-dog, turned into a donkey which is beaten and nearly drowned, twice threatened with being cooked and eaten, and twice eaten by fish). While he endures these disasters, he also suffers from knowing that his "mamma" and his "papa" disapprove of him.

> In the midst of his stupefaction and apathy his heart was pierced by a cruel thorn—the thought that he would have to pass under the windows of the good Fairy's house between the carabineers. He would rather have died.

The lesson of his worthlessness is never lost on him; he believes that he deserves everything that happens to him, even though he never meant any harm.

> If I had been a good little boy as so many are; if I had been willing to learn and to work; if I had remained at home with my poor papa, I should not now be in the midst of the fields and obliged to be the watchdog to a peasant's house. Oh, if I could be born again!

His capacity for remorse is his most valued moral trait, as the Blue-Haired Fairy tells him: "I saw from the sincerity of your grief that you had a good heart."

Pinocchio is brought to self-hatred through the time-honored devices by which parents browbeat children, only slightly embellished with fantasy and magic. Geppetto's main message to his "son" is that he has sacrificed everything for him, wanting nothing but the boy's well-being in return. Throughout the main part of Pinocchio's adventures, Geppetto's only role in the story is as a "victim" of Pinocchio's unintended treachery, suffering somewhere off in the distance, a constant source of guilt-feelings for the son.

Pinocchio's "mamma," the Blue-Haired Fairy, breaks Pinocchio's spirit more ingeniously. Her best trick is to die of grief over his misbehavior, and leave on her tombstone the epitaph:

Here Lies
The Child with the Blue Hair

Who Died from Sorrow
Because She Was Abandoned by Her
Little Brother Pinocchio

Elsewhere she toys with him, holding out the image of her goodness and her protection as a tantalizing goal for him to reach, but leaving him to stew in his own frustration and the attacks of his antagonists until his misery is complete. Pinocchio says,

> She is my mamma, and she resembles all other good mammas who care for their children, and who never lose sight of them, but help them lovingly, even when, on account of their foolishness and evil conduct, they deserve to be abandoned and left to themselves.

She has let him be changed to a donkey, beaten, and thrown into the ocean. But "as soon as she saw that I was in danger of drowning, sent immediately an immense shoal of fish, who, believing me really to be a little dead donkey, began to eat me." As a symbol for loving maternal care, this is perhaps as suggestively grotesque as anything literature provides.

The story's conclusion, where Pinocchio becomes at last "a real live boy," is a perfect image for the self-hatred and repression of his natural energies that he has been learning. He literally achieves a new self; the old one is cast aside. As a newly created "good boy," Pinocchio asks

> "And where has the old wooden Pinocchio hidden himself?" "There he is," answered Geppetto, and he pointed to a big puppet, leaning against a chair, with its head on one side, its arms dangling, and its legs so crossed and bent that it was really a miracle that it remained standing.
>
> Pinocchio turned and looked at it; and after he had looked at it for a short time, he said to himself with great complacency:
>
> "How ridiculous I was when I was a puppet! And how glad I am that I have become a well-behaved little boy!"

Pinocchio's place in the mainstream of nineteenth-century European moral psychology is easy to recognize, even from the brief description we've given here. The story frankly assumes that a person is born with a disposition to disobedience and folly, and finds the way to decent behavior only through stern education. In Freudian terms, it is the story of conflict between id-characters who urge Pinocchio to seek pleasure (the Fox and the Cat, Candlewick and the other schoolboys, the polecats, and others), and superego characters who preach work, obedience, and delayed gratification (Geppetto, the Blue-Haired Fairy, the Talking Cricket, and others). In Collodi's scheme, a worthy ego or self comes from listening to and internalizing the dictates of superego, and driving out or suppressing the impulses of the id.

But the question is, where is the fun in this for the modern reader who does not subscribe to that Victorian moralism and who doubts that pleasure should be so thoroughly denounced as it is in *Pinocchio*?

It cannot be that readers fail to see Collodi's didactic purpose. The story is too full of explicit lectures for that, on the evils of sloth and the necessity of work, the folly of disobedience, the value of school, and so forth. Apparently many readers accept the notion that this kind of moral preachment is valid children's entertainment if it is decorated with weird, surrealistic, "nonsensical" events and characters. The fun is supposed to lie in the fairy-tale grotesquery.

Thus (so this theory goes), in *Pinocchio* we have a situation the reverse of what happens in ordinary dream-life. In dreams, the unconscious releases thoughts and wishes which the conscience-governed mind cannot approve of. In order to avoid censorship, the mind entertains these thoughts and wishes in coded or symbolic form. Dream-events are weird in order to hide their naughty meanings and render them conscionable. But Collodi has the most righteous purposes in *Pinocchio*; he need hide none of his explicit theses, since his moral censor is in charge of the whole proceeding. Instead, devices normally used to make naughty thoughts seem nice—i.e., translating them into grotesque images—are now employed to the opposite purpose: to make nice thoughts seem not so infernally stuffy and righteous, and to give the book a spice of frivolity. That at least seems to be a standard argument by which people give *Pinocchio* credit for gaiety and high-spiritedness despite its heavy moralism and explain its continued popularity.

But the theory is out of touch with the reality of *The Adventures of Pinocchio*. *Pinocchio* does not turn out to consist of good advice sugar-coated with holiday spirits and naughty humor. Its humor is not spiced with the enjoyment of forbidden freedom, egotism and irreverence. What's fun and funny in the story is that a boy is extravagantly, grotesquely punished. *Pinocchio* really depends for its effect on the pleasure one can take in exorcizing and castigating the wicked. Ultimately, its surrealism does come from the same source as dream-symbolism—the need to hide objectionable feelings—because the moralism of *Pinocchio* goes too deep for comfort. It has real animosity in it. Collodi's surrealism is there to cover up the malevolence.

It is after the first few chapters (where the fun is the fun of naughtiness) that Collodi's real fantasy takes hold. From that point on, the essence of fun will not be Pinocchio kicking up his heels and having a forbidden good time, but rather Pinocchio getting clubbed and hounded and dangled and tantalized and frustrated. These things will happen to him primarily because he is young and gullible and inexperienced.

But *Pinocchio* is supposed to be a children's book. How can it be that a tale which amounts to little else than a fanciful story of child-abuse passes for a classic especially enjoyed by children? If the core-psychology of the book's humor is what we have said, how can children fail to sense it, and reject it?

Many children, of course, do reject *Pinocchio*; its currency as a classic owes more than many children's classics do to the parents, librarians, teachers, and merchandisers who keep it in print and in the movie theaters. Certainly it is easy to see that *Pinocchio* is a very parental story, showing the problems of maturation from a most grown-up viewpoint, magic and other irregularities notwithstanding.

But one really need not assume that children find nothing to like in *Pinocchio*, or even that they are automatically excluded from sharing in its cheerfully sadistic fantasy. Youngsters can believe very avidly in stiff punishment. They often love to inform on one another in hopes of seeing sinners punished; many a stuffed animal has borne the brunt of entirely righteous indignation. There is no reason why children in such moods cannot enjoy the thought of Pinocchio hanged from a tree for staying out late or chained by the neck for having wandered into a grape-arbor where he doesn't belong. The trick to enjoying this, of course, is to avoid identifying with Pinocchio. As long as the ordeals happen to a character safely at a distance from the reader, there is potentially some fun to be had in seeing him ingeniously tormented.

Besides, there is considerable imaginative richness to some of his adventures. Because of its obvious and conventional thesis and the openness of its plot, *Pinocchio* yielded Collodi ripe psychological expression on an unconscious level. Within the very general idea that Pinocchio is wild and almost incorrigible but that in the end he will reform for good and all, Collodi was free to improvise casually, and to follow unexamined whims wherever they led. He could indulge in some sharply suggestive imagery, arising from sources to which presumably his readers' unconscious interests can respond.

For example, twice in the story this situation occurs: Pinocchio flees in terror through darkness, pursued by villains, and reaches up to the Blue-Haired Fairy for help. In the first of these two episodes, the Fairy, "her face as white as a waxen image; her eyes closed and her hands crossed on her breast," announces that she is dead, and gives him no help; hooded assassins seize him. In the second, she is a blue goat, standing on a white marble rock; she "bleats lovingly" to the fleeing Pinocchio, "stretches out her forelegs to help him out of the water"—but again fails to save him, and he is swallowed by a sea-monster. Both scenes have some religious connotations; the Fairy is a version of the Madonna and Pinocchio the supplicant sinner begging to be taken out of a dangerous and sinful world. Evil, here, is something outside oneself, a force to be escaped. Good, too, is outside oneself, a blue-and-white image raised on high.

The scenes contain feelings about the maternal figure that are easy to recognize. Mother here is a distant, unattainable ideal of righteousness; she is pure and radiant and above the sea of tempestuous feelings. The perfection she represents is associated with death: In one scene she says she is dead, in the other she is standing on a kind of altar or gravestone. It is only by dying that one can achieve the perfection she stands for, the renunciation of selfish energies. Pinocchio will achieve this renunciation in the story's final scene, when his puppet-self stands dead in the corner.

Whether one recognizes these implications or not, the sense of deep meaning behind the scenes' strangeness surely contributes to their impact.

Consider one other example of the way Collodi's "nonsense" gravitates toward symbolism: the episode in Chapter Twenty in which Pinocchio encounters "a horrible Serpent." Here Pinocchio is hurrying toward the Fairy's house, in a proper Collodi state of mind—anxious, guilty, eager to get back in his parents' good graces.

> How many misfortunes have happened to me . . . and I deserved them; for I am an obstinate, passionate puppet. . . . Will the Fairy forgive me my bad conduct to her? . . . Would it be possible to find a more ungrateful boy, or one with less heart than I have!

Suddenly before him in the road is a huge serpent. "Its skin was green, it had red eyes, and a pointed tail that was smoking like a chimney." It scares Pinocchio and blocks his way. Pinocchio pleads humbly: "You must know, Sir Serpent, that I am on my way home, where my father is waiting for me, and it is such a long time since I saw him last! . . . Will you therefore allow me to continue my road?" The serpent, "who up to that moment had been sprightly and full of life, became motionless and almost rigid," feigning death. Pinocchio decides to risk jumping over the body. "But just as he was going to leap, the Serpent raised himself suddenly on end, like a spring set in motion"; Pinocchio, terrified, trips over his own feet and falls awkwardly in the mud with his legs in the air.

> At the sight of the puppet kicking violently with his head in the mud the Serpent went into convulsions of laughter, and he laughed, and laughed, and laughed, until from the violence of his laughter he broke a blood vessel in his chest and died. And that time he was really dead.

Pinocchio sets off running for home.

What does this scene mean? Why did Collodi include it? Imagine Collodi, turning out this month's installment of *Le Avventure di Pinocchio*, improvising along: Pinocchio is hurrying home, full of self-criticism and apprehension over whether his parents will take him back; he looks up and . . . what does he see this time? Oh, say . . . a serpent. Yes, that has promise. Collodi's instinct tells him that Pinocchio has not yet reached the bottom of his fall from pride. There's more fun to be had with him. In comes the serpent. It has some Biblical connotations, of course. The red eyes and smoking tail suggest Satan. This is no Garden of Eden serpent, talking in honeyed tones; it's Leviathan, the great dragon, waiting by the side of the road for sinners who try to pass by. This serpent is to be overcome not by courage or resolution, but by Pinocchio's falling on his face and making such a ridiculous spectacle that the serpent laughs himself to death. Despite all Pinocchio's soliloquy of self-reproach, Collodi feels he needs another notch of humiliation. He should fall on his face in the mud.

It is an intuitive comment on pride, in a pattern that is repeated in *Pinocchio* over and over: Pinocchio's statements of internal guilt are balanced with grotesque physical mistreatment at or near the same time—being hanged in a tree to swing like a bell-clapper, being covered with flour to be eaten like a fish, growing the ears and tail of a donkey, having his nose sprout to ridiculous length when he lies, and so forth.

One thing the serpent episode suggests is that, in Collodi's imagination, the force in Pinocchio which must be broken is masculine sexuality, and that the headstrong impulses which offend the fatherly viewpoint are the impulses toward developing manhood in Pinocchio. It is appropriate that Pinocchio's virtuous wish, the one he will finally have granted, is not to become a real man, but a real *boy*; this is a story about good–boy-hood, not manhood. Signs of his wickedness are often manifest in changes in his body: his growing nose is twice mentioned as being connected with "the most disgraceful fault a boy can have," and his transformation into a donkey is reminiscent of the physical changes of adolescence: his voice cracks, he begins to grow hair on his body, and he finds shocking protruberances growing on his person—his ears.

On this level, one can understand more clearly why Collodi pairs Pinocchio's frequent apologies and confessions with instances of his bungling and ineptitude, and the resultant pratfalls. From the standpoint of a father who sees his son growing into a man, confessions and apologies are hardly enough; the son's emerging manhood is, in itself, a threat to the father's authority.

The serpent scene makes sense. Pinocchio is, inwardly, repentant and apologetic and eager to please, hurrying back to his father. But there is still a dragon for him to pass—the phallic beast of male sexuality. How is Pinocchio to demonstrate that he is no rival to the paternal masculinity? By behaving like an infant, scared and defenseless, and by falling in the mud, his legs waving helplessly in the air. At this sight the serpent, archetypal specter of sex and Satan, muscular male potency, can be allayed. Pinocchio's humiliation "breaks a blood vessel in its chest," and it dies.

One can only speculate about how much of this unconscious meaning the typical reader glimpses and appreciates. We assume that some of it comes through to most readers, and that it might help to explain the story's durability, despite its rickety plot and its unfashionable moralizing. Certainly there are a few things "everybody knows" about *Pinocchio* that suggest it has some agreed-upon psychological impact. Everybody knows that Pinocchio wanted to get over being a puppet and become a real live boy; that he had to learn to "let his conscience be his guide," but that he also needed magic from a blue-haired fairy, a chilly and idealized figure of far-out fantasy. Above all, everybody knows that when Pinocchio told lies, his nose grew. Thus the world has distilled the story's meaning into a blunt moral thesis and a couple of weird physical images, the growing nose and the odd-colored hair. This seems, in a way, fair enough. Collodi's tale has entered the mythology of modern Western culture with its psychological core intact. It apparently speaks to fundamental feelings, however little we may wish to endorse the values those feelings promote.

14

JOHANNA SPYRI

Heidi

Of all the children's literature that has survived well and long enough to be considered classic, *Heidi* by Johanna Spyri (1827–1901) stands more solidly than any other in the old tradition which encouraged its readers to be good little girls—innocent and cute and complaisant and self-effacing. The cherubic Heidi is as extreme an embodiment of feminine love and generosity as our literature provides. And even though most of the assumptions about femininity which went into making her an ideal have been examined and criticized in recent years, *Heidi* continues to be printed and sold and read at as great a rate as ever. The social and moral vision upon which her story is predicated may be demonstrably old-fashioned and unliberated, but recognition of this seems to have impaired the story's popularity very little. Millions of little girls, like their tradition-bound grandmothers before them, apparently still delight in imagining little Heidi as she languishes in cold and stony Frankfurt, worries over her friends, and romps on the mountainside with Peter and his goats. To look more closely into why that might be is to understand a little better something of the way a popular story like *Heidi* both expresses and rises above the moral values of its author and its age.

It's customary to think of *Heidi* as a confection of sentimental optimism, an effusion of sweetness and light; and, as far as that description goes, it's fair enough. What is perhaps not so generally understood is that the story is Spyri's imaginative response to pain, of a definite, peculiar sort. At its deepest level, *Heidi* is a book for and about, not just nice people, but people who suffer from the need to be nice. The psychic stress inherent in the habit of sacrificing one's own interests to those of other people is the story's reason for being. A fantasy of health and freedom in the Swiss mountains is the medicine which Johanna Spyri offers for that distress.

There is a scene toward the end of the story that shows explicitly the essential dilemma that inspired Spyri; the scene reveals, too, the fact that she really finds no way to resolve that dilemma except by opting for the prerogatives of fantasy and wishful thinking. The episode takes place after Heidi has suffered her year of imprisonment in Frankfurt, and then been allowed to return to her grandfather's hut in the mountains. There she has regained the health she lost in the city; and her friend the doctor, like other characters in the story, has found Heidi's innocent good cheer a restorative for his own shattered spirits. But he must return to his practice in Frankfurt. As he takes his leave, he says off-handedly, "Now, Heidi, you must go back, and I must say good-bye! If only I could take you with me to Frankfurt and keep you there!"

His unconsidered remark throws Heidi into terrible turmoil. "The picture of Frankfurt rose before the child's eyes, its rows of endless houses, its hard streets, and even the vision of Fräulein Rottenmeier," the spinster house-keeper under whose tyranny Heidi has suffered. "I would rather that you came back to us," she says to the doctor.

> "Yes, you are right, that would be better. But now good-bye, Heidi." The child put her hand in his and looked up at him; the kind eyes looking down on her had tears in them. Then the doctor tore himself away and quickly continued his descent.
>
> Heidi remained standing without moving. The friendly eyes with the tears in them had gone to her heart. All at once she burst into tears and started running as fast as she could after the departing figure, calling in broken tones: "Doctor! doctor!"
>
> He turned round and waited till the child reached him. The tears were streaming down her face and she sobbed out: "I will come to Frankfurt with you, now at once, and I will stay with you as long as you like, only I must just run back and tell grandfather."
>
> The doctor laid his hand on her and tried to calm her excitement. "No, no, dear child," he said kindly, "not now; you must stay for the present under the fir trees, or I should have you ill again."

Heidi, here, is suffering profoundly—from the need to be nice. "She could not bear to see anybody unhappy, especially her dear doctor," says Spyri, and means it. She cannot bear to disappoint or offend people, even if her life depends on it. This fact comes out soon after she has been taken to Frankfurt, become homesick, and told Fräulein Rottenmeier that she wants to go home. The fräulein rebukes her for being an ingrate, and Heidi takes the rebuke utterly to heart.

She...understood that Herr Sesemann [Clara's father] would think it ungrateful of her if she wished to leave, and she believed that the grandmother and Clara would think the same. So there was nobody to whom she dared confide her longing to go home, for she would not for the world have given the grandmother, who was so kind to her, any reason for being as angry with her as Fräulein Rottenmeier had been.

As a result, she suppresses her discontentment as best she can, and begins to sicken.

Heidi would go and sit in a corner of her lonely room and put her hands up to her eyes that she might not see the sun shining on the opposite wall; and then she would remain without moving, battling silently with her terrible home-sickness until Clara sent for her again.

This is all to avoid giving any offense to her captors.

Only at great and costly effort can Heidi beat down her desire to be free on the mountainside; the emotional strain in her unselfishness is immense. If she were a real girl in a real world, presumably the wise thing for her to do would be to come down a little from her ideal of total obedience and self-abnegation, and to assert her own selfish wishes a little, in some tolerable balance with the wishes of other people. But Heidi's is a fictitious world, predicated on the idea that Heidi's selflessness is both good and necessary (necessary in the sense that those principles upon which one's personality has been built as squarely as Heidi's has been built on unselfishness are no longer really open to dispute in one's own mind). On one level, Spyri is preaching that one ought to be good, like Heidi. On another, she is comforting those who are caught in the trap of being like Heidi, by fabricating a wonderful story in which that is a very satisfying way to be. Spyri's imagination has constituted the world of *Heidi* so that Heidi can have her cake and eat it too. She can be an ideal embodiment of self-renunciation, and at the same time find happiness and self-fulfillment.

Put most generally, the question Heidi's homesickness raises is "What should one do when her desires are being painfully frustrated?" Johanna Spyri's explicit answer is a theological one: Trust and wait patiently on God's will. "God is a good father to us all, and knows better than we do what is good for us," she has the wise old grandmother say. "If we ask Him for something that is not good for us, He does not give it, but something better still, if only we will continue to pray earnestly and not run away and lose our trust in Him." That is Spyri's intended thesis. But the turn of events in the story by which she puts her thesis into action reveals an implicit thesis which Spyri may or may not have been entirely aware of.

Racked with misery though she is, Heidi accepts the grandmother's advice. She complains to no one, and prays that God will help her. Her mental distress is driven inward. She begins to walk in her sleep, and when her white-clad figure moves through the darkened house the servants think she is a ghost. Herr Sesemann and the doctor investigate and discover her plight. Sesemann sympathizes with her completely.

> "What!" he exclaimed, "the child a sleep-walker and ill! Home-sick, and grown emaciated in my house! All this has taken place in my house and no one seen or known anything about it!... Take the child in hand ... make her whole and sound, and then she shall go home."

In this solution to Heidi's problem, what exactly becomes of the argument that one should never complain or demand, but only pray for God's help? Heidi does get what she wants, to return to the mountains. But from Herr Sesemann's reaction we see that she could have had that all along, if she had just spoken up; the obstacles have been small or imaginary, and her keeping silent has actually prolonged her suffering.

Yet nevertheless we are clearly intended to feel that it is to Heidi's credit that she does not complain. The fact that from a practical point of view it would have been better for Heidi to take her problem directly to grandmother or Herr Sesemann is glossed over and absorbed into Spyri's unanalytical sense that patient and docile is the best way to be. Heidi has adhered to her selfless ideal of never imposing her wishes on anyone. Her conscience has bravely stifled her desire for freedom, leaving her unconscious mind and her ailing body to make the gesture that attracts Herr Sesemann's attention and brings relief. And that, according to the belief in selflessness by which Spyri's imaginary world operates, is for the best.

In this central episode, Spyri has said that the child should suffer adversity without protest—even though she has shown that suffering could be legitimately allayed if one just let the benevolent authorities know about it. This is not an inconsistency on Spyri's part; it simply indicates the paradox which lies at the base of her fantasy world. In that world, selflessness has a kind of magic power to bring rewards. One might suppose that in an ordinary real-life situation a person with Heidi's single-minded desire to help others would be taken advantage of or ignored, since she demands so little for herself. But in the story she stands as a kind of goddess to the other characters. Only the perverse Fräulein Rottenmeier tries in any sense to exploit her; almost everyone else adores her and seeks to serve her and enjoy her company. The crusty old grandfather takes her into his hut and his life, Peter becomes devoted to her, Clara and the servants in Frankfurt fall in love with her and do everything they can to help her, the doctor and Clara's grandmother press upon her food and money and affection. Peter's blind grandmother speaks for them all when she laments, "Alas! all our happiness and pleasure have gone with the child, and now the days are so long and dreary! Pray God, I see Heidi again once more before I die!"

Consider what a direct, undiluted fantasy Spyri is offering here. Imagine what it would be like to have people say about *you*, "all our happiness depends on you; pray God we see you before we die." It is a primal thought indeed, this dream that your self-effacement could blossom as if by magic into a radiance that everyone would see and appreciate. In sheer boldness, it is a fantasy similar to the scene where Tom Sawyer and his friends turn up at their own funeral and stride proudly down the aisle to the applause of the astounded congregation. At full volume, both these fantasies shout, "Am I not special?"

But if the two fantasies are similar, they are not identical. The Tom Sawyer fantasy dramatizes a stereotype of the male psychology; he arouses shock, excitement, admiration, and considerable envy. He doesn't care if people like him, so long as they are impressed by him. The Heidi fantasy is a female stereotype, this dream of a little girl who through innocence, purity, and self-sacrifice arouses the yearning love of everyone around her. Heidi in her world evokes feelings of desire so blatant as to seem almost frantic. People in that world are filled with a kind of innocent, unsexual lust for Heidi's goodness and sweetness. The way they yearn for her is caught in a scene early in the story, where her grandfather is just standing and watching her sleep.

> Just now the moonlight was falling through the round window straight on to Heidi's bed. She lay under the heavy coverlid, her cheeks rosy with sleep, her head peacefully resting on her little round arm, and with a happy expression on her baby face as if dreaming of something pleasant. The old man stood looking down on the sleeping child until the moon again disappeared behind the clouds and he could see no more, then he went back to bed.

A part of Spyri's mind recognizes that this fantasy of people needing and loving and desiring you has a sinister aspect. To be as nice as Heidi is, and to have people competing for your company as avidly as people compete for Heidi's, is perilously close to being not just their friend but their prey. Implicit in their love is the possibility that they will possess, consume, and even destroy you. The concept of love that Spyri is writing about contains, by its own logic, that possibility. But in her story she contrives to disarm any such threat, and to lay to rest the anxious suspicion that to be too nice is suicide.

In the standard fashion of fantasy and romance, Spyri tackles the problem by sorting out the pleasant and unpleasant aspects of her theme and assigning the one to a kind of heaven (which, in the story, she envisions in the mountains), and the other to a kind of hell (Frankfurt). Her Frankfurt is an exquisite torture-chamber of love and sociability gone sour and poisonous. Heidi wants people to ask of her, but in Frankfurt, people don't just ask; they demand and tyrannize. Heidi cares greatly about the feelings and opinions of people around her, but in Frankfurt, such sensitivity has long been frozen into rules and manners and social decorum. The need for love has turned into a demand for prestige; obedience has turned to slavery. Frankfurt is stone walls and harsh commands, nightmare counterparts for the embracing arms that the *Heidi* dream is all about.

If Spyri's picture of Frankfurt shows social feelings decayed into oppressive rules and systems, her picture of the Swiss mountains shows them completely cleansed and purified of all restricting or stultifying tendencies. In Spyri's mountains, love is Heidi handing out her food, her hymns, her cheery conversation, and her sympathy to her grandfather and Peter and the blind grandmother and the goats, and they loving and appreciating it, but not coercing her. The essence of wisdom in this pastoral world is submissiveness, acceptance, humility. The tone there is set not by strong, aggressive people in the prime of their lives, as it was in Frankfurt, but by children and old people for whom the struggles for social advancement are either impossible or meaningless. In Heidi's society on the mountains, people are not ambitious or self-assertive, or never more than temporarily so. Two characters— Heidi's grandfather and the doctor from Frankfurt—learn during the course of the novel that willfulness is folly, and thus learn how to enter Spyri's blessed inner circle. The doctor has suffered tragedy when his wife and his only daughter die. In keeping with his (misguided) view of himself as someone who makes decisions and controls his life, he resents and resists this assault on his happiness. He holds that "it is God Himself who has sent the trouble," and cannot accept it. His hardness of heart (i.e., his belief in the importance of his own desires) does not break down until Heidi tells him "things which she alone knew," little lessons on how to acquiesce in one's fate. Her teaching makes him emotionally into a child again.

> His thoughts had carried him back to a long past time; he saw himself as a little boy standing by his dear mother's chair; she had her arms around his neck and was saying the very verses to him that Heidi had just recited—words which he had not heard for years.

The doctor thus reaches the state of docility which is the key to life in Spyri's imaginative world. "It is good to be up there, good for body and soul," he says to himself, "and a man might learn how to be happy once more."

The grandfather's hard-heartedness has a different background, but his conversion is roughly the same. He has lived a riotous youth and manhood, wasting his inheritance in high living. He has had a son who married, fathered the baby Heidi, and, with his wife, promptly died. The grandfather has lived as a hermit on the mountain for many years, bitter toward society because it had been suspicious of him. The turning point comes when Heidi reads him the parable of the prodigal son, a story which touches his own situation exactly. He accepts its lesson of submission and repentance. "Father, I have sinned against Heaven and before Thee, and am not worthy to be called

Thy son," he finally prays. "And two large tears rolled down the old man's cheeks." He gives up defiant and self-assertive manhood and becomes a dutiful son, crying for his father's forgiveness. In learning to be a child, he learns to be an acceptable old man. He submits to a will beyond his own. Whether it is the will of God or society doesn't really matter very much; the resignation and submission are what count.

All this changing of heart takes place in the mountains, which is a point worth pausing over. Traditionally, mountains have often been associated with pride, strength, ambition, self-reliance, "masculine" virtues of risk and exertion as distinct from such "feminine" qualities as snugness and security; so in some ways it seems odd that mountains should have so conspicuous a part in a story devoted to teaching submission, humility, and obedience. Of course, Spyri has done quite a lot to domesticate her mountains, and to make them friendlier and more cooperative than many mountains are. She does what she can, for instance, to suggest that when Heidi runs off to the mountainside by herself, she is not really turning her back on society as one might suppose. What Heidi finds on the mountain, says Spyri, is not isolation, exactly, but new friends. Consider this description of Heidi playing alone, and notice how sociable an isolation hers is:

> Heidi was at home again on the mountain, running backwards and forwards in her accustomed way, not knowing which spot was most delightful. Now she stood still to listen to the deep, mysterious voice of the wind, as it blew down to her from the mountain summits, coming nearer and nearer and gathering strength as it came, till it broke with force against the fir trees, bending and shaking them, and seeming to shout for joy, so that she too, though blown about like a feather, felt she must join the chorus of exulting sounds. Then she would run round again to the sunny space in front of the hut, and seating herself on the ground would peer closely into the short grass to see how many little flower cups were open or thinking of opening. She rejoiced with all the myriad little beetles and winged insects that jumped and crawled and danced in the sun, and drew in deep draughts of the spring scents that rose from the newly awakened earth, and thought the mountain was more beautiful than ever. All the tiny living creatures must be as happy as she, for it seemed to her there were little voices all around her singing and humming in joyful tones, "On the mountain! on the mountain!"

Thus we are invited to believe that in going off by herself Heidi is really entering a loving and harmonious society of another kind. With such description as this, Spyri can evoke the great happiness Heidi might feel in going off alone, without giving up the claim that she is unceasingly warm, friendly, and solicitous of others.

Furthermore, says Spyri, there is social benefit to be gained from going to the mountains. The mountains give one strength, and the purpose of having strength is to help other people be happy. Therefore, getting away from society is a way of contributing to society.

> And Clara found a strange new pleasure in sitting all alone like this on the mountainside, her only companion a little goat that looked to her for protection. She suddenly felt a great desire to be her own mistress and to be able to help others, instead of herself being always dependent as she was now. Many thoughts, unknown to her before, came crowding into her mind, and a longing to go on living in the sunshine, and to be doing something that would bring happiness to another, as now she was helping to make the goat happy.

In the world of *Heidi*, one becomes "one's own mistress" not so she can exult in her own freedom, but "to be able to help others." That is the order of things in Spyri's moral perspective.

But the moral perspective is only part of the story; and when all's said and done, there stand those mountains, freighted with meaning that is not caught by calling them "friends," or talking of how one learns altruism under their influence. Whatever Spyri may say about the rightness of being a good little girl, you cannot mistake the feeling she has for the strong, deep-voiced winds and crags outside grandfather's hut. In the context of her dutiful thoughts on being a loving and helpful female, the mountains refer to a world utterly apart from the social demands to which the good little girl is constantly subjected.

> The thing which attracted [Heidi] most, however, was the waving and roaring of the three old fir trees on these windy days. She would run away repeatedly from whatever she might be doing, to listen to them, for nothing seemed so strange and wonderful to her as the deep mysterious sound in the tops of the trees. She would stand underneath them and look up, unable to tear herself away, looking and listening while they bowed and swayed and roared as the mighty wind rushed through them.

With their connotations of force and alienness and indifference, the mountains are a crucial part of the *Heidi* fantasy. They are the antithesis, the necessary antidote to the indoor world of obedience and responsibility which is the native habitat of the good little girls this story is for. The mountains bear witness to the selfish needs and energies that have no comfortable place in the strict philosophy of niceness, and they speak compellingly to those who believe in being nice, and can thrill to the thought of a good little girl whom everyone loves—but who feel, too, the allure of a mountain fastness where love and responsibility can be blown away in a mighty wind that shakes the firs like toys.

15

LEWIS CARROLL

Alice's Adventures in Wonderland

Charles Lutwidge Dodgson (1832–1898) was born in Cheshire and was the eldest of eleven children. His father, a cleric, hoped that his son would enter the Church and provided him an exemplary education. At Richmond Grammar School, Rugby, and Christ Church, Oxford, the young Dodgson (pronounced "Dodson") proved himself a fine student, particularly in mathematics and classics, but though he was ordained deacon in 1861, he never took holy orders, and he chose to teach mathematics at Oxford rather than to minister to a parish. Apparently, he also had some scruples of conscience concerning his ineradicable love of theatrical and other entertainments. At Oxford, Dodgson had formed the habit of attending music halls, and he delighted in their combinations of plays, skits, patter songs, parodies, and comic dialogues. At about the same time, he began publishing his own skits and verses, and, from the Latinized reversal of *Charles Lutwidge*, he coined the pen name *Lewis Carroll*.

Carroll was shy, deaf in one ear, and had a stammer. He made friends perhaps most easily with young girls, whom he liked to amuse, photograph, and occasionally kiss. Though he did, infrequently, photograph and draw young ladies in the nude, and though his attachments undoubtedly had an erotic component, Carroll was never accused of any indecency or impropriety.

The dean of Carroll's college, Henry Liddell, had three daughters—Lorina, Alice, and Edith. On July 4, 1862, when Alice was nine, Carroll and a friend accompanied the three girls on an excursion and picnic, during which Carroll recounted a version of "Alice's Adventures Underground." Alice asked for a copy in writing, and Carroll completed a manuscript with his own illustrations in February of 1863. Several adult acquaintances—including Henry Kingsley and George MacDonald—saw it, and Carroll was urged to publish it. A revised version, with drawings by the noted illustrator and cartoonist John Tenniel, was printed in July of 1865. The work sold well, and Carroll added *Through the Looking Glass* seven years later.

The *Alice* books did much to revolutionize the themes and forms of children's literature. Carroll traded conventional edification for thought-provoking entertainment, and his mixtures of wordplay, nonsense, adult-baiting, violence, nightmare, and comedy pushed the whole concept of writing for children light years ahead of the generally safe and sentimental didacticism of the earlier literature. *Alice's Adventures in Wonderland* constitutes a perennial enigma for all readers. Is it primarily funny or primarily frightening? Is Alice to be thought of as little, overpolite, easily cowed, too focused on manners, snobbish, often bored, often in tears? Or is she to be thought of as courageous, in love with adventure and fun, indomitably seeking self-understanding and her own maturity? The creatures Alice meets are mostly "mad," yes, but by *mad*, does Carroll mean senseless or angry? What is he saying about the nature of language and logic, reality, and growth and time? In *Alice* what are rules, manners, and social conventions for? What makes the creatures of Wonderland so original and so fascinating? Does Carroll make a case for linking creativity and perverseness? What is the basic human image that emerges from the book? To these and related questions readers will frame divers answers, but there will always be agreement on the central fact: the astounding brilliance of Carroll's tragicomedy.

No parent, teacher, or critic can really "do justice" to *Alice in Wonderland*. The work is far too dense and multivalent to be explicated and interpreted at all satisfactorily, and the work now has become surrounded by so much mystification and hoopla that interested readers must pick their way carefully through a mass of theories and countertheories about Carroll and *Alice* if they wish to guide themselves or any children to sensible understanding and judgment of the work.

It may be best to begin by attempting a "naive" reading of the text. One might usefully chart for oneself what happens in the twelve mock-epic chapters, keeping special track of Alice's changes in size. It is an open question whether the basic sequence of adventures suggests a progression in knowledge and mood. Alice might be seen as moving from a kind of birth trauma—falling down the tunnel, the long low hall, the amniotic pool—through meeting little animals (mouse, rabbit, lizard, caterpillar, pigeon) to meeting larger animals and adult humans. Her adventures intensify in the sense that the Duchess and plight of the baby seem more powerful and threatening than the Caucus Race or Caterpillar, and the tea party picks up the pace of madness while the Queen of Hearts and the Mock-Turtle adventures introduce increased fear and nostalgia ("off with her head," songs of voracious shark and panther). Then comes the final trial, a full social event in which Alice reaches the limit of her frustration and anger, asserts herself aggressively, yet wakes to "dead leaves" and "dull reality." Alice is in one sense "socialized" but with decidedly mixed results (just as in *Through the Looking-Glass* she becomes Queen all right yet finds it is not all "feasting and fun").

Another way to approach the same sequence of adventures is to note that Alice is engaged in a romance quest for her own identity and growth, for some understanding of logic, rules, the games people play, authority, time, and death. How each adventure contributes to or deepens the multiple quest is something each reader may answer variously, yet each time with keen connection to the work. Certainly as children's literature, the adventures are entertaining, but within the playfulness lies another dimension in which Alice repeatedly cries, is treated rudely, fears for her safety or life, and becomes genuinely angry. The book would not have fascinated millions if it were superficial fantasy. When the Caterpillar asks Alice, " 'Who are *you*,' " and Alice can barely stammer out a reply, " 'I—hardly know,' " then Carroll is exposing the quintessential vulnerability of the child whose growth and knowledge of self and the world vary so greatly from day to day that a sense of answerable identity becomes highly precarious if not evanescent.

An obvious and crucial feature of Alice's meetings with the animals is that she, unlike the heroes in tales of the Brothers Grimm or Hans Christian Andersen, is rarely aided by the creatures she meets. Whereas in a tale of Grimms or Andersen or John Ruskin, the protagonist's meeting with a helpful bird or beast would signal his or her charity toward the world or nature, and signal a concomitant abandoning of pure self-interest or pride (often represented in greedy siblings), in the *Alice* story, the animals do not represent nature responsive to innocence, good will, and charity, but rather they are masks for roles and attitudes of humans in a society based upon competitiveness and pride. Alice does not go out into nature but down into dreams and the sub- or un-conscious. No wind, wave, or mountain appears in Wonderland to provide a breath of feeling tone or a sense of living nature. The focus is relentlessly closed, societal, and sophisticated. The animals are chosen largely for incidental associations (mouse with long tail/tale, grinning Cheshire cat, crazy March hare, etc.) that allow for puns or eccentric personalities and behavior. Alice enters a world of intensely insecure but aggressively defensive adults whose narrowness of outlook expresses itself continually in attacks upon the reality or propriety of Alice in her appearance and behavior. Alice's consequent bewilderment is the subject of much mirth, but always ambivalence abounds because of the grotesque disparity in power and politeness between Alice and those she meets.

Carroll's introductory poem or proem sets up a paradigmatic set of conversational vectors and power relations governing the book. The story is told on a "leisurely," "golden," "dreamy" afternoon, but the relations between storyteller and listeners are not equally relaxed or reciprocal. The listeners are "cruel," "imperious," issuing "edicts," and constantly interrupting. The storyteller is "weak" and "weary." His wells of fancy are "drained." "What," he asks, "can one poor voice avail / Against three tongues together?" Admittedly this is all tongue-in-cheek, but still it invites us to see oral exchange in the book as struggle, as expression of power relations. What can Alice's one poor voice avail against all the tongues amassed to confront and confound her? Then again, Carroll appears ambivalent about the nature of the story and its telling. He admits the wonders to be "wild," yet says the "chat" with bird or beast is "friendly." But how many of Alice's conversations really are friendly? Carroll also says that his storyteller's breath is "too weak / To stir the tiniest feather," but later in the poem he says that the events of the tale were "hammered out." Here is a perhaps characteristically British ambivalence between the leisurely style and surface of deportment and fiercer struggles of the character within. As the poem ends, we are invited to think of Alice's adventures as a "childish story" placed among "childhood's dreams," yet also the story is compared to a "withered wreath of flowers." At the heart of *Alice* may be a simultaneous defense of the dream of childhood's spontaneous, gentle, innocent beauty assailed by adult stuffiness and pride and also a wistful recognition of the imperious nature of the child who demands growth and accepted entry into that very adulthood which will eclipse childish innocence.

Some readers will resist seeing *Alice* not just as silly happy fantasy adventures but also as satire, sometimes hard-driving satire, directed at unruly egos everywhere, at adult attitudes toward children, at the foibles of various social classes, at our pretensions to logic and to manners, and at the child's absorption in self and in the gyrations of its developing personality. Certainly in the very first chapter we are asked to be amused at Alice's opinions and behavior. She does not see the use of books without pictures; when she pops down the rabbit hole she "never once" considers how to return; she likes "showing off her knowledge" and saying "nice grand words" without the "slightest idea" what they mean; she does not want to be thought "an ignorant little girl"; she lets the question "Do cats eat bats?" reverse itself, suggesting that she is quite susceptible to bouts of illogic. In the second chapter she mocks "Mabel's" lack of knowledge and her "poky little house" and her few toys in a way that obviously leaves Alice the target of our amusement. But then when she begins meeting the generally rude and eccentric creatures in Wonderland, the equation of satire shifts from bemusement at Alice's ignorant innocence (her unintended insults to the mouse, for example) toward a special combination of laughter at antics of the brusque, logic-chopping creatures and sympathy for the plight of Alice who is forever fearful lest one of the creatures be offended in some way. We should take note of the number of times Alice cries, or does "not dare to laugh," or finds herself treated harshly. Once one notes the prevailing dynamics of her interchanges with the creatures, then one may recognize what a delicate matter it becomes to be confident of the tone in which various exchanges and comments should be read. What, for example, should be the kind and degree of sympathy or pity we feel for Alice when Carroll writes: " 'I didn't mean it!' pleaded poor Alice. 'But you're so easily offended, you know!' "? Or "And here poor Alice began to cry again, for she felt very lonely and low-spirited"?

Once we recognize that Alice is easily and often dispirited, we may see better the significance of the fact that she is also very resilient and re-buoyant. She consistently comes back for more. In this portrayal of her endurance and comic bounce of spirit, Carroll sides with many writers of children's classics such as Andersen in "The Snow Queen" or Ruskin in *The King of the Golden River* or Robert Louis Stevenson in *Treasure Island*, all of whom reveal youth's incredible capacity to endure the shocks of local defeat and yet keep coming on for final gain. Children's literature in this sense becomes a recognition that *life is on their side*, and the literature also becomes a celebration of that fact.

One source of Alice's lively resiliency is her curiosity. We are told in the third paragraph of the book that Alice follows the rabbit because she is "burning with curiosity." Soon she finds things becoming "curiouser and curiouser." In Carroll's world, curiosity leads toward that which is curious, and the curious borders on the very strange, and the very strange borders on the mad ("we're all mad here"), and the mad borders on the angry. There is a surprising amount of violence, real and threatened, in *Alice*, and readers owe it to themselves to note its occurrences and to reach some conclusions as to its meanings. Does it appeal to children (who often experience violent emotions and behavior as part of daily life)? Or does it frighten them? Or both? We know from amusement parks that fun and fear are sometimes compatible for children. When is Alice said to be frightened? How does she respond to her fear? How often is she delighted? When does she laugh? Does she ever give in to the nonsense and argument? Enjoy it? " 'It's really dreadful,' she muttered to herself, 'the way all the creatures argue. It's enough to drive one crazy!' " The violence of the cook and Duchess produces "an agony of terror" in Alice, but how seriously does she take her own suffering? How seriously do we? Notice how often Alice faces a fear of death, such as by shrinking away to nothing or in threats of headchopping or just growing ever older. There are implicit connections in *Alice* among youth, curiosity, and time. Alice's curiosity is allied to her desire to learn to grow. In *Through the Looking-Glass*, she wants to become and does become a Queen. In *Alice*, she asserts her larger being at the end. But the way of curiosity or growth leads also to eventual extinction, and much of the nonsense seems designed to baffle curiosity and stop time, as if to provide an antidote to death:

> "Would you tell me, please, which way I ought to go from here?"
> "That depends a good deal on where you want to get to," said the Cat.

"I don't much care where—" said Alice.

"Then it doesn't matter which way you go," said the Cat.

"—so long as I get *somewhere*," Alice added as an explanation.

"Oh, you're sure to do that," said the Cat, "if you only walk long enough."

Alice is ridiculed for trying to actually get somewhere or do something with her time.

Alice sighed wearily. "I think you might do something better with the time," she said, "than wasting it in asking riddles that have no answers."

"If you knew Time as well as I do," said the Hatter, "you wouldn't talk about wasting *it*. It's *him*."

"Perhaps not," Alice cautiously replied; "but I know I have to beat time when I learn music."

"Ah! That accounts for it," said the Hatter. "He won't stand beating. Now, if you only kept on good terms with him, he'd do almost anything you liked with the clock."

Certainly *Alice in Wonderland* fairly bristles with odd characters and conversation fit to fascinate anyone from eight to eighty. The varieties of fascination can be understood partly in terms of the kinds of wit, play, amusement, and nonsense present in the book. Selected examples of puns, parodies, and put-downs should be readily recognizable, such as *non sequiturs* like "It was the *best* butter, you know," and perverse literalisms, such as the Hatter's about "beating time," and capital rude remarks such as the Gryphon's about "uglifying." Then there are the gnomic tags such as the Duchess's "morals," the riddles, and the sheerly inventive wordplay as in the Mock Turtle's account of his school subjects. Once the variety and detail of Carroll's "nonsense" are noted, one is in a much better position to discuss some of the implications of the kaleidoscopic wordplay. Is Carroll reminding us that language, knowledge, and communication are not the clear, pragmatic, purposeful tools we generally assume? Is he drawing connections between game and bafflement or between play and non-purposiveness? Is he exposing his and our delight in using language to confuse and ridicule others? Is he suggesting that sense is balanced precariously close to nonsense in a highly volatile or "reversible" world of double-meanings and looking-glass effects? Undoubtedly many readers will want to extend such questionings in directions of their own choosing. At some point, they may find it helpful to consult a few books on *Alice* such as the Norton *Alice*, edited by Donald Gray, or the *Annotated Alice*, edited by Martin Gardner. Each of these is readily available in paperback, and each has an extensive bibliography on Carroll and the *Alice* books.

Working back and forth between a fairly simple-minded reading or discussion of *Alice* and then a less simple-minded reading or discussion is one productive way to appreciate the humor and fun and yet move on to note the residual tartness and thoughtfulness. Carroll wrote an epilogue poem to *Through the Looking-Glass* and ended it with the lines: "Life, what is it but a dream?" In *Alice*, life is both a dream and a joke. We need, perhaps, to "get" and enjoy the joke but also to realize that Carroll is saying the joke of life is on us (though still funny), just as the joke most of the time is on Alice. Alice offers to readers who are relatively new at the serious study of literature a splendid opportunity to learn respect instead of suspicion for one of the great modes of literature, satire. Satire seems duplicitous and overly sophisticated to some readers who are easily put off by it. But *Alice* provides such genuine delight as well as mystification that such readers may be willing to work with their distrust and modify it. Tenniel's illustrations may be studied in this connection to underline the sense of grotesque vivacity that animates the creatures. We need to ponder why Tenniel drew Alice as he did, making her look somewhat mature and severe. How does Tenniel's version of Wonderland compare to Disney's? Why would Carroll want a political cartoonist to illustrate the book? What qualities in the text are emphasized by Tenniel? Certainly Tenniel's drawings belie the cuteness and sentimentality sometimes associated with Alice and even promoted to some extent by Carroll's own framing commentary.

After being considered "for itself," *Alice* should be brought back into contexts of genre and of historical development in children's literature. Carroll mocks the conventions of quest stories such as the Grimms' tales in which the hero or heroine penetrates strange lands to win a consummate reward. Carroll mocks, furthermore, the tradition of didactic literature for children as in his parodies of supposedly edifying poems. He attacks also the vein of Romantic and Victorian sentimentalism that sees the child as savior of society and nature, Ruskin's Gluck pushed to the extreme. At the end of *Alice*, Alice shouts: "Who cares for you? . . . You're nothing but a pack of cards!" Allowing for a lurking pun in "cards," this finale may sum up part of Carroll's attitude to social organization and "fellowship." A sometimes reclusive bachelor who never married or formed much in the way of close and lasting friendship, Carroll's motto would hardly have been "only connect." Whom should Alice care for and why are questions the book may be asking. It comes up somewhat empty-handed. This is the world of Victorian doubt and isolation in which the little lame Prince must bear his own sufferings in a lonely tower. The fatuous Duchess remarks:

> " 'Oh, 'tis love, 'tis love, that makes the world go round!' "
> "Somebody said," Alice whispered, "that it's done by everybody minding their own business!"
> "Ah well! It means much the same thing," said the Duchess.

Love, then, becomes a matter of minding your own business, a kind of self-love. Alice's adventures tell us why. Yet we may be thankful that Carroll so honestly portrays our universal, if laughable, insistence upon minding each other's business.

16

LOUISA MAY ALCOTT

Little Women

Although Louisa May Alcott (1832–1888) drew heavily and uncalculatingly on her own childhood memories for material in *Little Women*, and although this novel is in some respects one of the most realistic of children's classics, yet it has come to serve for many readers—including perhaps some of its earliest readers—as a myth or enduring fantasy. Alcott's intense devotion to her vision of sisterhood and the family prompted her to create in *Little Women* a world which is, in its way, as compellingly imaginary as the world of the riverbank animals in *The Wind in the Willows* or the world of high-sea adventure in *Treasure Island*. Long after Alcott's social and moral and psychological attitudes have become old-fashioned and unstylish, readers continue to read *Little Women* for the vivid sense it gives of a certain kind of life, a certain moral and emotional ambience which they find not quaint but positively magnetic.

Little Women contains numerous moral maxims; they as much as anything give the book its old-fashioned flavor: "Work is wholesome, and there is plenty for everyone; it keeps us from ennui and mischief, is good for health and spirits, and gives us a sense of power and independence better than money or fashion." "When you feel discontented, think over your blessings and be grateful." "Learn to know and value the praise which is worth having, and to excite the admiration of excellent people by being modest as well as pretty." "Don't you feel that it is pleasanter to help one another, to have daily duties which make leisure sweet when it comes, and to bear and forbear, that home may be comfortable and lovely to us all?" Taken out of context like this, they can seem smug and self-righteous. Even in context they strike some readers that way; but for others, those who find in Alcott's book a strong and bracing sense of how to look at life, the moral sententia are part of that earnestness and definiteness of purpose and effort that make the March girls' lives such a pleasure to participate in.

In her opening chapter, Alcott seems intent on setting up a kind of mechanical schema for teaching moral lessons in her story, when she invites the reader to consider it a kind of real-life *Pilgrim's Progress*. Each of the March girls confesses to a character fault, a "bosom enemy" that she resolves to overcome, in the manner of Bunyan's Christian ridding himself of his spiritual burdens. Meg cares too much about her looks and too little about work; Jo is too "rough and wild" and high-tempered; Amy is selfish; Beth is shy. And, indeed, several succeeding chapters focus on how these faults figure in the girls' lives. Meg mingles with the rich and glamorous at a house-party, and receives a comeuppance of sorts; Jo loses her temper at Amy, Amy almost drowns as a consequence, and Jo learns a sobering lesson about controlling her anger; Amy goes through a "Valley of Humiliation" at school because of her selfish treatment of another schoolgirl; and Beth has to overcome her shyness in order to enjoy the pleasure of playing the splendid piano next door in the Laurence manor.

It soon becomes clear, however, that Alcott is not really going to reduce the story of the March family to a series of fables preaching a selfless docility or the totalitarian suppression of unruly appetites that lies at the root of *Pilgrim's Progress* (or, to mention other moralistic works among children's classics, *Struwwelpeter* or *The Adventures of Pinocchio*). Meg's appreciation of her own beauty may be her "bosom enemy" in Bunyan's terms, but it is also what makes her interesting. Jo may be an undisciplined tomboy who ought to control her rambunctiousness better, but her energy keeps the family spirits afloat. Amy is the spoiled and pampered baby of the family, but her heartfelt unwillingness to accept the ideal that she should live only for others gives her a spark of vitality that circulates through the household. And the idea that Beth's shyness (so extreme that in a real-life situation it would have to be called pathological) is a moral failing—well, that notion is hardly given even the pretense of a hearing. Beth is the household goddess to whom the other Marches pay regular and passionate adoration as a central part of demonstrating what values they really live by.

A basic difference between *Little Women* on the one hand and *Pilgrim's Progress* or *Pinocchio* on the other is that those didactic allegories are absolutist and mechanical and suggest that moral solutions can be final, whereas *Little Women* does not. *Pilgrim's Progress* is a story about learning, with God's grace, to eschew evil and reach the Celestial City, which Christian does. When Pinocchio finally becomes a real boy, his old, fallible self is cast off, and he becomes a new creature, good instead of bad. Alcott flirts with this kind of happy moral ending in *Little Women* when she has Mr. March, returned after a year away from his family, appraise the success of his daughters in making themselves good: He commends Meg for having made a "burnt offering" of her vanity and having learned the unglamorous skills that will make her a worthy wife; he praises Jo for having become "a young lady who pins her collar straight, laces her boots neatly, and neither whistles, talks slang, nor lies on the rug as she used to do." He pronounces that Amy "has learned to think of other people more and of herself less, and has decided to try and mold her character as carefully as she molds her little clay figures." But this is a false conclusion. As with so much else in this novel, Father here really does not know what is going on; he is essentially an outsider to the inner circle of females, and his appraisal of them is conventional and ultimately irrelevant.

It is Marmee who knows how the inner life really goes, and she reveals the truth when Jo asks for her help in controlling her temper. Marmee discloses the fact that she herself used to have a violent temper—and still has it. "I have been trying to cure it for forty years, and have only succeeded in controlling it. I am angry nearly every day of my life, Jo, but I have learned not to show it; and I still hope to learn not to feel it, though it may take me another forty years to do so." Seen in other contexts, this systematic denial of one's spontaneous feelings would have to be called repressive and unhealthy. But in *Little Women* it comes across as a kind of female heroism, a strength of character and purpose which is courageous enough to be admirable but not so idealized as to be inaccessible to the reader. In the end, Alcott holds out no promise of Scrooge-style radical conversions from bad to good, and settles instead for a hard-headed New England code of fighting the good fight without ever expecting it to be over.

Little Women is a book about dealing with life-sized problems; some of them are moral, but not all of them; some are practical; some are simply emotional. Throughout, it shows the value of life lived in a continual awareness of desirable objectives striven for but not quite possessed; admirable resolutions made and kept, but at a price that one has to keep paying.

The usual condition of children's classics—even moralistic ones like *Pinocchio* and *Struwwelpeter*—is unrealism and wonder and magic and exotic settings and fanciful symbols: kings and queens and fairies and pirates and monsters and flying through the air and descending into dark caves and magic spells and talking animals. *Little Women*, by contrast, is about the workaday world—about money and its absence; about housekeeping, cooking, mending one's clothes, working; about tending the sick, writing letters, planning an outing, having a headache. The trappings of *Little Women* are, in almost every sense of the word, *homely*: unfashionable, commonplace, and domestic.

Plot, in this book, is a casual, ambling affair. Most of the events it recounts are minor, incidental things, mundane: The March girls decide to give their Christmas breakfast to a poor family; they stage a home-made operatic melodrama for some of their friends; Meg and Jo attend a New Year's Eve dance;

Jo goes to call on Laurie, the rich boy next door; Beth makes friends with rich old Mr. Laurence, who gives her a piano; Amy is caught with contraband pickled limes at school and is publicly humiliated; Jo refuses to take Amy along to a play, Amy retaliates by destroying Jo's manuscript book of stories, and later falls through the ice on the river when the angry Jo fails to warn her off; Meg spends two weeks with the Moffats, members of worldly high society who flatter Meg and dress her up and make her temporarily forget her sober upbringing; the March girls hold a meeting of their *Pickwick Club* and, at Jo's urging, admit Laurie as a member; the girls experiment with neglecting their household chores and learn how unsatisfying a life of idleness is; they go on a picnic with Laurie and his guests from England; they talk about their dreams for the future; Jo gets a story published in a newspaper; Marmee is summoned to Washington, D.C., where Father lies dangerously ill; Jo sells her hair to a wig-maker to help finance Father's care; Beth contracts scarlet fever while ministering to a poor family; with Beth hovering near death, Amy writes her will; Marmee and then Father return home, and Beth improves; John Brooke, the Laurences' tutor, proposes to Meg, and Meg accepts.

Little Women is not much given to surprise or high drama or tricky plot-sequences. Its more sensational events happen off-stage (Amy burning Jo's stories, Jo selling her hair, a baby dying in Beth's arms), or are only antic-ipated (Father almost dies but recovers; Beth almost dies but pulls through; Meg decides to marry John Brooke but has not done so when the story comes to an end). It's not so much what happens to people that matters in *Little Women*; it is the spirit, the attitude, and, above all, the camaraderie with which one faces what happens.

Many classic children's stories are about gangs or cliques or inner circles of characters all the same sex (usually male): Rat, Mole, Toad, and Badger in *The Wind in the Willows*; Mowgli, Bagheera, Baloo, Kaa, and the Grey Brothers in *The Jungle Books*; Tom Sawyer, Huckleberry Finn, and Joe Harper in *The Adventures of Tom Sawyer*; Hazel, Fiver, Bigwig, and their comrades in *Watership Down*; Bilbo Baggins, Gandalf, and the dwarves in *The Hobbit*; Pooh, Piglet, Eeyore, Owl, and Rabbit in *Winnie the Pooh*; Peter Pan and the Lost Boys in *Peter Pan*; Robin Hood and his merry men; and so on. A basic appeal of such stories, it seems, is to a young person's appetite for membership in a strong, definite, close-knit community of like minded characters who may disagree among themselves enough to make life interesting but who are fundamentally loyal to one another and give the adventuring impulse a social aspect.

Sisterhood in *Little Women* is related to these gangs and chumships. The March sisters club together easily enough: They have their Pickwick Club and their Busy Bee Society, their theatrical troupe for staging *The Witch's Curse* and other home-made dramas, their communal let's-pretend acting out *Pilgrim's Progress*. Still, there is a very different dynamic or feeling to their group from that of Tom, Huck, and Joe Harper playing pirates on Jackson's Island in *Tom Sawyer*, or Badger, Rat, Mole, and Toad throwing a victory dinner in *The Wind in the Willows*.

One basic difference, of course, is that the March girls are literally sisters; their mutual ties are innate and biological before they are social. This is unusual in a classic of late-Victorian children's fiction. For the most part, the subject of siblings gets into canonical children's fiction through the older, earthier channel of the folk and fairy tales, and there it is often seen as murderous rivalry and conflict rather than solidarity: Cain and Abel, Jacob and Esau, Cinderella and her stepsisters, Big Claus and Little Claus, the good and bad sisters in "Mother Hulda," Gluck and his cruel brothers in "The King of the Golden River," and so on. For the most part, late-Victorian and early-modern children's fictionists (males in particular) seem leery of making their characters blood relations. Indeed, sometimes they go so far as to project them as being of completely different species (e.g., in *The Wind in the Willows*, the Mowgli stories, *The Hobbit*, *Winnie the Pooh*). Many authors' imaginations shy away from the emotional complications of family connectedness, and celebrate a sense of community that is higher or purer or maybe only more comfortably abstract than blood kinship can ever be.

But Alcott takes her readers right into the web of sisterhood. When she sat down to write the book in 1868, she made no bones about the fact that she was going to write about her own family. She characterized the project this way, in her journal: "Mr. N[iles, a Boston publisher,] wants a *girls' story*, and I begin *Little Women*. Marmee, Anna and May all approve my plan. So I plod away, though I don't enjoy this sort of thing. Never liked girls or knew many, other than my sisters; but our queer plays and experiences might be interesting, though I doubt it" (Commire 1: 19). Grudging and dogged as her interest in the project sounds here, and hastily as *Little Women* was written (it took a mere two and a half months), Alcott nonetheless managed to convey in her novel the devotion she had to the family circle of her girlhood. To a great extent, she incorporated material virtually unchanged into the novel: The activities, the conversations, the very poems and letters of the March girls are taken more or less directly from the real-life Alcott girls. The issue of the *Pickwick Portfolio* that Alcott reproduces in chapter ten, she assure us, "is a *bona fide* copy of one written by *bona fide* girls once upon a time."

Of course there is nothing magic about basing one's fiction closely on one's own personal history; authors have been doing it for centuries with all degrees of success and failure. The point is that Alcott approached the subject of sisterhood here with a wide, inclusive grasp—not with a grievance to air or a case to prove or a theory to advance. She had not solved sisterhood; she had not pinned it down to a single set of issues or feelings. She sentimentalizes sometimes, no doubt. Her tributes to the way adversity draws people together, or how work and discipline and resolute good spirits can overcome all problems are no doubt prettified. But of a few fundamental things she seems unself-consciously certain beyond question and they form the foundation of her belief in her family of sisters: (A) Love between sisters is like good manners—habitual, civilizing, and good for all occasions; (B) A family circle teaches you who you really are, and lets you be yourself as no other community will do; (C) Your family of origin represents the precious stability that is always passing away.

More than any other classic work of children's fiction, *Little Women* is a tribute to the family circle. The spirit of family cohesiveness, and the moral and emotional nourishment that spirit provides are the ultimate foundation of Alcott's vision. Beth is the apotheosis of that ideal. When she and the other girls are describing their favorite "Castles in the Air" in Chapter Thirteen, Beth says, "Mine is to stay home safe with Father and Mother, and help take care of the family. . . . I only wish we may all keep well and be together, nothing else."

It is not simply that Alcott believes that family solidarity is good and should be fostered (although obviously she does believe that). Even more, *Little Women* projects the sense that life *is* the family circle, and that when disaster threatens, it can usually be seen as some sort of threat to the family. Time after time in the novel, the basis for suspense is "Will the family circle survive this test intact?" It begins with the proposition that the family circle has been disrupted: Father has gone off to war and Marmee and the girls yearn to have him back. Various forces threaten further disruption: Poverty is a threat; being poor, the elder March girls must go out and work, and the possibility of the real collapse of the family's finances makes the wealthy Mr. Laurence and Aunt March especially magical in this story.

Death threatens to break the circle: Beth comes down with scarlet fever and almost dies; Father is hospitalized with pneumonia, and Marmee must be sent for. "How dark the days seemed now, how sad and lonely the house, and how heavy were the hearts of the sisters as they worked and waited, while the shadow of death hovered over the once happy home." When Marmee goes off to nurse Father, the emotional trauma is cataclysmic: "I feel as if there had been an earthquake," says Jo. "It seems as if half the house was gone," says Meg.

The undisciplined passions of the family members themselves can also threaten the family constellation. Jo's anger at Amy for having burned her book almost leads to Amy's death. Meg's passion for glamor and the high life draws her temporarily away from the hearth and its bonds, to "Vanity Fair." Even the family's devotion to charity can contribute to the danger, leading as it does to Beth's contracting scarlet fever.

But the deepest, most insistent threat, the threat that ultimately cannot be avoided, is men. The heart of *Little Women's* vision of family solidarity is the all-female household of Marmee, Meg, Jo, Beth, Amy, and the servant Hannah. They form, as it were, the precious inner circle. (Most readers notice, if they think about it, how little a real part Father plays in the emotional life of the family; even after he returns from the war, he is hardly more than a disembodied voice speaking airy abstractions, not a person on whom others really depend.) The seeds of that circle's destruction are within: The daughters grow up, become women, and go away with husbands. Young Laurie makes the first inroads in the female sanctuary in Chapter Ten when Jo puts him up for membership in the Pickwick Club. "We don't wish any boys," Amy protests. "They only joke and bounce about. This is a ladies' club, and we wish to be private and proper." Meg adds, "I'm afraid he'll laugh at our paper, and make fun of us afterward." Laurie is accepted nonetheless, on the condition that he accept membership on the girls' terms. (This process is repeated in Chapter Thirteen when he is admitted to the Busy Bee Society.) But the real invasion of the family circle comes when the courtly John Brooke overcomes Meg's maidenly reticence and extracts a promise that she will marry him. It is symbolically appropriate that he makes his appearance as a suitor in company with Father, the two men coming together to stake their rightful but subtly oppressive claims on the world of the females.

Jo, the fictional version of Alcott, voices the appropriate reaction. "I just wish I could marry Meg myself, and keep her safe in the family," she says. "I wish wearing flatirons on our heads would keep us from growing up. But buds will be roses, and kittens, cats—more's the pity!" Even the wise and stoical Marmee must agree with Jo's complaints:

> It is natural and right you should all go to homes of your own in time, but I do want to keep my girls as long as I can; and I am sorry that this happened so soon, for Meg is only seventeen.

At this point, Alcott ends her original story. The ebullient Laurie invites Jo to think about what might become of them all in the next few years, but she declines. "I think not, for I might see something sad; and everyone looks so happy now, I don't believe they could be much improved."

Meg's approaching marriage has the ambiguous emotional meaning that marriage often has in children's literature. On the one hand, in what might be called the official or programmatic sense, marriage is the point of it all, the fulfillment for which the March girls have worked so hard to become "little women." Marmee has said,

> To be loved and chosen by a good man is the best and sweetest thing which can happen to a woman, and I sincerely hope my girls may know this beautiful experience. It is natural to think of it, Meg, right to hope and wait for it, and wise to prepare for it, so that when the happy time comes, you may feel ready for the duties and worthy of the joy.

But, on the other hand, both she and Jo regret when "the happy time" actually approaches, and they are the reigning intelligences in *Little Women*, the eyes and minds through which the story is understood. Ultimately, marriage, in *Little Women*, feels like a kind of submission to mortality; one of the rewards of growing up, but reluctantly accepted; a giving-in to the right and healthy life-forces that pull men and women out of their youths and toward one another. On a certain deep level, not fully acknowledged, the idyl of *Little Women* suggests that with marriage "the shades of the prison-house begin to close."

This is why the sequels to *Little Women* (beginning with *Little Women, Part II*—or, as British editions accurately title it, *Good Wives*) are a different story, a different kind of fiction with subtly different appeal. They move abruptly away from the primary core of feeling for the original sisterhood: Beth dies; Meg marries John Brooke, bears a pair of twins and has little wistful-comic domestic adventures; Laurie proposes to Jo, is rejected, and marries Amy instead (a marriage which had no real-life counterpart); Jo marries the kindly, older Professor Bhaer (again, a marriage with no real-life counterpart), establishes a boys' school (something about which Alcott had ideas but no real firsthand experience), and is provided with two sons of her own by an author who has astoundingly little belief or interest in them. After *Little Women, Part II* came *Little Men*, *Jo's Boys* and the six-volume *Aunt Jo's Scrap-Bag*. These had some popularity and contain items of interest for fans of Alcott; but nothing else she wrote has ever had the immortal appeal of her story of the four young March sisters and their Marmee.

17

MARK TWAIN

The Adventures of Tom Sawyer

Like other work by Mark Twain (Samuel Langhorne Clemens, 1835–1910), *Tom Sawyer* is a wandering, unplanned, improvisational and episodic book, mixing its moods and its literary effects freely, always happy to interrupt its own flow with a choice comic turn, a folksy observation on human nature, a bit of stage-melodrama, or a satiric shot at Sunday schools, bleeding-heart sentimentalists, and people who put on airs. *Tom Sawyer* is several kinds of book all at once. For one, it is fictionalized autobiography in which Mark Twain (as he announces in his preface) indulges in some nostalgic imaginative re-living of his own childhood. For another, it is an affectionate satire on small-town life, an act of fanciful self-liberation in which Mark Twain demonstrates that he has outgrown his provincial beginnings and attained a height from which he can laugh at them. For another, it is one of several "bad boy books" that came out in the United States in the nineteenth century, sportive reactions against the exemplary and cautionary tales that children were given to read as moral and religious instruction. For another, particularly in the contrast it shows between Tom Sawyer's character and Huck Finn's, it is a rather probing comparative study of value-systems or philosophies of life. Finally, it is an adventure story engaging central themes that figure in many such children's stories: individualism versus conformity, risk versus security, pleasure versus duty, and youth versus maturity.

Everything ultimately revolves around the title character in this story, so a natural starting point is with a consideration of Tom's nature. "He was not the Model Boy of the village," Twain proclaims. "He knew the model boy very well though—and loathed him." We meet the model boy several times in the story: He is Willie Mufferson, "taking as heedful care of his mother as if she were cut glass. He always brought his mother to church. . . . His white handkerchief was hanging out of his pocket behind, as usual on Sundays—accidentally." He is Tom's half-brother Sid, who always says his prayers, never plays hooky, and likes to tattle on Tom. He is the "boy of German parentage" who had memorized three thousand verses from Scripture and won four or five Bibles ("but the strain upon his mental faculties was too great, and he was little better than an idiot from that day forth"). He is the citified boy whom Tom meets and whips in the first chapter, the boy with the cap and pantaloons and necktie.

The Model Boy, in short, is the boy who foregoes the esteem of other children and cultivates adults' approval by stupidly conforming to the rules the adults say they wish him to conform to. Tom, a "bad" boy, understands better the real sources of admiration and appreciation in St. Petersburg. He knows there is more to be gained from challenging and bending and mangling the official rules than from thoughtlessly obeying them. "Tom, Tom, I love you so," says Aunt Polly, "and you seem to try every way you can to break my old heart with your outrageousness." But the minute he leaves off his outrages, she brings out the tonic to get him started again.

The truth of the matter may be that, as Twain pictures it, boredom is the biggest and most fearful threat to life in St. Petersburg, and Tom is a specific corrective for that. The "sleepy atmosphere" that eternally threatens to settle in is only partly the lassitude natural to warm summers. Sleepiness is a quality of the town's mental life, an inevitable offshoot of St. Petersburg's docile, unimaginative cult of respectability. Respectability in *Tom Sawyer* translates into everyone doing the settled, traditional, routine thing—and doing it exactly the way every other respectable person does it. The town's social life is typified by the Rev. Mr. Sprague, who

> turned himself into a bulletin board, and read off "notices" of meetings and societies and things till it seemed that the list would stretch out to the crack of doom—a queer custom which is still kept up in America even in the cities, away here in this age of abundant newspapers. Often, the less there is to justify a traditional custom, the harder it is to get rid of it.

The minister, "regarded as a wonderful reader," reads every line of verse or hymn in exactly the same way. The Examination Day exercises held annually at the school are always exactly the same, culminating in the compositions by young ladies of the school.

> No matter what the subject might be, a brain-racking effort was made to squirm it into some aspect or other that the moral or religious mind could contemplate with edification. The glaring insincerity of these sermons was not sufficient to compass the banishment of the fashion from the schools, and it is not sufficient today; it never will be sufficient while the world stands, perhaps. There is no

school in all our land where the young ladies do not feel obliged to close their compositions with a sermon; and you will find that the sermon of the most frivolous and least religious girl in the school is always the longest and the most relentlessly pious.

All respectability in St. Petersburg has been reduced to precisely the same formula: people who do not really feel it or mean it going through stiff routinized motions and quietly dying inside themselves, hoping for some interruption but afraid to instigate any, lest they draw scandal on themselves. When Tom's pinch-bug sends a dog into frantic fits during a church service, everyone, not just Tom, is delighted:

> the whole church was red-faced and suffocating with suppressed laughter, and the sermon had come to a pass where even the gravest sentiments were constantly being received with a smothered burst of unholy mirth, under cover of some remote pew back, as if the poor parson had said a rarely facetious thing.

What this means is that the town is a perfect audience for just such a creature as Tom Sawyer: dying of boredom with the routines they themselves perpetuate, and secretly in love with the prankish, irreverent behavior they are afraid to commit. Tom is not a rebel against the values or the psychology they live by, really; he has a definite and appreciated role in their society. He is the town's chief scapegrace. "There were some that believed he would be President, yet, if he escaped hanging." The key to Tom's character is that he is as sensitive to and concerned with other people's opinions of him as is anyone in town—he is theatrical, willfully sensational, incorrigibly audience-conscious. All his schemes lead (with the conspiratorial help of Mark Twain) inevitably to the same pay-off: "Tom was a glittering hero once more—the pet of the old, the envy of the young."

For Tom, during seven-eighths of *The Adventures of Tom Sawyer*, sensation is the great desideratum. It doesn't ultimately matter a great deal to him whether the sensation he causes brings prizes (as when he horse-trades his way to a prize Bible in Chapter Four) or opprobrium (as when he announces that the first two disciples were David and Goliath), whether it gets him a medal or a beating. To him, being the child who ushers in Isaiah's millenium (Chapter Five) is essentially the equivalent to being the Black Avenger of the Spanish Main (Chapter Thirteen), since both hold the spotlight.

His imagination is deeply dependent on the books he reads, a definite indication that his mentality is rooted in his culture and not in fundamental rebellion against it. Ideas of gentility pervade his storybook games: his Robin Hood speaks in elevated archaisms, his pirates "don't kill women—they're too noble," his Languishing Lover (Chapter Three) thinks in the language of Victorian sentimental fiction. For all his supposed outlawry, Tom is a character who goes by the book.

And he has a conscience, in fact a very active one. When the boys run off to be pirates, Joe and Tom have trouble getting to sleep because they have stolen some meat, "and there was a command against that in the Bible." It is conscience that prompts Tom to take the blame for the torn anatomy book (because one should protect distressed females), and to come forward at Muff Potter's murder trial, and to turn "white as a sheet" when he hears that McDougal's cave has been sealed with Injun Joe inside. But it is also conscience that makes him "not care to have Huck's company in public places" and to threaten him with ostracism unless Huck agrees to become respectable. This conscience is a spotty, quirky, and not particularly humane force that raises no objections to his tricking his friends into whitewashing the fence for him, his throwing Amy Lawrence over for Becky Thatcher, or his cruelly allowing Aunt Polly to believe he's been drowned. Withal, Tom's conscience is more of an indication of his sense of place in the community (certain things are expected of a fundamentally respectable boy) than of any substantial moral ideal. It is a manifestation of Tom's deep-seated feeling that, for all the liberties he may take with the rules of society, those rules do matter to him, because society matters to him, in that only society can give the applause and attention that validate his achievements.

The depth of Tom's allegiance to St. Petersburg society is evident when one compares his character to Huckleberry Finn's. If Sid Sawyer, Willie Mufferson, et al., are the "good boys," and Tom (and Joe Harper and Ben Rogers) are "bad boys," Huck is the boy who exists, for most purposes, outside the town's moral categories. The town has labeled him according to its down-at-the-heels code of respectability. They have declared him anathema, proclaimed his shabbiness evil, and set him off-limits to their children.

> Huckleberry was cordially hated and dreaded by all the mothers of the town, because he was idle and lawless and vulgar and bad—and because all their children admired him so, and delighted in his forbidden society, and wished they dared to be like him. . . . Huckleberry came and went, at his own free will. He slept on doorsteps in fine weather and in empty hogsheads in wet; he did not have to go to school or to church, or call any being master or obey anybody; he could go fishing or swimming when and where he chose, and stay as long as it suited him; nobody forbade him to fight; he could sit up as late as he pleased; he was always the first boy that went barefoot in the spring and the last to resume leather in the fall; he never had to wash, nor put on clean clothes; he could swear wonderfully. In a word, everything that goes to make life precious, that boy had. So thought every harrassed, hampered, respectable boy in St. Petersburg.

Twain's point of course is that the respectable world—both mothers and sons—judged Huck without in the least understanding either him or their objections to him. Huck is neither evil, as the mothers say, nor a "romantic outcast," as the boys think. He is Mark Twain's version of natural man (or "natural boy"), a creature as close to being unaffected by the demands and blandishments of society as Twain could realistically imagine. Insofar as Huck thinks of himself in relation to society at all, he is inclined to accept society's judgment of him, that he is a low-down no-account. He makes a few little forays into respectability: Twain says he catches the "religious fervor" that sweeps St. Petersburg in Chapter Twenty-Two and quotes Scripture at Tom Sawyer; he tentatively tries to master the (to him) absurd rules of the literary games Tom Sawyer proposes, though he's a rather skeptical and incredulous student; and in the last chapter of the novel he vows to submit to civilizing by the Widow Douglas though he has already tried that once and found it intolerable.

Basically, however, Huck exists outside the matrix of social rewards and punishments that play so large a part in Tom Sawyer's life. He steals food, cusses, smokes, stays dirty, and loafs, not because it is forbidden to do so (as Tom Sawyer does), but in healthy indifference to whether other people like it or not. For Tom, one of the main pleasures of running off to play pirates is to imagine "What would the boys say if they could see us?" Huck's response to that is, "anyways I'm suited. I don't want nothing better'n this. I don't ever get enough to eat, gen'ally—and here they can't come and pick at a feller and bullyrag him so." Huck operates according to a very simple and practical view of life. Being a boy on his own, without much in the way of care, sustenance, or protection from family or village, he is cautious and literal-minded. Since the public attention he has received has consisted mainly of disapproval, the spotlight has no pleasures for him, and he prefers to stay out of it. (When he and Tom and Joe march into the church for their own funeral, the other two are exultant, but "poor Huck stood abashed and uncomfortable, not knowing exactly what to do or where to hide from so many unwelcoming eyes.") He is a friendly, gregarious person, though, who gets lonesome, and he is unfailingly glad when boys invite him into their games, as Tom does. "Huck was always willing to take a hand in any enterprise that offered entertainment and required no capital, for he had a troublesome superabundance of that sort of time which is not money." And the closest he comes to having a moral principle is that he feels loyal to people who are nice to him. It troubles him to think that Muff Potter might hang: "He's kind of good—he give me half a fish, once, when there warn't enough for two; and lots of times he's kind of stood by me when I was out of luck." But his sense of being outside the pale makes him unable to see any way to help Muff. Tom, the establishment boy, will come forward in court and testify against Injun Joe. But that path really isn't open to Huck. Injun Joe would drown him if he did, he knows that nobody would believe Huck Finn anyway, and he is thoroughly intimidated by the kind of public attention this would bring on him.

The same pattern occurs later in the story when Huck overhears Injun Joe's plans for revenge on the Widow Douglas.

> His thought was to fly. Then he remembered that the Widow Douglas had been kind to him more than once, and maybe these men were going to murder her. He wished he dared venture to warn her; but he knew he didn't dare—they might come and catch him.

In this case, he manages to act anyway, by going and telling the Welshman Jones in secret, thus serving both his caution and his sense of loyalty.

Later in Mark Twain's career, in *The Adventures of Huckleberry Finn*, this combination of unpretentious fellow-feeling and down-to-earth good sense will establish Huck as a moral hero, a character felt to be profoundly good by contrast to society's shallow, mechanically conventional ideas of respectability. But that is another kind of book than *The Adventures of Tom Sawyer*. In *Tom Sawyer*, the brash theatrical style is the right style, the approach to life toward which plot and event are shaped. In *Tom Sawyer*, rash and impetuous risk-taking is drastically better than the grown-ups' habit of reducing every activity to sterile routine, and also substantially better than Huck's habit of lying low and taking facts literally. In a story like this, Huck's kind of prudence comes off seeming agreeable enough, but distinctly lacking in flair and style. In this imaginary world, boys run away from home not to disaster but to a hero's welcome back; going to a graveyard at midnight brings justice, salvation for an innocent man, and applause for Tom; setting off into an unexplored cave brings not death but riches and acclaim. Deep in its foundation, *Tom Sawyer* is built upon the same philosophy as *Treasure Island* is built upon: Do the rash, high-spirited thing, show a youthful, sportive, and heroic disregard for sober advice and practical expediency, and the highest rewards will be yours.

Tom Sawyer, of course, is comic, where *Treasure Island* is more sober. Tom is no Jim Hawkins, and his author frequently treats him as a comic butt, an example of the absurdities of youthful play. Unlike Jim, Tom is capable of pratfalls, gaffes, and buffooneries at which the reader is broadly invited to laugh. Tom lies swooning beneath Becky's window in Chapter Three, and gets doused with a bucket of water; or he proclaims that David and Goliath were the first two disciples (Chapter Four); he acts the tragic death of Robin Hood (Chapter Eight) and "would have died, but he lit on a nettle and sprang up too gaily for a corpse"; he tries smoking a pipe with Huck Finn in Chapter Sixteen and makes himself sick. But this quality diminishes as the story turns more serious and melodramatic, moving more deeply into the plot concerning the return of Injun Joe and the descent into the cave. By the time Tom is laboring manfully to comfort Becky and either find his way out of the labyrinth or face death bravely, the idea that he is a posturing boy has receded pretty completely.

From that point on to the end of the novel, Twain indulges in no more laughter at the expense of Tom's rattle-headedness. Treasure now is not the imaginary "brass pot with a hundred dollars in it, all rusty and gay, or a rotten chest full of di'monds" that Tom pretended to look for back in Chapter Twenty-Five; now it is $12,000 in cold, hard gold. What jokes remain to be made are at the expense of the flabbergasted community:

> So vast a sum, all in actual cash, seemed next to incredible. It was talked about, gloated over, glorified, until the reason of many of the citizens tottered under the strain of the unhealthy excitement. Every "haunted" house in St. Petersburg and the neighboring villages was dissected, plank by plank, and its foundations dug up and ransacked for hidden treasure—and not by boys, but men—pretty grave, unromantic men, too, some of them.

The novel ends on one last glimpse of Tom Sawyer playing let's-pretend. Here the meaning of what he is doing has definitely changed. Under the influence of having become a man of property, and consequently having won the sober approval of Judge Thatcher and the other town dignitaries, Tom is well on his way to renouncing the scapegrace side of his character. He trots out the old robber-gang fantasy, this time to coerce Huck back to the regimen at the widow's house which Huck has found so painful.

> But Huck, we can't let you into the gang if you ain't respectable, you know . . . what would people say? Why, they'd say, "Mph! Tom Sawyer's Gang! pretty low characters in it!" They'd mean you, Huck. You wouldn't like that, and I wouldn't.

It is on this note that Mark Twain abruptly ends the story. "It being strictly a history of a *boy*, it must stop here; the story could not go much further without becoming the history of a *man*." He doesn't elaborate on what he understands *becoming a man* to mean, but if we apply the pattern of St. Petersburg generally, it is fair to say that it means a withdrawal into a hardening shell of safe, routinized, insincere but respectable behavior. (One is free to assume, of course, that Tom will have other options than this. Judge Thatcher has proposed sending him to the National Military Academy and then to law school, prospects that would get him out of the St. Petersburg orbit. Or one might speculate that what he has before him is the career of Mark Twain; certainly his love of the hoax, the fanciful tale, and the spotlight could be said to point that way.) Insofar as adulthood is presented in the novel itself, the prospects of maturation are pretty bleak—a kind of subsiding into the cultural half-consciousness that pervades St. Petersburg like the "drowsing murmur of bees."

It would be wrong, though, to treat *The Adventures of Tom Sawyer* as a grim warning against growing up. Late in his life Mark Twain will adopt a more tragic tone in speaking of the loss of youth, as when at the age of 65 he writes in a letter,

> I should greatly like to re-live my youth, and then get drowned. I should like to call back Will Bowen and John Garth and the others, and live the life, and be as we were, and make holiday until 15, then all drown together (Paine 2: 188).

But that is not the tone of *Tom Sawyer*. Here the tension between Tom's coltishness and the adults' hidebound rigidity is seen mainly as bracing and salutary, in that it provides that most precious of combinations for Twain, a performer and an appreciative audience. It is on this feature of the child-adult relationship that the vitality of *Tom Sawyer* most deeply depends.

18

JOEL CHANDLER HARRIS

The Uncle Remus Stories

The place of the Uncle Remus stories by Joel Chandler Harris (1848–1908) among the classics of children's literature is problematic in the extreme. On the one hand, there is no denying that they have had great impact on child audiences over the past century. Clearly Harris meant them for children (in the framework he contrived for them, Uncle Remus tells his stories to a little boy), and they have been both immensely popular and praised by critics ever since the first publication of the book *Uncle Remus: His Songs and His Sayings* in 1880. In 1946 the Walt Disney Studio adapted Uncle Remus and some of his stories for a popular movie, *Song of the South*.

On the other hand, Harris's rendering of the Uncle Remus stories is so thoroughly entangled with the moral and emotional implications of slavery and racism that it may be impossible for the general reader in the late twentieth century to read and enjoy them simply and directly. Not only is the Southern black dialect in which they are written sometimes difficult for a modern reader to understand, it is unhappily reminiscent of minstrel-show humor; furthermore, Harris unmistakably intends a kind of defense of Old Southern racial hierarchy in his portrayal of Uncle Remus as a simple, genial old black who happily serves as a plantation laborer and entertainer to the son of the white folks he works for.

It is in this last connection that the Uncle Remus books can be offensive. Harris thinks of Uncle Remus and the little boy as two child-like personalities in charming communion with each other and through a rich stock of folk-tales. Within limits, Uncle Remus sets the rules in the friendship: He some-times scolds the little boy for misbehaving, takes umbrage when the boy asks impertinent or skeptical questions about the stories, and manipulates the boy to pilfer pies and cakes and other treats from the big house. But essentially Uncle Remus and his little companion meet on equal terms, two simple, idle people who both like stories. The stories themselves may show that Uncle Remus, the teller, has wit and perspicacity far beyond those of a seven-year-old; but his dealings with the little boy otherwise do not.

The reason for this, of course, is that Harris invented the exchanges between Uncle Remus and the boy; he did not invent the tales. And it is the tales—authentic folklore, reaching back to Africa and other Old Worlds and shaped by American slave culture—that make the Uncle Remus books worthy of consideration.

The world of Uncle Remus's tales is populated primarily by animals, though they are animals in only a few incidental respects: Brer Rabbit was born and bred in a briar patch, Brer Tarrypin lives in a shell, the characters are capable of eating one another, and a few stories claim to explain about tails—why rabbits have short ones, why possums have hairless ones, and why the ends of foxes' are white. Mainly, though, these animals are people (more or less of Uncle Remus's own social class) going by animal names: They talk, wear clothes, live in houses, cook and clean, and fight over money, food, women, and status in purely human ways.

Compared with the folktale societies of the Brothers Grimm or Joseph Jacobs, the characters in Uncle Remus's world show a remarkable degree of social involvement. Their principal form of livelihood is farming (they are apparently sharecroppers or squatters who spend a certain amount of their time clearing new ground), with a little hunting and fishing on the side; but visiting is what they do most, often dropping in on "Miss Meadows en de gals," an undefined circle of females who sponsor candy-pullings and other soirees, courting, and gossip. "Society" is all around these characters. Even Brer Fox and Brer Rabbit feel some obligation to invite each other to dinner and to accept such invitations.

Enemies or not, the critturs practice good manners.

> Co'se, atter w'at done pass 'twix um dey wa'n't no good feelin's 'tween Brer Rabbit en old Brer B'ar, but Brer Rabbit, he wanter save his manners, en so he holler out: "Heyo, Brer B'ar! How you come on? I ain't seed you in a coon's age. How all down at yo' house?"

Quite a lot of Uncle Remus's narrative is devoted to such courtly greetings. " 'Heyo, Brer Tarrypin, whar you bin dis long-come-short?' sez Brer Fox, sezee." "How duz yo' sym'tums seem ter segashuate?" Brer Rabbit courteously asks the Tar Baby. "Howdy, Brer Bull-Frog, howdy!" says Brer B'ar. "En how yo' fambly? I hope deyer well, Brer Bull-Frog."

Each one of these friendly greetings is prelude to a violent physical attack by the speaker against the one he is greeting. For, despite all this socializing, the world of Uncle Remus's tales is no happy, loving community, no A. A. Milne Hundred Acre Wood; lions do not lie down with lambs here. On the contrary: The elaborate sociability and good manners of the Brers and Sisses ornament a world of great competitive ferocity, treachery, and brutality. Long John Silver would feel right at home here, as would Injun Joe and the giant at the top of Jack's beanstalk. The courtesy of Uncle Remus's characters is like the courtesy the wolf shows Little Red Riding-Hood just before he devours her. It is a system of pretense, a habitual means of keeping people off-guard. One of the politest conversations in *Uncle Remus: His Songs and His Sayings* takes place between Brer Rabbit and Brer Wolf, when Brer Rabbit has tricked Brer Wolf into hiding in a chest, and is in the process of methodically scalding him to death:

> "W'at you doin' now, Brer Rabbit?"
> "I'm a bo'in' little holes so you ken get bref, Brer Wolf."
> Den Brer Rabbit went out en get some mo' wood, en fling it on de fier.
> "W'at you doin' now, Brer Rabbit?"
> "I'm chunkin' up de fier so you won't git cole, Brer Wolf."
> Den Brer Rabbit went down inter de cellar en fotch out all his chilluns.
> "W'at you doin' now, Brer Rabbit?"
> "I'm a tellin' my chilluns w'at a nice man you is, Brer Wolf."
> En de chilluns, dey had ter put der han's on der moufs fer ter keep fum laffin'. Den Brer Rabbit he got de kittle en commenced fer to po' de hot water on de chist-lid.
> "W'at dat I hear, Brer Rabbit?"
> "You hear de win' a blowin', Brer Wolf."
> Den de water begin fer ter sif' thoo.
> "W'at dat I feel, Brer Rabbit?"
> "You feels de fleas a bitin', Brer Wolf."
> "Dey er bitin' mighty hard, Brer Rabbit."
> "Tu'n over on de udder side, Brer Wolf."
> "W'at dat I feel now, Brer Rabbit?"
> "Still you feels de fleas, Brer Wolf."
> "Dey er eatin' me up, Brer Rabbit," en dem wuz de las' words er Brer Wolf, kase de scaldin' water done de bizness.

Society is important in these stories, because society confers status, and the desire for status, to the Uncle Remus characters, is on a par with the desire for survival, money, and food. Most of the stories in *Uncle Remus: His Songs and His Sayings* center on pranks of one sort or another. The prankster may get his pay-off in taking somebody else's string of fish, or somebody else's crop, or somebody else's life; but whatever the trophy, an important part of his victory is in having looked smarter or quicker or more deceitful than his rival in the eyes of the community. To be the butt of a prank is to feel outcast; to lose a contest of wits is to feel "mighty lonesome," unable to hold one's head up in company.

Much of the imaginative force of each of these stories (and they probably should be judged and appreciated one by one, each as a separate idea, rather than as "chapters" in a "novel") depends on the artfulness or ingenuity or inherent suitability of the pranks they contain.

By all odds the most famous of the Uncle Remus stories is "The Wonderful Tar-Baby Story," a yarn with a concept as compact, economical, and inevitable as "The Three Billy Goats Gruff" or "Little Red Riding Hood." The basic idea is that anyone as clever, sassy, and impressed with himself as Brer Rabbit is, is most vulnerable not to an antagonist who matches him maneuver for maneuver, but to one who just sits there—who isn't even alive. Being the embodiment of impudence and brash vitality, Brer Rabbit demands that the world react to him, either to challenge him or pay him respect. The Tar-Baby, of course, will do neither. Brer Rabbit is a counterpuncher who depends on his opponent's misguided momentum for his victories. He is therefore frustrated by an opponent who won't talk and won't hit back and won't let go.

The story's humor depends on our seeing it from Brer Fox's point of view. We are supposed to laugh with Brer Fox as he lays low in the bushes and watches Brer Rabbit's progression from sprightly sociability ("Mawnin'! . . . Nice wedder dis mawnin' ") to irritation ("Youer stuck up, dat's w'at you is") to anger ("Ef you don't take off dat hat en tell me howdy, I'm gwineter bus' you wide open") to panic ("Tu'n me loose, fo' I kick de natal stuffin' outen you"). The pleasure we take in this is the primitive, amoral pleasure of an appropriate trick well-played (comparable to the scene in which Puss in Boots gets the ogre to turn into a mouse by appealing to his pride, or to Hans Christian Andersen's rogues getting the vain emperor to walk through the streets naked). For the duration of this one story, there is no use thinking of Brer Rabbit as "the good guy." Here he is just the cocky guy, and the plot simply spells out one of the comic implications of his cockiness.

"How Mr. Rabbit Was Too Sharp for Mr. Fox" is a symmetrical counterpart to "The Wonderful Tar-Baby Story." At the end of that first tale, Uncle Remus said a number of things could possibly have happened after Brer Fox caught Brer Rabbit. Even so, there is a neat balance or sense of completion in this account of how Brer Rabbit saves himself and recovers his dignity.

If "The Tar-Baby" showed the folly of cockiness, "How Mr. Rabbit Was Too Sharp for Mr. Fox" shows the folly of blind vindictiveness. Brer Fox is too incensed at Brer Rabbit, too resentful of his boasting and his uppityness, to think straight.

> You been runnin' roun' here sassin' atter me a mighty long time. . . . You bin cuttin's up yo' capers en bouncin' roun' in dis neighborhood ontwel you come ter b'leeve yo'se'f de boss er de whole gang.

If Brer Fox had any proper selfish use for Brer Rabbit—if he wanted to eat him, say, or make him his slave to do his work for him—this would be an entirely different story. But all Brer Fox wants is to "hurt Brer Rabbit bad ez he kin," and that, in effect, leaves the choice of punishments up to Brer Rabbit himself, since only he can really know what he would hate worst. Once this logic is established in the story, Brer Rabbit is master of the situation. All he has to do is name his preferred treatment, and the furious Brer Fox is obliged to give it to him.

The tale leaves one with the odd double impression that Brer Fox knows Brer Rabbit both too well and not well enough. He's fully aware of the legend of Brer Rabbit—the legend Uncle Remus refers to in introducing the story, of Brer Rabbit's dominance as "a monstus soon creetur" who was "at de head er de gang w'en any racket wuz on han'." But Brer Fox doesn't know, or doesn't remember, that Brer Rabbit comes from the briar patch— a fairly obvious fact about him. This may not be strictly realistic, but in a sense it is appropriate. Brer Fox hates Brer Rabbit impersonally, as it were, for his position in the neighborhood. He is hypnotized by Brer Rabbit's reputation and so plays right into Brer Rabbit's hands, never realizing what he would know if he were thinking personally about Brer Rabbit, i.e., that he was bred and born in the briar patch.

Perhaps more distinctly than the previous two tales, "The Sad Fate of Mr. Fox" shows what a primitive level these folk-tales rest on, if by "primitive level" we mean a patent disregard for moral decency. In the context of all the Uncle Remus stories together, one might argue that Brer Fox deserves to die by Brer Rabbit's trickery, since in a number of other tales Brer Fox initiated hostilities against him. But to look at the story in this way really distorts Uncle Remus's meaning as he tells it here. He makes no references to any past crimes of Brer Fox's by which Brer Rabbit could justify his behavior. In fact, as his answer to the little boy's final question shows, he is inclined (here as elsewhere) to let the story stand by itself, regardless of its antecedents or consequences.

> Some tells one tale en some tells nudder; some say dat from dat time forrer'd de Rabbits en de Foxes make frien's en stay so; some say de kep on quollin'. Hit look like it mixt. Let dem tell you w'at knows.

In and of itself, "The Sad Fate of Mr. Fox" is simply a raw celebration of Brer Rabbit's spirit of getting ahead of those he lives among and staying there. Positive social impulses like gratitude, loyalty, and cooperation (Brer Fox's willingness to give Brer Rabbit fire and tell him where he procures his beef) are seen as foolish.

Two kinds of story "The Sad Fate of Mr. Fox" emphatically is not. It is not a story where a villain comes after the hero in open or dangerous hostility and earns himself a comeuppance (it is not, that is to say, of the pattern of "Little Claus and Big Claus" or "Snow White"). Neither is it a story where the hero hatches an elaborate scheme whereby to cheat the world and make it give him what he wants (it is not, then, of the pattern of "Puss in Boots" or "Jack and the Beanstalk"). What Brer Rabbit manifests in this story is neither innocence attacked nor flashy ingenuity. He bungles repeatedly — cuts the cow's haslett, fails to trick Miss Fox into eating her husband's head, gets himself cornered in a hollow tree, lets Miss Fox come up and catch him while he's talking to Tobe. He merely succeeds in being not quite as dumb as his rivals, a little quicker to see a crack of daylight and to make for it. Obviously at some level audiences are supposed to take vicarious delight in Brer Rabbit's realizing that, when Mr. Man discovers his slaughtered cow, it's a little bit smart to hide, but it's smarter to step forward and direct the blame away from oneself. There is a similar crude cunning in his offering Tobe a dollar to fetch him a drink, and his convincing Miss Fox she ought to grind his nose off so he won't smell after he's dead and then sending her for water to cool the grindstone. This is not masterful planning by any means. It is just keeping one's feet under him once trouble is in motion, and taking whatever little advantages offer themselves.

It may be instructive to consider how the view of life projected in "The Sad Fate of Mr. Fox" might be appropriate to the slave-culture Uncle Remus comes from. Although there is a kind of glee to be found in Brer Rabbit's getting away with stealing from "Mister Man" (a rough correlative to the white boss), blaming the theft on his pal, and escaping revenge from the pal's family, it is a triumph of a very limited, sordid kind. It carries with it a sense that, even if he manages to come out ahead of his rival, even if he kills him, the struggle goes on indefinitely into the future (those who say the foxes and rabbits "kep on quollin' " obviously have the best grasp of reality). There are no "happily ever afters" in the Brer Rabbit cycle.

There are, however, good spirits—zest, humor, and verbal wit—in these stories, no matter how brutally or sordidly the characters behave. The tone in which they are told is one of rakish delight. Uncle Remus's humor manages to be both proverbial and nonsensical, both worldly-wise and frivolous, developed by folk usage into sharp patterns of rhythm and balance and metaphoric ornamentation. It is verbal play of a most exuberant kind, play carried on by a master player.

For instance, when Uncle Remus introduces a man into one of his stories, and the little boy asks the man's name, Uncle Remus doesn't just make up a name, or say that he isn't named in the story as Uncle Remus has heard it. He says:

> Dish yer man mout a had a name, en den ag'in he moutn't. He mout er bin name Slip-shot Sam, en he mouter bin name old One-eye Riley, w'ich ef 'twuz hit ain't bin handed roun' ter me. But dish yer man, he in de tale, en w'at we gwine do wid 'im? Dat's de p'int, kase w'en I get ter huntin' 'roun' 'mong my 'membunce atter dish yer Mister W'atyoumacollum's name, she ain't dar. Now den, less des call 'im Mr. Man en let 'im go at dat.

Some of his rhetorical formulae are general-purpose figures, good for emphasizing any detail. If such-and-such a grand claim isn't true, "den I'm de ball-headest creetur 'twix' dis en nex' Jinawerry wuz a year 'go, w'ich I knows I ain't." "Well, ef dis don't bang my times," says Brer Fox, "Joe's dead and Sal's a widder." A character proud of his hunting declares, "I'm ole man Hunter from Huntsville." When the little boy claims that Uncle Remus has said that rabbits have long bushy tails, Uncle Remus says he never even dreamed such a thing—"w'ich goodness knows ef I'd a dremp' it, I'd a whirl in en *un-dremp'* it." Characters don't just feel good, they feel "des ez scrumpshus ez a bee-martin wid a fresh bug" or "ez sassy ez a Moggin hoss in a barley-patch"; they don't just feel humiliated, they feel "tampered wid twel plum' down ter de sap sucker'll set on a log en sassy me"; when they get scared, they "walk weak in de knees a mont' afterwuds." Beatings are administered liberally throughout these stories, but Uncle Remus seldom settles for saying one character thrashes another; he "showers down on 'im," he "lams 'im," he "fa'rly wipe up de face er de yeth wid 'im." When Mr. Man catches Brer Fox who's been stealing his geese,

> He lit inter Brer Fox wid de hick'ries, en de way he play rap-jacket wuz a caution to de naberhood. Brer Fox, he juk en he jump, en he squeal en he squall, but Mr. Man he shower down on 'im, he did, like fightin' a red was'-nes'.

This humor is not a shell detachable from the tale itself, not a coating laid over a kernel of some other substance. The heart of Uncle Remus lore is the trickster tales, the ingenious, surprising, acrobatic judo maneuvers of adversary against adversary, and humor is the appropriate tone for telling them. Stories of all kinds are about struggle, to be sure; but struggle in a Brer Rabbit tale takes place in a psychic arena different from that, say, between Snow White and her stepmother (where youthful beauty and bitter self-love contend against each other), or that between Mowgli and Shere Khan (where honorable pride contends against mean-spirited envy). Brer Fox and Brer Wolf may die, but there is nothing tragic or pathetic about them; Brer Rabbit may win the hand of "one er de gals," but there is nothing romantic about him; and he may show a subtle grasp of psychological motivation equal to Solomon's in the story of the two mothers, but there is nothing wise or profound about him. He is, as Uncle Remus says, "the soones' man ez ever wuz," and the mood in which to talk of him is anarchistic joy.

19

ROBERT LOUIS STEVENSON

Treasure Island and *A Child's Garden of Verses*

Treasure Island is in many ways the quintessential work of children's literature. Not only is it crammed with adventure that is written in an impeccable style, making it a book guaranteed to please the most fastidious child or grown-up reader, but it also remains, like many another fine children's book, a still undiscovered masterpiece. For it is relegated to the child's bookshelf when it truly demands and deserves mature scrutiny. It raises dark and intriguing questions that a lifetime may not be enough to answer.

Robert Louis Stevenson (1850–1894) was born in Edinburgh, an only child and one of ever delicate health. Often confined to bed, he lived for the most part at home and attended a variety of nearby schools. One predictable result of his Calvinist upbringing was that he formed "an extreme terror of Hell." In 1867 he entered Edinburgh University to study engineering and embarked upon a rebellious phase—dressing outlandishly, playing pranks, frequenting bohemian taverns, and declaring his atheism. Then he studied law and was called to the bar in 1875. He never practiced law, however, for at about the same time he began writing essays and stories for periodicals, and he read Whitman's *Leaves of Grass*, which, he said, "blew into space a thousand cobwebs of genteel and ethical illusion, and . . . set me back again upon a strong foundation of all the manly virtues" (Commire 2: 230).

He attracted a group of literary supporters, including Andrew Lang, W. E. Henley, and Edmund Gosse, and on a trip to France in 1879 he met and fell in love with Fanny Osborne, an American ten years older than Stevenson, who had three children and had been deserted by her husband. She divorced her husband, and Stevenson traveled to San Francisco (crossing America by immigrant train) to marry her. In 1881 Stevenson, to amuse his twelve-year-old stepson, Lloyd Osborne, embellished a map of Treasure Island. He next wrote and read to the boy a chapter each day and began publishing the story in serial form in *Young Folks* magazine. He halted for a time at Chapter Sixteen but eventually got underway again. A somewhat revised version of the whole was put in book form in 1883, and it was an instant success. Stevenson wrote *The Black Arrow* in the same period, *A Child's Garden of Verses* (partly inspired by the work of Kate Greenaway) in 1885, and *Kidnapped* and *Dr. Jekyll and Mr. Hyde* in 1886. In 1887, seeking a healthful climate, Stevenson took his family on an odyssey that included residences in upstate New York, California, and eventually Samoa, where he happily lived out his few remaining years.

Stevenson was, apparently, a delight to be with. He loved to argue, was a brilliant conversationalist, favored salads and horses, and kept his friends in laughter. He shared his short life with others fully and well.

Treasure Island deserves study not only for its stylistic brilliance and structural perfection but also for its insistent probing of certain existential doubts. In Stevenson's hands the material world emblematically reflects unseen realities. The physical mutilations of the pirates suggest the parallel deformities of their moral natures. They sing so often of the devil out of pained awareness that their destiny may be hell, and they drink to secure momentary oblivion. Set against the pirates' world of smear, dissolution, dream, fever, fog, and darkness is the world of Dr. Livesey and Captain Smollett: neat, quick, bright, disciplined, governed by rules and courtesies. Yet in Stevenson's Calvinist scheme, where damnation and election are predestined, honesty and upright dealing are no guarantees in themselves of salvation. All are equally "gentlemen of fortune." All are in the hands of a deity whose intents are indecipherable, and Stevenson's concentration on strange hands—Black Dog's talon, Flint's fist, Pew losing his hand guides, the black spot passing from hand to hand, the sailors as untrustworthy "hands," Israel Hands, and so on—may reflect his sense of tenuous connection between all handiworks and the heart of moral judgment.

Only Long John Silver and, to a lesser degree, Jim Hawkins participate in camps of both the upright and the wicked. Silver is a pirate but not dark and bleared, never drunken or feverish. He shares attributes of Dr. Livesey and Squire Trelawney even as he schemes against them. Silver seems to transcend the piratical guilt in an effusion of Falstaffian vitality; he is able to live life for its own sake, without undue concern for the morrow. As a man who incorporates within himself much of humanity's moral ambiguity, as a comic version of Jekyll and Hyde, a man who faces his own evil, dares damnation, and just possibly wins, Long John Silver epitomizes the daring reach of Stevenson's moral speculations and the high rewards of his art.

In *Treasure Island*, the central burning image of the golden horde of coins invites readers to think "profitably" about the kinds of fantasy that tend to dominate that basic form of children's literature known as quest-romance. Treasure, to find and to hold, is the goal in Stevenson's tale. Treasure becomes the goal in Mark Twain's *Tom Sawyer*. Greed for gold is basic in John Ruskin's *King of the Golden River*, in Joseph Jacobs' "Tom Tit Tot," and in many other children's tales. But the goal of gold, or what is goaled, in these stories tends to shift its meaning and value depending upon the sort of person who seeks it and the purposes pursued. There are generally both good and bad people in the tales who seek the same treasure, and there are good and bad motives and good and bad things to do with the treasure. Men such as the pirates in *Treasure Island* or Injun Joe in *Tom Sawyer* or the bad brothers Hans and Schwartz in *King of the Golden River* would spend their ill-gotten gain on drink—they are all specifically depicted as drunkards—so that the gold stands for their ungovernable appetite, the thirsty greed that leads to "drink and the devil" and to dark isolation: Having spurned the thirst of others, Hans and Schwartz end as two black stones surrounded by rushing waters; Injun Joe dies seeking the water that drips from a stone; and three pirates at the end of Stevenson's story are left with little food, marooned on an island in the sea. Those who live for self alone become selves alone.

As money, treasure can of course be put to good use. At least it need not be spent on drink. The treasure that Tom and Huck get is invested at interest. Long John Silver carefully puts his "haul" in the bank. Sometimes, however, the stories suggest that the true goal lies beyond the treasure or through the metamorphosis of the treasure into something else. For Gluck, the River of Gold becomes the water of life pouring down once more into Treasure Valley. Success in such tales belongs to those who are pure in heart, to those who, like Gluck, Huck Finn, and Ben Gunn, are far from being commercial acquisitors. The treasure hunts teach that life is to be valued more in its persons and activities than in its things. Even Squire Trelawney shifts his sights from product to process: "Hang the treasure! It's the glory of the sea that has turned my head." None of the tales, moreover, dwells long on the satisfactions of having the treasure. It is not in the nature of some—like Huck Finn or Ben Gunn—to savor the delights of gold, and for the reader, in any event, the search has been the real treasure.

No doubt youthful readers or listeners are specially attuned to the fantasy of treasure hunting, because it promises something for nothing, or at least a reward vastly disproportionate to the effort expended to get it, which is the hallmark of infant gratifications and child wish fulfillments. People search for treasure because they think they want easy money, unearned rest, a haven or heaven for the asking. In *Tom Sawyer* and *Treasure Island*, such treasure seeking turns partly into nightmare, perhaps suggesting the guilt or the truly appropriate reward for such dubious desires. What child and other readers find in these stories is that we rarely can force unearned rewards from the world. Treasure hunting turns out to take a lot of work, albeit exciting work.

Through the psychological approach to literature we may fairly assign a variety of meanings to the treasure and the search for it in these youth-stories. Why, first of all, does treasure occupy haunted ground? "They most always put in a dead man when they bury a treasure under a tree, to look out for it," Tom Sawyer opines (Chapter Twenty-five), and of course the actual treasure search in *Treasure Island* is suffused with references to the spirits that seem to haunt the treasure ground: "The terror of the dead buccaneer had fallen on their spirits" (Chapter Thirty-one); " 'Belay there, John!' said Merry. 'Don't you cross a sperrit' " (Chapter Thirty-two). In one sense the gold in these tales belongs to the dead, and treasure hunting is robbery. In another sense the gold and the dead both belong in and to the ground, the earth, and the gold becomes associated with corpses and death. But, again, gold (like the earth) seems to have a magical regenerative property: It produces new goods. Food and other things can be bought with it just as food springs from the earth, life out of death. In *Treasure Island* and *Tom Sawyer* alike, the gold is not obtained by the heroes when it lies in the haunted place of death. Instead the gold is taken away by others, in each instance to a cave which is also associated in each story with food—the picnic and hunger of Tom and Becky and Injun Joe in *Tom Sawyer* and the food stored up by Ben Gunn in *Treasure Island*.

The hunt for gold leads, then, to mysteries of death, darkness, and finality out of which come life, bright shinings, and sustenance or new beginnings. In the oldest of literary cliches, tomb becomes womb, and life is saved from almost certain death. The gold, like its proverbial associations dust and feces, is treated as if it were fertilizer yielding new life out of decay. The child's nearest analogy may be the treasure hunt for Easter eggs on the ground, at a time of death and re-birth of god and a turning of old season to new, a hunt for the mysterious sources of generation.

The pattern of deflection or detour—the treasure must be re-sought in a new place—is of course common through romance and indeed all narrative. In formalistic terms there must be some blocking forces to prevent a pre-mature conclusion to the story: few of us seem much interested in the details of what happened when "they lived happily ever after." In terms of content, however, the deflections and detours suggest not only that the wish vies with its fulfillment for final interest, that the active means may prove more valuable and memorable than the passive ends, but also that delayed grat-ifications are superior and even superior precisely because they are delayed. Thus children, through such stories as *Treasure Island*, *Tom Sawyer*, and *Alice*, may be helped to sense the interdependence between achievement and patient striving and so to apprehend at least one more meaning of maturity.

Many of the quests in children's classics involve a search for renewal: the water of life, the golden river, a bride, a garden. Alice follows a rabbit, emblematic of generativity, who is hurrying not to lose time. Even Peter Rabbit is in search of food when he enters the interdicted place. Insofar as the renewal which is sought would enhance only the life interests of the individual quester, then the atmosphere of admonishment against greed in the tale is likely to be intensified. Peter Rabbit's invasion of the garden leads him back toward savagery—he loses his clothes, goes on four feet—and gives him a tummy ache in the bargain. The search for gold, unless and until the gold is transmuted or associated with creative forces, is likely to be similarly dark. In northern mythologies like *Beowulf*, imitated in *The Hobbit*, the quested gold is presided over by the dragon of death. Quests for the water of life or for the holy grail tend to suggest less personally greedy, more benevolent and transcendent aims, and are less likely to carry a burden of parental or religious interdiction. Certainly the search in *Treasure Island* is suffused with an atmosphere of profaneness as the greed and domination of the pirates swell and subside.

In *Treasure Island*, as in much of Stevenson's other writing, evil encroaches upon innocence and gradually threatens to overmaster it. Billy Bones comes to Benbow Inn; in Stevenson's emblematic scheme "Bones" and death invade the sequestered "hamlet" and the "Benbow" suggestive of benevolence, beauty, security, sea-worthiness. Billy Bones, described as tarry, soiled, black, and dirty, carries a chest in a "barrow," and this chest becomes associated with the "dead man's chest" of the song that runs refrain-like through the story. It is from the dead Bones's anatomical chest that the key is taken to open his sea-chest from which the treasure map is extracted. If we speculate on the semi-allegorical meanings of the pirates' names, their mutilations, their associations with the devil, their ritual of the black spot, their tearing the Bible, and so on, it becomes more apparent how significant in *Treasure Island* is the whole scheme of Calvinist insistence on the horror of damnation and the single importance of salvation. Stevenson had this scheme drummed into him by a nurse and remained deeply affected by it.

Billy Bones, Black Dog, Blind Pew: These names all smack of the grave and decay. As the characters are successively introduced, their mutilations increase from scars to missing fingers to blindness, and their evil intensifies as well. The sense of their connection to a profane, material view of death is caught not only in the putrefying tenor of "blind pew" (if not the anagrammatical play latent in Dog/God—cf. Faustus summoning the devil: "Within this circle is Jehovah's name, / Forward and backward anagrammatized"). In Stevenson's cosmic paradigm, what is profane and monstrous lurks at the edge of death since it is there that man's journey splits to the radical paths of damnation for the many, salvation for the few. Given the hellish destiny of the many and the elevation of the few elect, it is not surprising that what is damnable in the human character, though it first seems only latent though potent, should seep to the surface, attempting to prove its domination just as the pirates mutiny in apparently overwhelming numbers.

The pirates, then, are like the infamous Mr. Hyde in Stevenson's story *Dr. Jekyll and Mr. Hyde* (written in 1885, two years after *Treasure Island* was written). Mr. Hyde is, of course, the savage, diabolical portion of Dr. Jekyll's personality that is unleashed in experiment and threatens to take over the whole person. Mr. Hyde hides, as do the pirates. He is also the "hide," the flesh that thirsts for "drink and the devil" and then dies to bring its owner to the jumping off place of ascent or descent. Hidden in the name "Jekyll" is the French/English combination "je kill"; Jekyll ultimately kills Hyde by killing himself, an act which, presumably, assures his damnation. In *Treasure Island*, the view of our entwined natures is less pessimistic, for neither evil nor good is portrayed in quite such harsh and absolutist terms. In *Treasure Island*, the chief antagonist to evil is also a doctor, again a person like Dr. Jekyll who deals with death, but this doctor's name is not "I kill" but rather "Livesey," or "lives he."

Dr. Livesey threatens death, to be sure: "If you do not put that knife this instant in your pocket, I promise, upon my honour, you shall hang at the next assizes"; "if you don't break off short, you'll die—do you understand that?—die, and go to your own place, like the man in the Bible." But the person he threatens is not himself, it is Mr. Bones, exemplar of devilry and death. Still, the Doctor so neat, quick, bright, confident, and correct, seems (like the Captain) almost attenuated in his rectitude, a little formal, a bit impersonal, somewhat smug and self-righteous. Livesey laughs at the fever-stricken pirates, looks on Jim Hawkins as a deserter, and coolly thinks his way to the treasure, never sweating in the hunt. He has his redeeming traits, plainly, and we are no doubt meant to like him, but he and Captain Smollett, though they condescend to seek the gold, remain a trifle aloof in rule and rightness, whereas the heart of Stevenson's interest and empathy lies with persons more thoroughly cross-grained in both lights and darks, rights and wrongs.

Foremost among the characters steeped in doubleness of values is Long John Silver. Though a pirate through and through, Silver shares none of the piratical propensities toward drunkenness, dirtiness, swearing, and fever. Unlike the bleared and smeared crew he commands, Silver is blond, tidy, vigorous, ingratiating, cheerful. The fact that he has such a winning "good side" makes him, like Dr. Jekyll or the similarly bivalent Alan Breck Stewart in *Kidnapped*, all the more horrifying in his "bad side," his willingness to lie, steal, and murder for his own ends. It is not very easy to say just what series of attitudes and what final attitude the book engenders towards Long John Silver. Are we alternately charmed and repelled by his blandishments and duplicities? How are we affected by witnessing the murder he commits? Do we still hope that he will escape the black spot ritual of his own crew? Do we want him to escape at the end? If so, why? In Stevenson's predestinarian world, Silver should be as doomed as the rest of the pirates; Jim Hawkins himself says of Silver: "his chances of comfort in another world are very small." But do we feel that? Do we care? Does not Silver make us admire his vitality and verve, the completeness of his commitment to this life with no thought for the other?

Not only his actions such as his command over the restless crew, his befriending of Jim, his efficiency in the galley, his incredible agility in spite of his crutch, his humor, his courage against odds, but also his ways with words mark Silver off as a special challenge to our usual moral evaluations. Silver has the brief-phrased, verbal energy of command:

> "Israel, your head ain't much account, nor ever was. But you're able to hear, I reckon; leastways, your ears is big enough. Now, here's what I say: you'll berth forward, and you'll live hard, and you'll speak soft, and you'll keep sober till I give the word; and you may lay to that, my son."

This passage typifies Silver's colloquial style and the content of his never-ending message. There is the confident put-down of Israel whose last name is "Hands" but whose head is of little "account." Like all the "hands" or sailors, Israel does physical labor better than mental, and Silver takes unerring aim, humorously suggesting that even Israel's listening may not be guaranteed by his big ears; hands and mind, ears and mind, material world and invisible have only tenuous connections. Then there is the intrusive ego of Silver's speech: "I reckon," "here's what I say," "till I give the word." The ego matches the power of the admonishment which demands such controlled and civil behavior from Hands, a ruffian. The ungrammatical "ain't" and "ears is big" give the flavor of living speech among unlettered men, and the repetitions of subject–verb–adverb in "you'll berth forward, and you'll live hard, and you'll speak soft, and you'll keep sober" typify the oral-formulaic quality of Silver's speech. We are told that Silver "had good schooling in his young days and can speak like a book when so minded," but he consistently prefers a very unbookish speech in which chopped phrases, sea-metaphors, and refrain-like assertions ("Dooty is dooty," "you may lay to that") crowd and tumble forth with a ferocious vivacity.

What Silver does is to talk people out of their own views, particularly their assertions of conscience or judgment. In his tavern he out-palavers Jim; aboard ship, he seduces good men to evil; at the stockade he wins the Doctor's leniency; when his own men revolt he puts them down with words. All with speech. "I give the word" is indeed his boast. The other pirates are destined where drink and the devil will take them. But Silver is never drunk. He never catches fever. The other pirates take their business of the black spot very seriously, but Silver doesn't. They may think to set up a kind of pagan ritual, but they cannot get out from under the supervening Christian one. They cut the black spot paper out of the Bible, the "Word" of God.

Against that "Word" Silver pitches his own un-bookish word. His hair is blond-silver, but his speech is silver, too, with the sound of money and the sea.

"You may lay to that" is what Silver says dozens of times, more often than anything else. It is his stamp, his character reference. He means, of course, "you can bet on what I say," though the word "lay" may reverberate with other associations: you may lay your life on what I say; you may lay to or sleep or rest assured I'm right; and, ironically, you may risk being laid in the grave in faith of what I say. Other crucial formulas in Stevenson's poetic tale have to do with money: "fifteen men on the dead man's chest"; "pieces of eight, pieces of eight." Through such formulaic repetitions, Stevenson draws us into the world of obsessional concern with the treasure. The first chapter gives us Billy Bones singing of the "dead man's chest" and promising Hawkins a "silver fourpenny" each month to look out for Silver who then haunts his dreams as "a monstrous kind of creature who had never had but the one leg, and that in the middle of his body." In Stevenson's mind, if not in the minds of most of us, Silver or money is associated with the phallic middle leg or Long John of sex. Silver is the only man in the book who has a woman. It is specified twice that she is black, as if forbidden, and at the end Hawkins speculates that Silver has found "comfort" with her as opposed to "comfort" in the next world. Money, the treasure, comes to stand for meanings of the material, secular, profane world, especially meanings of sex, the grave, and food. Upon seeing the treasure map, Trelawney exults: "We'll have . . . money to eat, to roll in, to play duck and drake with ever after." Money to eat, to play Mrs. and Mr. with. Of course the "ever after" part is the catch, because Stevenson sees the treasure hunt as a guilty commitment to the pleasures of this life in an attempt to ignore the perils of the next. The money represents secular, material, generational appetite in guilty conflict with the dutiful heavenward longings of the soul. Jim "paid pretty dear" for his silver piece in the shape of haunted dreams. As the pirates approach the treasure pit, they are assaulted with a dread of spirits and with Ben Gunn's song "Fifteen men on the dead man's chest," but "the thought of the money, as they drew nearer, *swallowed up* their previous terrors"; "their whole soul was bound up in that fortune, that whole lifetime of extravagance and pleasure." The "whole *soul*" is sold for a "whole *life*time" of pleasure. Soul versus life: The treasure hunt is a search for total worldliness that will "bind up" the demands of the soul.

In Stevenson's view, the appetite for worldly life, for material wealth, cannot easily "swallow up" the terrors of death and damnation. Indeed, the search for the treasure itself becomes seen as a kind of feverish dream in which the pirates are haunted by the fact and knowledge of death. As they approach the treasure, Silver curses "like a madman" at the flies, Dick babbles "both prayers and curses," Jim is "haunted" by thoughts of "ungodly" tragedy, and Silver moves "like one possessed." Over the treasure of life broods the nightmare of death. Jim's final words in the book concern "that *accursed* island": "the worst dreams that ever I have are when I hear the surf booming about its coasts or start upright in bed with the sharp voice of Captain Flint still ringing in my ears: 'Pieces of eight! Pieces of eight!' "

Jim had been betrayed earlier, of course, by the same parrot's refrain:

> My foot struck something yielding—it was a sleeper's leg; and he turned and groaned, but without awaking.
> And then, all of a sudden, a shrill voice broke forth out of the darkness: "Pieces of eight! Pieces of eight! Pieces of eight! Pieces of eight!"

Often in the book, nightmares have to do with money—the fourpenny piece, the pieces of eight, the feverish and dreamlike search for the cursed treasure itself—as if men are to be shown that they may not imitate heavenly rest in innocent sleep so long as they are determined to think on and seize only the treasures of this life. Yet Silver insists, over and over, "You may lay to that." He, of all the characters, is most thoroughly committed to the world of calculation: A person's head is of "no account," Silver "reckons," "I don't care two coppers," "I laid by nine hundred safe, from England, and two thousand after Flint," and so on. His incessant calculation and greed reflect his commitment to the quantitative and material side of life as opposed to the spiritual. When the other pirates tear a piece from the Bible to make their "black spot," Silver mocks their superstitious fears. When the voice of Ben Gunn horrifies them on their way to the treasure site, Silver refuses to give in: "Still Silver was unconquered. I could hear his teeth rattle in his head, but he had not yet surrendered. . . . 'I'm here to get that stuff, and I'll not be beat by man or devil.' "

Through a combined exploration of character, action, and language such as suggested here, readers can make more real for themselves the terrific tension Stevenson engenders in *Treasure Island* between this-worldly and other-worldly demands. In one sense Silver's impious hedonism comes to nought; the treasure has been spirited away by the pious Ben Gunn who laments that his troubles began "with chuck-farthen on the blessed grave stones," again pitting money against the afterlife. But look at Ben Gunn. He is a witless noddy, no match for attractiveness with Long John Silver. (Ben Gunn's names could suggest a country-accented "been gone" referring to the lifted treasure; in Stevenson's associational mind, moreover, the curve of the action may be seen as from the Benbow Inn to Ben Gunn's cave, from ben-bow to ben-gun, from the map in Bones's chest in the Inn to the gold from Flint's hoard in the Cave.) Ben Gunn's piety is half-mocked by Stevenson who has Gunn dreaming of cheese, longing for rum, " 'the first chance I have,' " and spending his thousand pounds in nineteen days. Once the book is over, we may well feel that, despite the brooding reminders of damnation for the worldly, the overwhelming act of courage has been Silver's defiant greed for the pleasures of this life.

Just where the pleasures of this life are best to be found remains somewhat ambiguous in *Treasure Island*. We never see, of course, the pleasures of high-living that the pirates imagine: the carriages, fancy clothes, women, and fine houses. Their drinking is shown to produce only a malarial nightmare. In general, the land-pleasures are dim or suspect; it is the sea-pleasure that is genuine. On board ship, the pirates do their work well; they are "capable seamen" and contribute to a "prosperous" voyage. Everyone in the story, from Trelawney on down, appears animated by "the glory of the sea." Even Billy Bones carries about with him in his sea-chest some "curious West Indian shells." The spell of the sea is upon them all as it is upon their author. Stevenson's nautical talk—not just the technical terms but the infiltrated metaphors and expressive sea-lingo in the jabber of Silver and the other seamen—constitutes perhaps the life blood of the book. To Long John Silver, of course, Stevenson gives the saltiest palaver:

> "Why, how many tall ships, think ye, now have I seen laid aboard? And how many brisk lads drying in the sun at Execution Dock?" cried Silver. "And all for this same hurry and hurry and hurry. You hear me? I seen a thing or two at sea, I have. If you would only lay your course, and a p'int to windward, you would ride in carriages, you would. But not you! I know you. You'll have your mouthful of rum tomorrow, and go hang."

The sea-terms supply a world of metaphors, and, as they mix with other features of Stevenson's style such as the short sharp phrases, the pronominal repetitions stressing personal speech, the colloquial idioms, the ever-desperate tone, the reader is drawn into a distinct presence of mind that comes to represent the realm of the sea.

The sea-glory in *Treasure Island* emerges as a style of freedom, energy, and self-direction that runs counter to the predestinarian gloom and fear associated with the land and law or civilization. Stevenson introduces the reader to a mind-set of the sea where, on the one hand, the tightly circumscribed world of the ship functions as a tool for man's direction and, on the other hand, the fluid indeterminacies of chance are continually emphasized, faced, and overcome. Once on board, Silver quickly establishes himself as leader of most of the crew, and he moves on the ship as easily, despite his wooden leg, as all the other men. Here, at sea, his nautical speech finds its native home. (Stevenson makes the overwhelming orality of his book into a kind of sea-sound.) But Jim Hawkins, too, becomes the fortunate benefitter of chance at sea. By chance he hides in the apple barrel and discovers the plot. By whim he jumps ship, goes ashore with the pirates, and eventually meets Ben Gunn. And by luck he reboards the *Hispaniola* from his little coracle and so commandeers the ship.

Jim and Silver share a freedom and indeterminacy denied the others. Silver's looks are blond and cheerful, but his purposes are dark; he appears handicapped by his crutch, but it proves to be a murderous weapon; he seems to take orders but is really more a leader than one led; he belongs neither before the mast nor behind it. Jim, too, seems weak but proves himself strong; appears law-abiding but is actually quite reckless; he is a boy/youth, without a father, on his own; Silver calls him "my son" in Chapter Ten, but Silver also calls Hands "my son," as we have seen; Jim learns not to lean on Silver but to take his fate into his own hands. When he does so, we get a peculiar conflation of the child's wild eye and the predestinarian view of things. Jim describes his notion to jump ship and explore the island as "the first of the mad notions that contributed so much to save our lives." Madness, whether that of Jim or Ben Gunn, saves. As a result of jumping ship, Jim witnesses the horrible murder committed by Silver, but he also meets Ben Gunn. A second time Jim strikes off on his own when he leaves the stockade: "This was my second folly, far worse than the first, as I left but two sound men to guard the house; but like the first it was a help towards saving all of us."

On a casual consideration of his character and behavior, Jim seems to be somewhat awe-struck and passive except for occasional whimsical acts. But, not only is the story seen through his eyes and heard through his ears so that we sense within the convention of the first person narrator a remarkably sensitive and acute intelligence, but also Jim comes to personify a force of will perhaps equal to Silver's in standing up to the buffets of fate. Jim's plight while in the coracle seems the very type of the child's (and the Calvinist's) helplessness: "It was plain she was not to be interfered with, and at that rate, since I could in no way influence her course, what hope had I left of reaching land?" But then Jim finds that he can dip his paddle in from time to time and influence the course of the little boat. The whole book is like that. Impossible burdens suddenly dissolve. Partly it is a fictional technique, the essence of romance, yet in Stevenson's hands it becomes a celebration of miraculous will against implacable destiny, as in, for example, the magnificent moment of self-assertion at the end of Chapter Twenty-four, when Hawkins leaps for the ship, stamping the coracle under water, and embracing his fate.

By the technique of first person narration, Stevenson filters most of what happens in the book through Jim's consciousness. Since most of the action takes place in the youth's presence, he seems in part to be a passive observer and recorder. His incredible accuracy of detail, however, together with his commanding knowledge of nautical terminology and his brave and reckless action, makes him the central presence in the book and blends the poetic orality with the child's-eye view of things. As much as Long John Silver, Jim Hawkins embodies, finally, an ethos of radical freedom from authority, a freedom that, for Stevenson, approaches a delightful profanation. Jim's father dies, and Jim takes up with men who admire the pirate Flint and are "proud he was an Englishman" and defied the Spaniards (the parrot "Cap'n Flint" is admired because she "sailed with England, the great Cap'n England, the pirate" and swears "blue fire"). At the climactic moment of his adventures alone, Jim confronts the pirate Israel Hands, lectures Hands on the Christian view of sin and salvation, and then hears Hands plainly declare his anti-Christian views: "I never seen good come o' goodness yet. Him as strikes first is my fancy; dead men don't bite." Jim then allows himself, at least for a time, to adopt a less pious perspective on the business of killing, for he coolly takes aim at Hands and pulls the trigger only to find the priming wet. Then he sees himself while dodging away from Hands as playing "such a game as I had often played at home," "it was a boy's game." When Hands at last approaches Jim who is seated on the cross-trees of the mast, Jim says, " 'One more step, Mr. Hands,' said I, 'and I'll blow your brains out! Dead men don't bite, you know,' I added with a chuckle." After killing Hands, Jim finds himself strangely undisturbed at the act. He heaves O'Brien's corpse overboard, explaining: "The habit of tragical adventures had worn off almost all my terror for the dead." And then Jim wades ashore "in great spirits," "in famous spirits."

Part of the quest, then, is for Jim's freedom from conscience and authority, from the father and the Father. It is a quest for Silver's freedom from Dick's Biblical superstitions and for Silver's freedom to mock principles of command with his ever ironic "Dooty is dooty." The forbidden quest for radical freedom finds its most persistent image in Stevenson's repetitive focus upon "hands." The main idea is that hand is hidden from eye (of conscience). The blind Pew intones: " Hold out your left hand. Boy, take his left hand by the wrist and bring it near my right.' " All through the book, we focus upon hands, discretely imaged and often violating established codes. When Silver persuades one of the hitherto honest seamen to join the pirate crew, the lad says, " 'I didn't half a quarter like the job till I had this talk with you, John, but there's my hand on it now.' " The sailors, of course, are called "hands." Job Anderson attacks the stockade with the cry: " 'At 'em all hands—all hands!' " Hawkins sees Israel Hands and O'Brien "locked together in deadly wrestle, each with a hand upon the other's throat." Later Jim sees the same two: "Red-cap on his back, as stiff as a hand-spike, with his arms stretched out like those of a crucifix . . . Israel Hands propped against the bulwarks, his chin on his chest, his hands lying open before him on the deck." The name Israel Hands reinforces the notion of unChristian hands. When Jim shoots Hands, he says, "my pistols went off, and both escaped out of my hands," as if the hands have no control over the forces of murder. What Hyde or hide is in *Dr. Jekyll and Mr. Hyde*, so Hands or hand is in *Treasure Island*: The embodiment of our hidden will acting in guilty freedom from the exercise of conscience.

We may consider the hand imagery in connection with other images to appreciate how Stevenson spins a seamless web of moral allusion and religious tonality. In Chapter Twenty-nine, the black spot once again passes "from hand to hand," but the spot has been cut from the Bible and all are dismayed. Then Silver shows them the treasure map, and it, too, is sent "from hand to hand." Meanwhile, Jim is handed the black spot to look at, and he notices that it was cut from the very passage in Revelation that includes the warning: "If any shall take away from the words of the book of this prophecy, God shall take away his part out of the book of life." Clearly Stevenson is playing artfully with relations between black spot and Bible. The same sort of play occurs in the passage quoted above in which images of "handspike" and "crucifix" are juxtaposed; it may be no accident that Jim, seated on the "cross-trees" first feels himself pinned to the mast by Hands's dagger and then shoot Hands. Does Stevenson see Israel as crucifier of O'Brien and Hawkins? Is all murderousness, then, but a shadowing of the murder of Christ? What we are to make of Silver ever moving on the cross of his crutch and even using it for a murder weapon remains even more problematical.

Treasure Island, when carefully reconsidered on its own and in the light of similar tales of quest-romance, can very directly and profitably challenge any reader to explore the psychological and religious as well as the stylistic and structural dimensions of great literature for "children." In Stevenson's hands, "all the old romance" turns out to have surprising resonance and depth.

A CHILD'S GARDEN OF VERSES

It is hard to believe that Stevenson wrote a good many of the verses for his *Child's Garden of Verses* (1885) at the same time that he was writing *Treasure Island*. The comforting charms of the poems contrast strongly, at first glance, with the often grim and frightening adventure story. Stevenson's dedication is to his faithful nurse, Alison Cunningham, who made, he says, his "childish days rejoice," and, true enough, the verses glow with the joys of children's days and ways. But the same hand that gave Long John Silver both a sunny and a sinister side gave these verses a resonance far beyond a nurse's kindly voice. Again and again, in reading Stevenson's lyrics, our vista opens out—from the rain on local umbrellas to all the ships at sea, the sea coming up in a child's sandy holes "till it could come no more," the wind riding "all night long in the dark and wet," a deserted city with "no spark of light," the "mountainsides of dream" with their "many frightening sights." Not only do we find the characteristic urge of Stevenson to explore—"If I could find a higher tree / Farther and farther I should see"; "Up in the air and over the wall / Till I can see so wide"—but also we find a willingness to "explore / The colder countries" and to admit "the breath of the Bogie" and "the wicked shadows coming."

Yet for all their recognition of realities that qualify the childhood dream of play—a recognition characteristic of the best in children's literature—these verses win through to a specially happy child's eye view of things. The sense of newness washing the world; the loosening of space-time relations toward a metamorphic flow of interevolving wonders; the interest in simple immediacies like wind, rain, sun, bedclothes, cows, and garden; the lulling sonorities of the easy, short-syllabled couplets and quatrains; the psalmic praise of life all contribute to Stevenson's triumph in these poems.

Stevenson's verses for children differ from the Mother Goose nursery rhymes and from the poems of Edward Lear in that Stevenson writes specifically from a child's perspective and makes his poems cumulatively define childhood. The adult's perspective on children is somewhat ostentatiously discarded in "Whole Duty of Children," as the speaker begins with the familiar adult admonitory tone only to cancel it in the final line. A child who hears that four-line poem is being told that what we are interested in here is not rules for the child but the child's real abilities. The rest of the poems explore the child's imaginative perceptions and projections and even combine to paint the portrait of a child fascinated with the elemental forces of wind and rain, sleep and light, landscape and creaturehood.

Sometimes a specific persona, "I," is brought forward who may have affinities with Stevenson as a child but who is made to stand for other children, too. The full text of the verses makes it clear that the world envisioned is one of upper-class or upper-middle-class gentility replete with nannies, tea-time, plenty of toys, and comfy beds. Still, the force of the poems resides partly in the fact that they so frequently open out to the realms of experience beyond cute and comfortable domesticity. In the poem "My Shadow," for instance, the speaker's shadow becomes a kind of darker shadow self "not at all like proper children," who makes a "fool" of the speaker, does not know how children "ought to play," and eventually refuses to mimic the I or ego, and remains lazily in bed. Sleep, as in "The Land of Nod," liberates the child to a realm where there are "none to tell me what to do" and where a "curious" music is heard that never can be remembered distinctly. The poems respect the child for being in touch with a substantial reality that does not await maturity but precedes it and perhaps even fades as maturity nears. Thus the summer sun looks down from "empty heaven" and then goes about, "the gardener of the World," to paint the rose and "to please the child."

Children, of course, are rarely skilled enough to write poems like A Child's Garden. Such poems are, of necessity, an adult's gift to children. The perennial question, endemic to all literature written for children, thus arises: Is there not really a double audience in Stevenson's mind as he writes? The "child" in the poems is often the adult's nostalgic view of a lost self, "a child of air / That lingers in the garden there." And so we hear, improbably, of children trying in the day to get back to the land of dreams, and we find the speaker imagining that when he's a man he will have great adventures but will wind up his journey, as in "Travel," in a deserted city and house contemplating in a corner "the toys / Of the old Egyptian boys." Stevenson's *Garden*, then, presents not only the child's-eye view of things but also the adult's reverential but nostalgic and distanced view of the child.

20

JOSEPH JACOBS

English Fairy Tales

In his *English Fairy Tales* (1890), Joseph Jacobs crystalized the folk-con-sciousness of a nation. Adapting and retelling (if sometimes pacifying) with precision and economy, Jacobs, a professional folklorist and ethnic historian, managed fairly to translate into literary form an essentially preliterary ex-perience, the art of the ancient storyteller. Even today, his versions of many a treasured tale ("Jack and the Beanstalk," "Henny Penny," "Lazy Jack," "Johnny-Cake") live in the memories of those who heard them as children throughout the English-speaking world.

Born in Sydney, Australia, Jacobs (1854–1916) emigrated to England, graduated from Cambridge in 1876, and swiftly embarked upon his varied career. At one time or another he wrote essays for periodicals, including a once-famous series in 1882 on Russian persecutions of Jews; edited the British journal *Folk-Lore*; wrote on folklore in learned and popular essays; collected numerous volumes of English, Celtic, Indian, and other fairy tales; wrote voluminously on Jewish history; helped edit the *Jewish Encyclopedia*; and latterly was Professor of English at the Jewish Theological Seminary in New York City. Father of two sons and a daughter, Jacobs struck his asso-ciates as unusually dispassionate, generous, witty, humane.

Jacobs tried his stories, as did Lewis Carroll, John Ruskin, Beatrix Potter, Kenneth Grahame, and A. A. Milne, on juvenile audiences, and, as is true of many classics that appeal to children, his stories first existed in oral, not written form. When one considers the high percentage of great works in children's literature that contain colloquial speech rhythms or some other pronounced oral appeal—the nursery rhymes and songs; the hearer-tested tales of Charles Perrault, the Brothers Grimm, and Hans Christian Andersen; the music-hall patter and desperate palaver of characters in *Alice* and *Treasure Island*—one observes that the best in children's literature seems to appeal to the most universal listener in us all, the preliterate listener. Certainly the outstanding quality of the memorial reconstructions and condensations by Jacobs is the use of the oral art of repetition and the sheer delight in many kinds of wordplay. Jacobs lamented that, in the nineteenth century, so many English folk stories were superseded by foreign ones: "The superior elegance and clearness of the French tales replaced the rude vigor of the English ones. What Perrault began, the Grimms completed" (Jacobs 239). Jacobs changed all that. He went beyond such contemporary collectors of tales as J. O. Halliwell and Andrew Lang to bring out the "rude vigor" of the folk yarn. Having once heard, few can forget the reverberating phrases echoing like refrains through Jacobs's collection: the sinister "Noo, 'tain't" of "that," the black impet in "Tom Tit Tot"; the "Fee-fi-fo-fum" of the Jack-giant stories and of "Molly Whuppie"; the "chiny chin chin" of each little pig; the formulaic chantings of names in "Henny Penny." Jacobs once said that he tried to get down his stories as a "good old nurse" would speak them to her charges. The triumph of his attempts is one of the triumphs of colloquial English, just as the intensity and ritual unalterability of the tellings attest to the high mastery of the storytellers of old.

By the time the oral folk-tale becomes written as children's literature, it has inevitably passed through the sensibility of one or more literate persons. Perrault adapted his tales in the direction of middle- and upper-class interests in fairies, riches, and romance. The Grimms were philologists intent upon catching with a species of accuracy the nuances of their tellers though the principal tellers hardly epitomized the folk. Jacobs was another scholar through whose sensibility the tales passed and were transmuted. He wanted to stress the rude vigor, emphasis on the colloquial, and the unromantic and humorous nature of the English tales. Yet still it should be remembered that these versions were collected and adapted by a scholar with a propensity to classify them as legends, beast fables, drolls, nonsense stories, and the like. Jacobs's high-powered reverence for the essence of the tales as he conceived them may help account for their extremely stylized nature and the evident delight in colloquial idioms.

"Tom Tit Tot" deserves comparison, of course, to "Rumpelstiltskin." Jacobs is obviously trying to give the flavor of a peasant telling as he opens artlessly and humorously with "Once upon a time there was a woman. . . . " We may profitably reflect on the nature of such humor. When the daughter fails to understand her mother's idiomatic expression, "they'll come again," is it simply because the daughter is "gatless"? Or is there, in this opening tale, the hint of a suggestion that the country-folk idioms of the older generation are quaint and incomprehensible to the younger? In other words, is the humor partly at the expense of the "folk-tale" genre?

"Well, the woman she was done": "done" in the sense of "finished supper"?
Or "fairly had"? Her daughter's literalism was too much for the mother?
Instead of becoming angry, she celebrates her daughter's deed in song, but
she does not want the king to know, suggesting again a consciousness of
double standards in behavior and in senses of humor. The king, however,
is given a rather unkingly exclamation, "Stars o' mine!" Royalty is being
conceived of through peasant mentality. The king's simultaneous proposal
of marriage, offer of spinning labor, and death threat seems a strange mix
of love and exploitation, if not aggression. Does the tale reflect true folk
standards of affectionless life? Or are emotional realities sacrificed for the
sake of the driving plot?

The tale is partly cautionary in that the daughter's greed in eating five
pies turns into the punishment of having to spin five skeins. Is she, addi-
tionally, threatened with cannibalism from the impet (as Rumpelstiltskin
may hint at cannibalism)? Or does his "you'll be mine" refer to her soul?
Or her as slave (including sex slave)? Those who seriously seek "answers"
to such questions, if there really are answers, may be directed to portions
of the voluminous literature on the study of folklore. They might begin, for
example, with Stith Thompson's *Types of the Folktale* and *Motif Index of
Folk-Literature* as well as Ernest W. Baughman, *Type and Motif Index of
the Folktales of England and North America* and Iona and Peter Opie's *The
Classic Fairy Tales*, to get an idea of how the tales can be varied and
recombined. Further study might proceed by way of Jan Harold Brundvand,
Folklore: A Study and Research Guide; Alan Dundes, *The Study of Folklore*;
V. Propp, *Morphology of the Folktale*; and Munro S. Edmonson, *Lore: An
Introduction to the Science of Folklore and Literature*.

Jacobs suggested in a note to "Tom Tit Tot" that Tom was called "that" because
his name was unknown throughout the story until the end, but the story teller
repeats "that" suspiciously often and plays with it in a tricksy way:

> "What are you a-crying for?"
> "What's that to you?" says she.
> "Never you mind," that said, "but tell me what you're a-crying for."
> "That won't do me no good if I do," says she.
> "You don't know that," that said, and twirled that's tail round.
> "Well," says she, "that won't do no harm, if that don't do no good."

"That" is at once a source of linguistic fun and a source of revulsion at the
unnameable, inhumane quality of the creature. "Tit tot" could be nonsense
or could suggest tit for tat or breast (tit) and baby (tot), as if Tom were
perhaps an ogreish child-eater? Jacobs also suggests that the tale makes use
of an ancient superstition that to know another person's name gave one
power over that person, but this superstition does not seem to have any
guiding force in the story. More interesting is the way the king overhears

two snatches of poetry, the one leading into the trouble and the other leading out of the trouble. The king remains somewhat shadowy in purpose and power. Why did he want the skeins? Why threaten death? Why did he relate the incident of overhearing Tom? We cannot definitively answer such questions, of course, and the tale does not, perhaps, invite the questions, yet the suspicion may arise for some readers that the king knowingly or half-knowingly let his wife "off the hook."

The world of Jacobs' English tales is firmly patriarchal. Indeed in that world women and children, or youth, tend to be dominated or threatened by kings, ogres, and men with magical powers. The stories are generally told from the perspective of women and youth who manage, in spite of the odds, to win over the adult male antagonist. This is true of the girl in "Tom Tit Tot" and of Molly Whuppie; the girl in "Master of All Masters" and the little old woman in "The Three Bears" both contrive to disturb and humiliate the male-dominated household. The youthful and diminutive "Jacks," similarly, take down pretentious male giants.

There is a wonderful formulaic jauntiness about tales such as "Jack and the Beanstalk." The many repetitions ("what to do"; "What shall we do, what shall we do?"; "what we can do"; "Take that! Take that! Take that!"; "he climbed and he climbed"; "he walked along and he walked along"; and "thump! thump! thump!") signal a much-told tale that knows exactly where it is going because it has been there so many times. We expect the outcome to be just right in consequence. Many of the repetitions, furthermore, depict motions of slapping, climbing, and stomping, so that the story makes use of enactive language which brings the hearer more firmly into its presence and a sense of it happening in present time. In this connection, moreover, one might usefully trace out the casual intermixture of past and present tense recitals in the story (as, for example, the way sometimes "says" and "said" are thoroughly intertwined). The story was then, is now, and forever will be.

There is a strange confluence in "Jack and the Beanstalk" of sharp, concrete, daylit dialogue and dreaminess. The "funny-looking" old man appears from nowhere knowing Jack's name and offering magic beans for the cow "Milky-White." The beanstalk grows while Jack sleeps, and the romance quest takes place in the clouds. Yet the concretizations of the story serve to make the dream seem true. There is the ironic folk-shrewdness of " 'You look the proper sort of chap to sell cows' " and the nifty humor of the exchange: " 'How much did you get for her?' 'You'll never guess, mother.' " The beanstalk casts a real shadow in Jack's room and the ogre's home is solidly physical, the realm of food, oven, copper, and heavy gold.

Underlying stories such as "Tom Tit Tot" and "Jack and the Beanstalk" is the theme of hunger. The "darter's" gulping of five pies gets her into trouble until she faces someone who would perhaps eat her; Jack, too, proclaims his hunger and is threatened by a cannibal ogre: "It's breakfast you *want* . . .

it's breakfast you'll *be!*" The seemingly ignorant protagonists who think to feed on five pies and five beans find that their hunger leads to trials which, when met successfully, lead to riches and "happiness ever after."

The first time Jack comes down the beanstalk he brings a bag of gold which eventually runs out. The second time he brings the magic back with him in the form of the hen who can supply all the gold they need. Why, then, does Jack go back a third time to the ogre's house? Because he is "not content." He wants "another try at his luck." Jack and the "darter" are both creatures of large appetite and much "luck." Each enjoys triumphing. Each represents the kind of energetic, tough-minded, greedy, devil-may-care boisterousness that it takes, apparently, for survival and success in that rough and tumble world.

"The Story of the Three Little Pigs" is the quintessential folk-animal tale; its orality is so pronounced (on many levels) that it almost insists on memorization the first time it is experienced. Not only is the incident of pig meeting man to get material for house thrice presented with confidently repeated words and phrases, but also the repetitions of individual words within each telling—little pig, little pig, no, no, chin, chin, huff, puff, puff, huff—so solidly structure it that the story's narrative line supports one's prediction of an orderly conclusion. The pattern of thrice-repeated incidents continues in the second half of the tale except that the three "expeditions" are capped by the solo venture of the wolf down the chimney. All the incidents are propelled by appetite and by attention to out versus in. First the sow sends the pigs "out" because she has no food; then they get "in" their houses; then two end in the wolf's belly (as if his is now the supervening appetite in the story); then, when the wolf cannot get the third pig, he and the pig exercise their appetites jointly out in the world; finally the wolf enters the pig's house and the pig's stomach, a dramatic conflation of the opposing forces (which neatly forgets the point that pigs are not predators?). This is a story of masterful precision, economy, balance, and humor.

It is interesting that "The Story of the Three Bears" can be told successfully both in the Goldilocks version and in the naughty old woman version which Jacobs relays from Robert Southey as told sixty years earlier. (Southey evolved the old woman from a fox in earlier versions.) Much of the fun of the Jacobs version is in sassing the old woman as bad, impudent, a user of wicked words, greedy, ugly, dirty, nosy, a thief, and a vagrant, whereas Goldilocks receives no disapprobation. The principal fun for small children, no doubt, is in the climax of the repetitions and the three differing voices. Again, it should be noted, hunger takes a central place in the adventure, and again the protagonist's hunger leads to a vague threat of being eaten. Sleep and dream are present here, too. In such tales, appetite, wish, and dream are associated in a wise generalization of desires.

"Jack the Giant-Killer" is terribly weak in its plot, being only a succession of similar episodes. The story celebrates Jack's "briskness" and "wit" which are, apparently, sufficient for all tasks. Much of the tale is taken up, once again, with defeating ogreish counter-appetite. ("Poor Jack" refers to cheap, dried and salted fish.) Jack's "wit" includes a brisk disrespect for demonry, and indeed the whole story is a kind of debunking of alleged supernatural powers and a paean of praise for English pragmatic shrewdness. All through, the combat runs between the heavy, dull, angry giants and the nimble, mocking Jack, as if two styles of power were being contrasted.

Of "Henny-Penny" Jacobs says, "the fun consists in the avoidance of all pronouns, which results in jaw-breaking sentences," but the names have to be amusing enough to bear repeating. The adding on of names builds the tension even as the repetitions stretch to exasperated tedium. The moronic politeness of the venturers matches their failure to recognize their natural enemy, the fox. Henny-Penny escapes only by chance, and quite unfairly, as she led them into the trouble. The final laconic comment, that the king never received the crucial message, is superb.

"Molly Whuppie" begins in the familiar fashion of "Hansel and Gretel" and Perrault's "Hop O' My Thumb" with the opening greatly abbreviated and the hunger passed, as it were, from parents to children to ogre. "Cleverness" is again the celebrated virtue. Note here the dry humor of "Molly thought it time" and the talk of "managing" murders and robbery. Such stories as this and the "Jack" stories suggest that great reward comes from the willingness of wit to risk all repeatedly against power. Marriage, as usual, is made the conclusion of adventure. After marriage in such stories, staid "happiness" sets in. Thus children's literature is probably like most literature in that the prevalent cautionary plots advocate peace and not trouble but show trouble as the only worthy excitement.

"Lazy Jack" depends for its perhaps middling interest on the varieties of ineptitude that Jack can pursue. The folk-tellers obviously thought it a great joke that the ignorant poor should win over the upper classes, and it is problematic whether such tales as "Lazy Jack" relieve or rather intensify class antagonism and, by association, generational antagonism.

"Master of All Masters" must be one of the strangest stories ever concocted. We know from earlier tales such as "Jack and the Beanstalk" that "funny-looking" old men are likely to be somewhat zany. Wanting to be called "master of all masters" suggests the pride that deserves a fall. The girl's willingness to call her master's things by "whatever" name he pleases is pushing the ideal of dutiful and pliable service to comic extremes. If new readers or listeners can find any systematic relation between the items' real names and the new names given them, they will have outwitted generations of scholars. Jacobs calls the story a "quaint droll" and asserts that it may be a "satire on pedantry." The suggestion then might be that the master is likely to perish in the flames for failure to understand his own piled-up phrases. Whether the story invites reflection upon other forms of pedantic overcomplication (as in interpreting children's literature), we leave it for others to decide.

21

L. FRANK BAUM

The Wonderful Wizard of Oz

L. Frank Baum (he hated his first name, Lyman, and always went by Frank) was born in Chittenago, New York, in 1856, seventh of the nine children of Benjamin Ward Baum, an oil man and theatrical entrepreneur. Delicate health ran in the Baum family; four of Frank's brothers and sisters died in infancy, and Frank himself suffered all his life from a heart condition. A frail and dreamy boy, Baum received most of his education at home from tutors. When he was twelve his parents sent him to Peekskill Military Academy, but he soon suffered a nervous or physical collapse and returned home. He took early to literature, reading popular Victorian novelists and trying his own hand at verse and fiction.

When he was eighteen, Baum tried to break into show business as an actor in a stock company; it was his first of a series of attempts to succeed as an entertainer, first as an actor, later as a writer and producer. He had some brushes with success. But when his father died in 1887, his fortune having disappeared in competition with the Standard Oil Company, Frank had to support himself and his young family (he was by now married and the father of the first of his four sons). He went west to Aberdeen, South Dakota, then to Chicago, finally to California. For ten years he worked variously as a storekeeper, a traveling salesman, and a newspaper reporter, editor, and columnist.

In Chicago in 1879 he published his first children's book, *Mother Goose in Prose. The Wonderful Wizard of Oz*, which appeared in 1900 with illustrations by William Wallace Denslow, was his third book for children. It was an instantaneous success. Some 90,000 copies of it were sold the first year, and since then it has firmly established itself as the best-selling children's book in the world.

Baum was later to write thirteen other Oz books: *The Marvelous Land of Oz* (1904), *Ozma of Oz* (1907), *Dorothy and the Wizard in Oz* (1908), *The Road to Oz* (1909), *The Emerald City of Oz* (1910), *The Patchwork Girl of Oz* (1913), *Tik-Tok of Oz* (1914), *The Scarecrow of Oz* (1915), *Rinkitink in Oz* (1916), *The Lost Princess of Oz* (1917), *The Tin Woodman of Oz* (1918), *The Magic of Oz* (1919), and *Glinda of Oz* (1920). All of them sold well, though none ever matched the meteoric success of *The Wonderful Wizard of Oz* (the title was later shortened to *The Wizard of Oz*). The series even continued after Baum's death. Ruth Plumly Thompson, commissioned by Baum's widow and publishers, wrote nineteen additional Oz books, and a number of other writers have added items to the series.

When *The Wonderful Wizard of Oz* came out in 1900, reviewers frequently called it "an American Alice in Wonderland," since Lewis Carroll's by-then-thirty-five-year-old masterpiece was in the full tide of its popularity. Now, though, some generations later, to speak of the two stories in conjunction with each other is to call attention to what a limited similarity they have. Alice and Dorothy are both little girls, about the same age; both are dropped, in natural/mysterious ways, into fairy lands of sorts, encountering there fantastic characters and challenging situations. Both stories are relatively unconcerned with overall plot-development (*Oz* has more plot than *Alice*), and focus more sharply on separable scenes and incidents, especially conversations among pairs or small groups of characters. Baum does some punning and witty play with logic, though compared with Carroll's best his word- and thought-games are of minor importance to his story.

Although it has some ideas in it that might fairly be called philosophical, neither is *The Wonderful Wizard of Oz* a philosophical fairy tale in the sense that "The Light Princess" and *The Little Lame Prince* are. Baum obviously had no kernel-thesis in mind when he sat down to write it. He inserts ideas into his episodes *ex tempore*, rather than framing episodes consciously to embody pre-conceived ideas.

One can list Baum's conspicuous themes briefly:

- Home is the place you are used to, and where you feel you belong; it is therefore more desirable than other places of greater glamor and excitement.
- Virtues such as intelligence, compassion, and courage are created by what you do; you "get" them by behaving as if you had them. Some people, though, mistakenly believe they are arbitrarily bestowed by some externalized process.
- Reality can be temporarily manipulated by a clever illusionist, but in the end illusions yield to the persistent inquirer, and "truth will out."

But these ideas aren't really what give *The Wonderful Wizard of Oz* its imaginative life. What sort of thing does Baum really seem to have been interested in in writing this story? Attempts to answer this basic question produce a list of a different kind:

- He is interested in scenes where characters confront simple, definite physical problems, and solve them. (Pursued by the Kalidahs, the Tin Woodman makes a bridge by felling a tree and then destroys it before they can follow. Faced with the question of how to move a 400-pound lion out of a poppy field, the Scarecrow mobilizes thousands of mice to pull a jerry-built truck. To fight off wolves, the Tin Woodman uses his ax; to fight off crows, the Scarecrow scares them; to fight off bees, the party covers its vulnerable members with straw and lets the bees destroy themselves against the Woodman's tin. To rescue the Scarecrow from the middle of the river, they enlist the aid of a friendly Stork. And so forth.)

- He is interested in the simple pleasure of moving through a foreign world and finding a place to sleep, a chance to wash up, and food to one's liking. (This scene occurs ten times in the story's twenty-three chapters.)

- He is interested in implications that would follow "realistically" from unrealistic fairy-land premises. (If a Scarecrow were alive, he would be most afraid of fire, but he would not need to eat or sleep. If a sentimental man were re-cast in metal, his tendency to weep would be a problem for it would make him rust. If people were made of china they would break easily, mend easily, but the cracks would show. If everyone wore green glasses inside a certain city, they would think everything in the city were green.)

- He is interested in setting up odd or striking phenomena and then explaining them. (The Scarecrow explains how he was made; the Tin Woodman explains how he came to be made of tin; the Winged Monkey explains the charm of the Golden Cap; the Wizard explains his hoaxes and illusions.)

- He is interested in problems that turn out to be a lot easier than they seemed. (To kill a Wicked Witch, all Dorothy has to do is let the mark of the Good Witch's kiss protect her and throw an ordinary bucket of water on the villainess. In order to grant the Scarecrow's, Woodman's, and Lion's wishes, all the Wizard has to do is give them any old thing and call it brains, heart, and courage. In order to get back to Kansas, all Dorothy has to do is click her heels and wish to be there.)

These recurrent situations or preoccupations do not convey any very formidable truth about life, nor do they seem to emanate from any deep inner core of psychological necessity. But they do winningly project an easy-going, comfortable, do-it-yourself, pragmatic American view of the world which many readers enjoy and which Baum found extendable over many subsequent books. Life in this Land of Oz is a casually linked series of medium-sized physical problems that yield to pedestrian, common-sense thinking and medium-sized discoveries that have explanations. Oz people do literal things, not symbolic ones. Nobody has to open a door by cutting off her finger, as in "The Seven Ravens." Nobody has to decide whether to save her own life by plunging a knife into the man she loves, as in "The Little

Mermaid." One either does things with wood, straw, cloth, and glue, or one does them with magic. But magic in Oz is essentially a different kind of force from that in the old fairy tales or "The Light Princess" or *Alice* or *King of the Golden River*. In those stories, magic grew mysteriously out of overwrought impulses of human psyches (a woman's love changed a beast to a man; a father's curse changed sons to ravens; a dreaming girl created a troublesome, surreal world; greed and cruelty changed two men to black stones). In *Oz* magic is mechanical and systematic, a parallel kind of technology. Dorothy has the magic kiss on her forehead, the Golden Cap on her head, and the silver shoes on her feet in much the same spirit as she has bread in her basket, or the Woodman has his ax: just because they are useful. She herself (and he too, for that matter) remains basically a natural and realistic character, unmodified and unexplained by the magic in her environment.

Characters in *The Wonderful Wizard of Oz* have simple, moderate motives and wishes. Compared with the Mole's passionate attachment to his home in Chapter Five of *The Wind in the Willows*, Dorothy's desire to go back to Kansas is a mere notion. Compared with the stepmother's mania for being the most beautiful woman in "Snow White," the Scarecrow's desire for brains is as normal as preferring steak to beans. The Lion's desire for courage would look like a careless whim if it were thrust into the blood-stained life-and-death tests of manhood in *Treasure Island* or the Mowgli stories.

At the core of Baum's vision in *Oz* is a kind of ordinariness, and Baum is proud of it. He announced in his introduction that "the time has come" to get rid of "the stereotyped genie, dwarf and fairy" from the "old-time fairy tale," and expressed thereby an impatience with old-world trumpery that genuinely does characterize *The Wonderful Wizard of Oz*. In its way, Baum's is quite a democratic story. Dorothy, the Scarecrow, the Woodman, and the Lion are all obviously "commoners," people of no particular blood-lines or breeding, plain, classless characters. They are born with the virtues they need; no growth or improvement in them is necessary as long as they just have confidence (the power of positive thinking) in themselves.

This is not to say that *The Wonderful Wizard of Oz* comprises an overt populist political tract. Actually its few references to political establishments are somewhat inconsistent. Baum obviously expects us to approve when the Munchkins and the Winkies are freed from serving the wicked witches. But he also assumes we will approve when the Scarecrow, Woodman, and Lion fulfill themselves by finding peoples to rule over. The Lion doesn't sound like a very good American liberal, for instance, when he says, "If I put an end to your enemy, will you bow down and obey me as King of the Forest?" But his tyrannical ambition isn't supposed to shock or offend us, either. The point is that Baum has no political point to make; he just assumes that the native good sense of farm-types like Dorothy and the Scarecrow or a working man like the Tin Woodman will be resource enough to see an adventure through. He is not interested in how that kind of sense could be converted into running a whole society.

Most people who read *The Wonderful Wizard of Oz* in this day and age will also have seen the MGM movie "The Wizard of Oz," and will inevitably make some comparisons in their minds between Baum's book and Victor Fleming's movie. It is probably well to sort out the major differences between them, in order to get clearly in view what the book actually contains. The movie does not really tell the same story the book tells. In the film, Dorothy's trip to Oz is a dream from which she awakens in the end. The characters of the Wicked Witch of the West, Dorothy's three traveling companions, and the Wizard himself are all anticipated by characters whom Dorothy knows in Kansas: the cross spinster who wants to kill Toto, the farmhands, and the traveling medicine-show doctor. The movie shows that Dorothy is unhappy at home (mainly because of the threat to her dog) and wants to go "Somewhere Over the Rainbow." Her journey to Oz is her own dream-making subconscious's way of granting her wish and of simultaneously teaching her that she is wrong. The dream shows her that, even in other worlds that you might flee to, your basic difficulties will be the same: The same enemy will be there to attack you; the same friends will be there to help you. Baum's book never suggests any such thing. Dull and grey as Kansas is, his Dorothy never expresses any discontentment with it; she is swept away entirely against her will, and what happens to her in Oz is not a product of her imagination. (Really, Baum seems to assume that Dorothy does not have much imagination.)

As for what takes place in Oz, the movie omits a great deal of Baum's material: Encounters with the Kalidahs, the field mice, the china people, the Hammer-Heads, the kingdom of animals are all dropped. The movie has nothing about the Woodman's building the raft or the ladder or the truck to move the sleeping Lion, nor the Lion's carrying his companions across the gully on his back or killing the spider, nor the Scarecrow's getting stranded in the river and being rescued by the Stork, nor the defeat of the Witch's wolves, crows, and bees. In short, the movie cares far less for all the incidental problem-solving which obviously pleased Baum and his readers. Likewise, the movie drops most of the explaining how things work: how the Woodman came to be made of tin, how the Winged Monkeys came to be enslaved, how you make a hot-air balloon.

In place of all this, the move sharply emphasizes the simplified romance-plot that arouses sympathy and suspense and resolves it in a standard melodrama pattern that fits conveniently into a two-hour movie.

In pointing out contrasts such as these, we do not insist that the book is better than the movie. In fact, some critics have argued that director Fleming actually improved on Baum's original, creating greater coherence and psychological urgency as well as providing music and spectacle appropriate to, but not provided by, Baum's kernel idea. Certainly Fleming was less concerned with eliminating "the horrible and blood-curdling incident . . . to point a fearsome moral" or "the heartaches and nightmares" than Baum was. The greater vividness of the movie, with its color, sound, and violent motion, has quite the contrary effect. Whether for better or for worse, Baum's matter-of-factness, his comfortable, unhurried, meandering, common-sensical attitude toward fairy lands is not the attitude Fleming took for his film.

22

KENNETH GRAHAME

The Wind in the Willows

Why is *The Wind in the Willows* a classic example of children's literature? The question deserves to be asked, for the book has no children as characters, nor does it deal primarily with childish pursuits. It contains a good deal of rather adult satire on courts and prisons; a long digression on international travel; an enigmatic encounter with a nature god seen from an adult perspective; a smattering of misogynist comments; and, most often, a pottering, bachelorish view of life. Its style, furthermore, borders more than once on the trite phrase, the cliche, the stock response: "the joy of living and the delight of spring," "flowers budding, leaves thrusting—everything happy," "I like your clothes awfully, old chap." We find overalliterative, purple prose: "the diffident and delaying dog-rose stepped delicately," "riot in rich masquerade." And the second half of the book extends itself interminably with the pufferies of Mr. Toad. Why, then, is the book hailed as a great one?

Part of the answer lies in a consideration of Grahame, his purposes, and his time. *The Wind in the Willows* is autobiographical, in that it celebrates an ideal moment in Grahame's childhood as well as the transmutation of that ideal moment into adult terms. Kenneth Grahame (1859–1932) lived in Scotland from his birth until the death of his mother when he was five. His father, an attorney, abandoned the family and died, an alcoholic, in France. Grahame, third of four children, spent three years, from age five to eight, with his grandmother in Cookham Dene, Berkshire, near the Thames and Windsor Forest. It was here that he developed, apparently, his lifelong fascination with rivers and here that the scenes of *The Wind in the Willows* were impressed on his imagination. Grahame went to school in Oxford but was not allowed by his relatives to attend the University. The rest of his life may have seemed to Grahame a detour or the occasion of regretful yearnings for a pastoral return, for he soon entered the Bank of England and worked there thirty years. Though he rose at an early age to one of the highest positions in the bank, he invested his principal imaginative energy in his writing career. He published essays in periodicals and then, in 1895 and 1898, came two books for adults, *The Golden Age* and *Dream Days*. These works tell the adventures of orphans who prefer servants and bachelors as friends instead of their kin, and they contain stories such as the famous "Reluctant Dragon." In 1899, Grahame entered what has been termed a "disastrous" marriage. The only child, a son, Alistair, was born the next year. He was partially blind and was destined to be run over by a train twenty years later, a possible suicide.

Grahame's life, then, was not one of unalloyed happiness. *The Wind in the Willows*, which began as bedtime stories to Alistair and advanced in letters to the boy when he was away for a time, qualifies as the most genuine sort of escapist fantasy: escapist for both teller and listener. In terms of literary history, it qualifies as a "Georgian" pastoral of the Edwardian era (it was published in 1908), a monument that stands in the gleaming twilight, the wistful gloaming, of English confidence before the War. That confidence for Grahame consists partly in a series of assumptions about the perfections of rural life; the happy innocence of children and animals; right patterns of domesticity; acceptance of male withdrawals into preadolescent (or middle-aged?) clubs or "chumships"; and the innate superiority of English middle-class values, activities, comforts, and idioms. The tensional center of Grahame's book lies in the characters of Mole and Rat, who are neither quite children nor quite adult; they are committed neither solely to home nor solely to adventure, neither to stability and rest nor to growth and change. Grahame tries to give them the best of both worlds, as so many children's authors do, creating for them lives of adult comforts and excitements without corresponding adult strains of childrearing and work. They live in childlike closeness to nature without experiencing true animal savagery or pain. One secret of the book's appeal as children's literature inheres in the deftness and completeness of the fantasy. Mole and Rat are specially tuned to hear the imperious calls of nature, yet they also enjoy "messing about in boats," picnics, afternoon tea, *dulce domum*. Like many another children's author, Grahame spends a lot of time mocking officious adults, with their pretension to Government, Society, and Culture; their fascination with cars, speed, technology. Child readers can be assured that they already share with the animals the essentials of enduring creaturehood. Says Badger, "People come—they stay for a while, they flourish, they build—and they go. It is their way. But we remain."

The Wind in the Willows celebrates most assiduously what "remains," equating it with a bedrock of child and animal goodness. The wanderlust of the Sea Rat, the egocentricity and dash of the Toad are celebrated, too, as if in recognition that what remains in the more homey lives and natures of the other animals may be a bit tame. Wild Wood and Wide World only sound, after all, nearly the same; they are not equally to be shunned. But the central images of the work have to do with peace subsisting at the heart of endless agitation; with "long summer evenings"; "a quiet, steady, respectable life"; "we fellows who remain"; "the sight of familiar things greeting us as long-absent travelers from far oversea"; and finally a child asleep in the arms of Pan, resting at the center of nature. All this is captured in Grahame's easy, limpid prose which, despite its occasional lapses, flows with the constancy and grace of the very river and wind whose comforting presence it so surely evokes.

The Wind in the Willows raises many of the best and most searching questions that run through the classics of children's literature. In what sense is a cautionary tale really cautionary? Do the brash adventures of Mr. Toad promote Mole-like modesties in child readers or listeners? Is the satire in the book against human adults and their "society" a light and forgiving sort of satire? Or is it a more thoroughgoing and seriously intended indignation? Do Grahame's views of humans as presented in the book border on misanthropy (beyond the bachelor misogyny)? Is Grahame presenting a retreat from active participation in the workings of society, a retreat that takes us simultaneously away to haunts of retired men, to childhood irresponsibilities, to animal nature as preferable to human, and finally to a nature worship that supersedes all fellowship?

If *The Wind in the Willows* offers, finally, a viable way of life alternative to urban and industrial patterns, then it is genuinely salvational and not merely escapist. But it is difficult to conceive how a valid salvational argument can be constructed for the book when the life depicted remains so utterly remote from the workaday concerns, the demands of commerce, earning a living, rearing children, and furthering governmental practices and ideals. One response to this sort of objection may be that Grahame addresses the heart and not the head or hands and asks us merely to accept his story as a metaphor for life lived at the level of the still small voice that counsels calm in the face of ambition, connection to springs of rest and refreshment in nature, and reverence for our instincts toward "home" and a community of fellowship.

A first reading of the book may yield a feeling for the plot and the characters and a general sense of the world they inhabit, but a more confident and profound grasp of what the book is saying may come only with more prolonged and thoughtful study of it. Many questions come to mind, questions that each may answer in unique ways. One may think, for instance, that the animals—Mole, Rat, Badger, Otter, Toad, and so on—are the only significant characters in the story, but, in truth, the title hints at a wider view, does it not? Instead of *Adventures of Mr. Mole and Friends* we have *The Wind in the Willows*. Is the Wind a character or at least an important presence in the work? What does the Wind whisper among the reeds? Is the River a similar presence? What other parts of nature are personified so as to speak to, smile at, or otherwise comfort the animals? What does it mean to say: "Spring was moving in the air above and in the earth below . . . with its spirit of divine discontent and longing"? What does "Spring" represent or call to mind? How can it move *in* the air and *in* the earth? What is divine about the discontent and longing? What are the forces that call Mole, Rat, and Toad both away from and back to home? How might one describe the music or voice or presence which is the subject of the seventh chapter? What is its significance? What is the relation of Badger and his "unseen influence" to the divinity of the seventh chapter and its status as "helper and healer?" Is the book presenting an unfounded optimism and religion of nature? Or is there a convincingness in the presentation of the good animals and the natural world as fundamentally kind, comforting, stable, sensible, properly valuing home and the familiar and friendship? What complex of attitudes and conduct does Grahame hope will remain or endure in life?

In his seminal essay, "On Three Ways of Writing for Children," C. S. Lewis asks us to: "Consider Mr. Badger in *The Wind in the Willows*—that extraordinary amalgam of high rank, coarse manners, gruffness, shyness, and goodness. The child who has once met Mr. Badger has ever afterwards, in his bones, a knowledge of humanity and of English social history which he could not get in any other way." One may agree with this description of Badger or not agree, but he certainly does repay our interest in characterizing him. To compare and contrast, moreover, the Mole, Rat, and Toad, and Otter with Badger and with each other is to learn for oneself something about the kinds of friendship and society they seek individually and, perhaps, collectively.

We say "*perhaps* collectively" because there appear to be essential contradictions in *The Wind in the Willows* that question the possibility of truly collective ideals for living among the creatures. A recognition, furthermore, of Grahame's own divided nature helps expose the divided nature of the book. Just as Grahame, when he worked in London, was active for a time in the Scottish Regiment, social work, and athletics like boxing and fencing, but eventually became reclusive and withdrew from urban life to inveigh against blights of industrialism upon the countryside, so *The Wind in the Willows* celebrates active fellowship, doing battle together, and even casts an appreciative eye on Toad's irrepressible love affair with technology, though the book as a whole satirizes the rituals and trinkets of mass society and appeals to our instincts for privacy and communion with nature as most fundamental in us. Grahame, too, impressed others with his extreme handsomeness of physique and manner, yet he was deeply diffident and held himself aloof for a complex of reasons. Thus, through a brief consideration of Grahame's own nature and career, one can better identify the tensions in *The Wind in the Willows* between conviviality and privacy, between Toad's dashing elan and Toad's contemptible pride, between the excitements of motor cars and trains and satiric dismissal of them in favor of nature's quiet, steady underlife.

Tensions similar to those mentioned above reside in Grahame's writing style and in his views of nature. On the one hand, Grahame, like Beatrix Potter, generally writes in a chastened style suitable for child listeners and readers. An accessible vocabulary, lots of conversation, attention to concrete details, a world of things and familiar acts, all this makes it a child's book. On the other hand, Grahame confessed that he considered a fine style an end in itself and often worked "to build a noble sentence." Some measure of what Grahame meant in the building of noble sentences is found in the passage where the Water Rat adumbrates his vision of foreign romance. The Water Rat's hypnotic vision both casts a rapturous spell and sounds suspiciously like a travel brochure. Grahame, it appears, can hardly decide if Nature calls more imperiously for brave and romantic action or for a more conservative delight in comforts closer to home. The "nobler" the sentence is the less true it is, often, to the unshowy, milder voice of wind in willow and reed, the voice that the book as a whole asks us to heed.

Chapter Seven, "The Piper at the Gates of Dawn," captures the same tension between an inflated or intoxicated style and vision of Nature and a chastened or detoxificated one:

> Perhaps he would never have dared to raise his eyes, but that, though the piping was now hushed, the call and the summons seemed still dominant and imperious. He might not refuse, were Death himself waiting to strike him instantly, once he had looked with mortal eye on things rightly kept hidden. Trembling he obeyed, and raised his humble head; and then, in that utter clearness of the imminent dawn, while Nature, flushed with fullness of incredible color, seemed to hold her breath for the event, he looked in the very eyes of the Friend and Helper.

Soon Rat and Mole receive the "last best gift" of forgetfulness,

> Lest the awful remembrance should remain and grow, and overshadow mirth and pleasure, and the great haunting memory should spoil all the after-lives of little animals helped out of difficulties, in order that they should be happy and lighthearted as before.

Seen in this light, *The Wind in the Willows* is largely an exploration of how we are to respond to the sublimity in nature and in our own natures. Are we to worship its full-throated "adult" power, its nobility in elemental forces and the glorious romance of adventure? Or should we rest content with transmuted versions of the power, let the "little breeze" waft in "oblivion," and bustle like the portly child unthinkingly in nature's minor dimensions and scenes? Grahame keeps trying to make up his mind in the latter direction, to counsel small-scale and childlike delights in a rural domesticity as the best and safest accommodation of higher, dangerous powers. The residual tensions in the book testify to the past century's struggles with or through romanticism, industrialism, and Darwinism as responses to changing views of Nature, and the book as a whole testifies to the greatness of children's literature as a vehicle for winning both truth and beauty out of these and other struggles. To reflect long and slowly enough on what is happening in the book so that one may grasp the wise confusion of its themes can afford one of the best chances to help one appreciate the depth and complexity not only of Grahame's vision, but of insights endemic to the stories that have held the attention of both children and grown-ups ever since "once upon a time." Like Chekhov's plays, *The Wind in the Willows* seems for the most part to be about somewhat fretful people who are doing nothing heroic. Yet one remembers them forever. They want what we want. They are where we are. They interpret us.

23

JAMES BARRIE

Peter Pan

Peter Davies, the boy whose name suggested "Peter" for James Barrie's hero, knew first-hand what went into the making of *Peter Pan*. He had watched the shy, moody, and oddly aggressive Barrie befriend him and his brothers more out of a need for playmates than for sons, and he had seen the story of Peter Pan emerge from Barrie's obsession with youth, play, and brittle, airy fantasy. Thus aware of both the charm and the emotional sources of Barrie's work, Davies called it a "terrible masterpiece" (Dunbar 165).

The work quickly came to be regarded as a classic, and this has meant, among other things, that most people have lost sight of what is terrible about it. Assisted by Walt Disney's movie-makers and uncounted editors, abridgers, and illustrators, the story of Peter Pan has been enshrined as a cheerful, whimsical celebration of childhood, a story about flying and swordfights and other adventures, with a little puppy-love interest thrown in on the side. But in the form Barrie himself gave to the story, it is more than that; it is a work of classic fantasy which insists on its very unreality and reveals the psychological sources from which such a deliberately insubstantial fantasy springs.

Barrie's fantasy world, "the Neverland," is first presented as part of "the map of a person's mind," created from the welter of conscious and unconscious material stored there. It is an ambiguous place: one part of the psyche desires and therefore creates it; another part denies and retreats from it, insisting it is only make-believe, when it threatens to become too real. The conflict of desire and fear which Barrie's characters feel may appear to be the classic dilemma of children's literature: the conflict between staying home and running away. And the adventures of the Darling family may seem similar to those of Jim Hawkins in *Treasure Island* or the children in the Narnia Chronicles. But the Neverland is, in a subtle way, much more dangerous. The worlds of Treasure Island and Narnia do not threaten or lure the characters in quite the same way. The Neverland is more disturbing in a sense because it is too desirable. And therefore Barrie must deny it all the more emphatically.

For, in Barrie's mind, the issue of whether to fly away or stay at home was really settled before the story ever began. Any biography of him shows that the idea of ever really detaching himself from his home and mother would have been unbearable. His imagination had committed itself absolutely to the image of the faithful child who would remain a child. Therefore the departures had to remain sheerest game and make-believe. Moreover, Barrie undercut the fantasy because he apparently could not bear its implications. For in the Neverland there exists for him a mother-wife figure whom he can't, even there, embrace, and a villain of a father he can slay. Such visions were very likely too frightening for him to stand by, so that as soon as he hinted at them he had to repudiate them. And since he could neither fulfill them nor get rid of them, he was immobilized.

This is why the fantasy of flying to the Neverland takes the form it does in *Peter Pan*. Barrie (1860–1937) was plagued all his life, and quite consciously, by an excessive concern for his mother's affection. When he was six years old, his thirteen-year-old brother David, his mother's acknowledged favorite among her ten children, died in an ice-skating accident, and as a result his mother suffered a nervous collapse. James set himself the impossible task of replacing his dead brother in her affections by "playing physician," as he put it, to heal her of her debilitating grief. From his seventh year on, his whole life resolved itself—again, quite consciously—into a prolonged campaign for his mother's love; the desire to please and amuse her was the first commandment of his existence. "Wait till I'm a man," he recalled crying to her, "and you'll lie on feathers" (*Margaret Ogilvy* 207).

She enthralled his imagination. The stories she told him about herself as a girl became the obsessive subject of his fantasies and his writing. In *Margaret Ogilvy*, the biography he wrote of her after her death, Barrie frankly admitted, "The reason my books deal with the past instead of the tale I myself have known is simply this, that I soon grow tired of writing tales unless I can see a little girl, of whom my mother has told me, wandering confidently through the pages. Such a grip has her memory of her girlhood had upon me since I was a boy of six" (25). He joked sadly about his utter inability to create any major female character in his fiction who did not directly resemble her. All his life, the women he liked best were young mothers with children. But the omnipresent image of his mother prevented his achieving adult sexuality and parenthood himself. His own marriage ended in divorce after fifteen childless years; his wife revealed to friends that Barrie was impotent and that their marriage had never been consummated.

Barrie's excessive attachment to his mother comes as no surprise to anyone who has read *Peter Pan*, with its rhapsodic effusions on the glory of mother love. The same exaggerated concern for his mother which generated those passages generated the fantasy of the Neverland—and generated, too, the need to insist that the Neverland was not real. For, on the one hand, the Neverland is the product of a half-hearted wish for a world away from the tempting, guilt-producing influence of a mother about whom one cares too much. In a fundamental way, it is conceived as a world without mothers; its basic business goes on without them: exploring, fighting, running risks— things which boys do away from home. Peter has come there to escape his own mother; the Darling children come as an elaborate way of teasing their mother by their absence. But, on the other hand, the fantasy of a motherless world is ultimately impossible for Barrie. Appealing as it might be to project an island free from the tensions of his relationship with mother, his attachment for her is still the greatest principle of his thinking and wishing. A world without the mother on whom his deepest desires are fixed is miserably incomplete; it is no fun at all. In short, a mother must be imported; and Peter immediately fetches one. Thus the primary intention of the Neverland—to be a world free from the anxieties of the mother-fixation—is immediately compromised, since Barrie's imagination is so thoroughly infused by that fixation.

Peter's own attitude toward mothers is a clear expression of this simultaneous wish to be free of their bothersome presence, and to have their unlimited devotion. "Now, if Peter had ever quite had a mother, he no longer missed her," says Barrie. "He could do very well without one. He had thought them out, and remembered only their bad points." When he meets Mrs. Darling at the beginning of the story, he gnashes his teeth at her; when he finds Wendy grown up and a mother at the end of the story, he gives "a cry of pain" and "[draws] back sharply." Yet at the same time he inarticulately craves a mother. He brings Wendy back with him in the first place to mother him and the lost boys; when he returns in the last chapter, he announces, "I came back for my mother, to take her back to the Neverland." "He does so need a mother," the new little girl Jane says. " 'Yes, I know,' Wendy admitted rather forlornly; 'no one know it so well as I.' "

The little girls Peter takes back to the Neverland are, of course, always to be his make-believe mothers, not his real one; that is important to Peter and to Barrie. Why this should be so is easy to understand. It is not simply that a real mother can boss you around and force you to grow up, as Peter says; in his very running off to the Neverland Peter has shown that real mothers don't have that kind of authority over him. There are differences more important than this between real and make-believe mothers; and Barrie makes it clear that they have something to do with sexual desire.

Sex is bound to be a worrisome subject for a person emotionally over-burdened by the love of his mother. He faces the terrifying possibility that his passionate feeling for her will shade toward erotic desire—and that is absolutely taboo. He knows he must not feel what he is afraid he does feel. Barrie's fantasy handles this precarious wish/fear with great ingenuity. He has Peter choose for his mothers a series of girls, not quite women themselves but on the verge of becoming so. He brings them back to the Neverland to be his mother—but, once there, they play house, with Peter taking the part of the husband. All along, Barrie reminds us that this is all in play; the girl is not really Peter's mother, nor is she really his wife. Hence the incest-taboo is not really broken. Barrie's fantasy does include a degree of eroticism, but it is assigned only to the girl/woman, never to the boy. His innocence is preserved, immaculate. Consider this exchange between Peter and Wendy, which occurs while they are pretending to be the parents of John, Michael, and the lost boys. Peter suddenly draws himself up.

> He looked at her uncomfortably; blinking, you know, like one not sure whether he was awake or asleep.
> "Peter, what is it?"
> "I was just thinking," he said, a little scared. "It is only make-believe, isn't it, that I am their father?"
> "Oh, yes," said Wendy primly.
> "You see," he continued apologetically, "it would make me seem so old to be their real father."
> "But they are ours, Peter, yours and mine."
> "But not really, Wendy?" he asked anxiously.
> "Not if you don't wish it," she replied; and she distinctly heard his sigh of relief. "Peter," she asked, trying to speak firmly, "what are your exact feelings for me?"
> "Those of a devoted son, Wendy."
> "I thought so," she said, and went and sat by herself at the extreme end of the room.
> "You are so queer," he said, frankly puzzled, "and Tiger Lily is the same. There is something she wants to be to me, but she says it is not my mother."
> "No, indeed, it is not," Wendy replied with frightful emphasis.

Peter and Wendy's dual relationship as son-and-mother and husband-and-wife is not the only one that needs to be safely insulated in make-believe. Peter's relationship with Captain Hook is another. The climactic event of the Neverland adventure, of course, is that Peter brings their ancient conflict to an end by killing Hook. On the face of it, there isn't anything especially taboo about a hero's killing a storybook villain like Hook. But if one observes how Barrie has imagined him, one sees that Hook's death at Peter's hands is indeed an event which must be kept make-believe.

For Barrie establishes a clear connection between Hook, the wicked, unfamilied man who "has no little children to love him," and Mr. Darling, Wendy's father, the only other man with any prominence in the story. Barrie stipulated that the same actor should play both Hook and Darling on the stage, and the two characters are crucially alike. In the first place, neither of them is really grown up. Darling "might have passed for a boy again if he had been able to take his baldness off"; and when Hook goes to his death in the duel with Peter, he is mentally a schoolboy still; in his mind he is "slouching in the playing fields of long ago." And not only are they boys, but they are bad boys—cheaters and sulks who lack good form and who try, by unfair means, to steal attention and respect. Darling is obsessed with having the good opinion of his neighbors, his children, and his wife, but he does nothing to deserve it. He throws a tantrum when he cannot tie his tie, he cheats in the medicine-taking treaty with Michael, he uses his remorse over the children's absence to get attention for himself by moving into the kennel. Hook, too, cheats and sulks (he calls it brooding) and behaves like a petulant child. In one episode, just after Peter has made the noble gesture of giving Hook a hand up so they can fight on the same level, Hook bites him. In another, he violates the unwritten laws of romantic warfare by attacking the redskins rather than waiting for them to attack him. Like Darling, he struts and fumes in an effort to make people look up to him, he postures, he dresses splendidly, and he lords it over his crew. But all his concern for good form is vain—for "was it not bad form to think about good form?"

Whimsically but insistently, Barrie emphasizes that these men compete with the boys for the mothers' favor. Darling rivals the children bumblingly and indirectly, pretending not to, revealing his jealousy only in sporadic outbursts; he wheedles and whines for the motherly attention that Mrs. Darling gives spontaneously to her children. Hook, who hates the boys openly and nakedly, tries to kill them, attempting to steal Wendy to be his own mother. And it is a great satisfaction in Barrie's fantasy to see Peter put the men's ridiculous aspirations to rout. Hook, of course, he kills, rescuing Wendy from his clutches and then spurning him with his foot. He registers his victory over Mr. Darling when he casually takes "the sweet, mocking kiss" from Mrs. Darling's lips, a kiss which Mr. Darling had tried and tried in vain to get.

Obviously Barrie is not as nervous about the fantasy of a boy killing the father-like rival as he is about the boy's becoming the mother's husband; he feels no need to render Hook's death doubly make-believe as he has done with the marriage of Peter and Wendy. It is sufficient that Hook dies in the Neverland. (Barrie does emphasize the unreality of his death by mentioning that, within a year of its happening, Peter has forgotten all about it.) The saving power of make-believe does its work. The boy may freely perform the deeds in the Neverland which would destroy him in the real world—because in the real world he would have to face the forbidden nature of his desires and feel guilty about them. That is the great magic of the Neverland: it is a place for people who are "gay and innocent and heartless"—that is, free of guilt.

What Barrie's Neverland demonstrates, then, is one of the primary values of make-believe. Make-believe is the power of the mind to create its own psychologically insulated place—"for the Neverland is always more or less an island"—in which one can act out, symbolically and therefore recklessly, the desires which the real world denies one. There is no penalty to pay, because make-believe actions don't count.

To call this an escape from the real world is accurate enough, in one sense; but in another it is exactly wrong, since ultimately those very concerns from which the mind most eagerly desires to free itself become the preoccupations of the fantasy world itself. In his eagerness to create a pleasing fiction, this kind of fantasist creates a mirror-image of the real world: the real world, that is, as it appears in his own mind.

Not all fantasy is of this sort, of course; the fantasy I am discussing is the kind produced by writers—like Barrie, Lewis Carroll, and Hans Christian Andersen—who create out of discernible need to arrogate the fantasy rights of children as a way of expressing, in sportive modes, their own troubled thoughts. For this purpose, the sportiveness is of special importance, since it is the means by which disturbing feelings can be made pleasurable. Such fantasy asks at every point not to be taken seriously, not to be believed in. It emphasizes the absurdity or the arbitrariness or the insubstantiality of its surface details, and thereby muffles its deeper meanings. In introducing a chapter on the mermaids' lagoon in the Neverland, for instance, Barrie writes:

> If you shut your eyes and are a lucky one, you may see at times a shapeless pool of lovely pale colours suspended in the darkness; then if you squeeze your eyes tighter, the pool begins to take shape, and the colours become so vivid that with another squeeze they must go on fire. But just before they go on fire you see the lagoon. This is the nearest you ever get to it on the mainland, just one heavenly moment; if there could be two moments you might see the surf and hear the mermaids singing.

Literally, this means that the lagoon is an optical illusion, but what Barrie is doing here is describing the quality of evanescence. All through his story, incidental details have the same qualities, which serve to make things diminutive and insubstantial. The mermaids play rugby with "bubbles made in rainbow water"; the lost boys wear animal skins "in which they are so round and furry that when they fall they roll"; the chimney of Wendy's house is made by knocking the bottom of John's hat out and clapping the hat on the roof; even Hook smokes two cigars at once "in a holder of his own contrivance." These and a hundred other minutiae emphasize how unserious, and therefore inconsequential, and therefore innocent, the events of the story are.

It is ironic that this kind of whimsy should be considered especially appropriate to children's literature, when children generally show less appreciation for it than adults. It is the rhetoric of lovers, stage magicians, and jolly uncles. Children don't indulge in it themselves very much, and they don't particularly seek it out in books. The most popular kids' fiction—like the Nancy Drew and Hardy Boys series, the Tarzan books, and so on—are notable for their rather ponderous seriousness, their avoidance of Barrie's arch "Let us now kill a pirate, to show Hook's method" kind of narrative. All the canny modernizers, abridgers, and popularizers of *Peter Pan* recognize this. They leave out the whimsical trimmings—the addresses to the reader, the entirely ornamental details—and keep the plot: the buffoonery and humiliation of Mr. Darling; Peter's taking Wendy to the Neverland to play at being wife and mother; the children's learning to fly; the feud with Captain Hook and his defeat; the children's triumphant return at last to Mrs. Darling's waiting arms. It seems that ordinary readers share enough of Barrie's interest in the fantasy of a child who defeats the father and plays house with the mother to be attracted by his story, but they don't need the camouflage Barrie provides. Barrie sensed the "wickedness" of his fantasy much more strongly than most of his readers do, and instinctively took steps to render the story exaggeratedly innocent. In *Peter Pan*, whimsy, wit, and fantasy are put to one of their most important psychological uses—rendering the unthinkable harmless.

Barrie's notorious remark that "Nothing that happens to us after the age of twelve matters very much" also means that everything that happens to us after the age of twelve matters too much. What made childhood so attractive to him was that children are permitted to make-believe. Done in the spirit of play, what they do doesn't have to matter at all. They need not be guilty. They are only playing.

24

RUDYARD KIPLING

The Mowgli Stories

The Mowgli stories in *The Jungle Books* by Rudyard Kipling (1865–1936) do what many classics of children's literature do: They begin with a psychological dilemma that lies near the heart of the author's sense of his own childhood—an unfulfilled yearning, an old frustration, a wrong unrighted—and generate from it a fantasy which fulfills that yearning, releases that frustration, rectifies that injustice. It is a mark of literary genius when such fantasies reach outside the author's private grievance and touch universal feelings which millions of readers can share. And it is a very high order of genius when the author can not only bring his fantasy to the world, but also bring the world into his fantasy, incorporating in the fiction itself the truths of human life which are the wise corrective to his own wishful thinking. The Mowgli stories achieve that high order of genius.

The essential dilemma underlying these stories is the theme of the song Mowgli sings at the end of " 'Tiger-Tiger!' " Here Mowgli, having been denied membership in either the society of wolves or the society of men, has killed Shere Khan, the reprobate tiger who has been his most conspicuous enemy.

> Waters of the Wainganga, the man pack have cast me out. I did them no
> harm, but they were afraid of me. Why?
> Wolf pack, ye have cast me out too. The jungle is shut to me and the
> village gates are shut. Why?
> As Mang flies between the beasts and birds so fly I between the village and
> the jungle. Why?

I dance on the hide of Shere Khan, but my heart is very heavy.
  My mouth is cut and wounded with the stones from the village, but my
  heart is very light, because I have come back to the jungle. Why?
These two things fight together in me as the snakes fight in the spring. The
  water comes out of my eyes, yet I laugh while it falls. Why?
I am two Mowglis, but the hide of Shere Khan is under my feet.
All the jungle knows that I have killed Shere Khan. Look, look well, O
  wolves!
Ahae! My heart is heavy with the things that I do not understand.

To understand the mysteries that Mowgli struggles with here—to understand why men and wolves have turned against him when he did them no
harm, and why he finds himself "two Mowglis," laughing and crying, with
heart both light and heavy; to understand why he dances on the hide of
Shere Khan before the watching eyes of the wolf pack; and to understand
why his moment of triumph leaves him with a heart "heavy with the things
that I do not understand"—is to understand the root-situation of the Mowgli
stories, and to fathom their urgency and depth of meaning, for Kipling first,
and next for his readers.

Classic children's literature contains a number of memorable outsiders,
characters who stand significantly beyond the pale of the culture upon which
their lives are a comment: Huckleberry Finn, St.-Exupéry's little prince,
Peter Pan, the child in Hans Christian Andersen's story who announces that
the emperor has nothing on. Mowgli is, in a general sense, one of them.
But he is different, too, in that he is not simply outside a culture looking
in; he is specifically between two cultures. An outcast from the society of
both men and wolves but in some sense a product of both of them, Mowgli
thinks and acts very differently from someone who, like Huck Finn, simply
has no place in ordered society anywhere, or someone who, like Peter Pan,
has looked on society and rejected it. That Mowgli flies "between the village
and the jungle" as "Mang [the bat] flies between the beasts and birds" is
essential to the drama of his life, and makes of the Mowgli stories something
very different from the tense personal fantasy of *Peter Pan* on the one hand,
or the social satire of *Huckleberry Finn* on the other. In these tales, Kipling
bridges the gap between solipsistic personal dream and detached, impersonal
social comedy. He was well qualified to do so.

Mowgli, as the boy between two cultures, is in an important sense Kipling
himself, whose whole life was spent in odd and excited suspension between
and among various societies. Born in India of English parents, he was very
early made aware that he was neither entirely English nor Indian. He was
raised by a native Indian nurse and spoke Hindi before he spoke English;
at the age of six, like many Anglo-Indian children, he was sent back to
England, away from his parents, to learn to be English. The experience as
he recalls it in his memoirs and in the short story "Baa, Baa, Black Sheep"
was profoundly traumatic; dropped from a world where, as the little *sahib*,

his every whim had been honored, into a foster home which he came to call "The House of Desolation," where a strict and Puritanical woman set about breaking his spirit, Kipling experienced a dislocation that was virtually absolute. Later, when he was twelve, he was sent to the United Services College, a public school established by a group of army officers to prepare their sons for the responsibilities of army commissions. But Kipling's father was not an army officer—he was an architect, a man of letters, and a museum curator, with no intention that his son should become a military man. Between the ages of twelve and seventeen, Kipling lived in unreconciled tension between two styles of life, which one of his biographers describes this way:

> The holidays he spent with his Burne-Jones and Poynter aunts, meeting the Pre-Raphaelite Brotherhood and their friends. He looked at pictures of delicate dream women set against backgrounds of hard bright detail. At school—and it must be repeated that it was a boarding-school with no week-ends away, an interminable thirteen or fourteen weeks at a stretch—he lived among budding subalterns under a headmaster he admired but assistant masters whom he regarded as enemies and in some cases disliked or despised. (Mason 46)

He returned to India in his eighteenth year and took up the trade of newspaper journalist and, later, local-color short-story writer, vocations which set him psychologically apart from the officers and civil servants among whom he lived and whom he observed as material for his writing. Finally, having escaped India on the strength of a prodigious early reputation as a writer of fiction and verse, he settled temporarily in Vermont, where he carried on a polite cold war with neighboring Vermonters, who did not know what to make of the celebrated and unsociable foreigner camping in their territory. It was here, in Vermont, that Kipling wrote the Mowgli stories, about a boy who yearns for membership in two social worlds but finds himself ill-suited to either of them. Kipling knew firsthand the dilemma he was writing about.

Part of what he accomplished in the Mowgli stories was a piece of wish-fulfillment, a consoling fantasy akin to Hans Christian Andersen's self-vindication in "The Ugly Duckling." Both Kipling and Andersen made up stories in which heroes are rejected by society not simply because they are different from ordinary people, but because they are better. In both stories, rejection is pictured not as the mark of inadequacy which it seems to be in real life, but as a badge of superiority. In the ironically titled story "Mowgli's Brothers," which tells of Mowgli's first dealings with the Seeonee Wolf Pack, the innocent, good-hearted little boy is at first nominally accepted in membership. He assumes that he really belongs. "I was born in the jungle," he says. "I have obeyed the Law of the Jungle, and there is no wolf of ours from whose paws I have not pulled a thorn. Surely they are my brothers." But he is wrong, as Bagheera the panther explains to him:

> Not even I can look thee between the eyes, and I was born among men, and I love thee, Little Brother. The others hate thee because their eyes cannot meet thine; because thou art wise; because thou hast pulled out thorns from their feet—because thou art a man.

They hate him, in short, because he can do things they can't. Later, the humans' reaction against him will be the same; they fear him because he is stronger, more sensible, and wiser in the ways of the jungle than they are. "Sorcerer!" they cry. "Wolf's brat! Jungle-demon! Go away!"

Rejected by two packs of mediocrities, Mowgli (something like Andersen's swan) joins instead an elite society which is much nobler than the societies from which he has been excluded. Baloo the wise old teacher-bear, Bagheera the model of masculine independence and power, Akela the statesman-leader of the wolf pack, and Kaa the ancient, mysterious and mighty python make up this lordly society, the preferable substitute for the societies that have denied Mowgli. Baloo, Bagheera, and Kaa are all loners, living apart from their own species; Akela, seeing the faithlessness of the wolf pack, virtually renounces his membership in it. "In truth, I have lived too long," he says. "I know ye to be cowards, and it is to cowards that I speak." All four are physically imposing, strong, and dangerous fighters; all are creatures of honor and high principle; all are indisputably expert, the best at what they do. Bagheera is "as cunning as Tabaqui, as bold as the wild buffalo, and as reckless as the wounded elephant." Akela is the embodiment of principled legality. Baloo is the sage of the Law of the Jungle, the scholar of civilized wisdom. Kaa knows more primal stuff, the distillation of age and sheer massive experience:

> Kaa, his head motionless on the ground, thought of all that he had seen and known since the day he came from the egg. The light seemed to go out of his eyes and leave them like stale opals, and now and again he made little stiff passes with his head to right and left, as though he were hunting in his sleep.

Just to be accepted by this exotic elite would be a great distinction; but Mowgli, even better, creates this heroic brotherhood, for it is only through their love of Mowgli that the four constitute a society at all.

Membership in that brotherhood is dependent on strength, cunning, charisma, personal merit; membership in the various packs that roam Mowgli's jungle—wolf pack, monkey pack, man pack, dog pack—is the merest accident of birth. Pack-thinking and pack-behavior are consistently vulgar, undiscriminating, mean, and petty. Ordinary membership in such groups is equivalent to personal mediocrity. To be purely logical, Mowgli should feel relieved that he has escaped the downward-leveling of wolf pack and man pack.

But of course the matter is not one of pure logic. We can readily understand why Mowgli seeks entry into such groups, inferior as they are; we can see that the Mowgli stories, unlike Andersen's one-dimensional little fable, are something larger than an extended version of the compensatory thought, "Who wants to belong to that crowd, anyway." Being rejected doesn't do much of anything to Andersen's swan; he simply undergoes the ordeal, grows up a little, finds a flock of swans to join, and prospers. Kipling knows, and the Mowgli stories show, that being rejected is not only a painful process but a deeply formative one, crucially affecting a person's sense of self, values, and habitual stance before the world.

The pattern of Mowgli's personality is simple and consistent: In the beginning, innocently, he wants and expects to be loved. The mother wolf, whose instincts are right, adopts him and loves him, and Mowgli assumes that everyone else will, too. But the wolf pack turns on him. By a plain and direct process of substituting an objective which can be reached for one which cannot, Mowgli becomes infatuated with power and dominance. In effect he says to the world, "You have shown you do not love me; very well, I cannot force you to love me. But I can force you to fear and respect me, and that will be good enough." Mowgli becomes preoccupied with revenge—with killing Shere Khan who has insulted him, with destroying the man village that has insulted him, with destroying the red-dog pack that has presumed to enter his jungle. The destruction of his enemies becomes a primary pleasure. When Kaa asks him, "So the jungle gives thee all that thou hast ever desired, Little Brother?" Mowgli answers, "Not all, else there would be a new and strong Shere Khan to kill once a moon."

On this vindictive energy Mowgli rises to be master of the jungle. "It was after the letting in of the jungle [where the native village had been] that the pleasantest part of Mowgli's life began," Kipling writes. "He had the good conscience that comes from paying a just debt [of vengeance], and all the jungle was his friend, for all the jungle was afraid of him."

Honor has become the great ideal in Mowgli's eyes: good reputation, the unsullied name; he values it because society has treated him as if he were not honorable. "They have cast me out from the man pack, Mother," he announces in " 'Tiger-Tiger!' " "but I come with the hide of Shere Khan to keep my word . . . Look well, O wolves. Have I kept my word?" Making and keeping personal oaths—particularly oaths of vengeance—are one of the clearest ways of demonstrating one's honor in these stories. He declaims in "Red Dog":

> I say that when the dholes come, and if the dholes come, Mowgli and the Free People are of one skin for that hunting. And I say, by the bull that bought me, by the bull Bagheera paid for me in the old days which ye of the pack do not remember, I say, that the trees and the river may hear and hold fast if I forget. I say that this my knife shall be as a tooth to the pack—and I do not think it is so blunt. This is my word which has gone from me.

The whole system of manly virtues follows from this idea of honor: pride, courage, discipline, loyalty, cunning, and physical strength.

The high style in which Mowgli speaks is intrinsic to the stance of defiant self-assertion that he has developed. We see this style most clearly in all the rhetorical occasions of chivalric combat: the taunt, the challenge, the boast; but its characteristics pervade virtually all the speech and manners of Mowgli and his circle: stately, ceremonious, self-conscious, designed to remind one's listeners of one's status and prowess. "A brave heart and a courteous tongue" says Kaa to Mowgli. "They will carry thee far in the jungle." And Kaa is exactly right; courtesy is itself a demonstration of bravery, a formal notice that one takes oneself seriously and demands respect from others.

The very Law of the Jungle itself, which embodies much that is basic to Kipling's attitude on many social subjects, is among other things a construction of principles and values ideal for the pursuit of power and dominion to which Mowgli is driven. Kipling does not present it primarily as that, of course. He presents the Law as the basic rule of survival, growing out of real-life natural history. It is "by far the oldest law in the world," he says; it "has arranged for almost every kind of accident that may befall the Jungle-People, till now its code is as perfect as time and custom can make it." The myth which the elephant Hathi relates in "How Fear Came" suggests that the Law has certain moral benefits, as a corrective to natural failings like laziness, petulance and irresponsibility—but that its primal foundation is the fear of death. "The first of your masters has brought Death into the jungle, and the second Shame. Now it is time there was a Law, and a Law that ye may not break. Now ye shall know Fear."

From what Kipling shows us of the maxims that grow out of this beginning, one sees clearly enough that they are mostly concerned with species-survival. The law provides rules within which death can be controlled, and the animals can release their impulses of hunger, ferocity and hostility without exterminating whole species. The occasion on which Hathi tells the story gives a clear example of what this means: He tells it to the animals—predators and grass-eaters together—assembled under "the Water Truce" which goes into effect during drought. The Water Truce forbids killing at the drinking-place, since if killing were permitted there the grazers would stay away from water and die quickly, of thirst, and the predators would then die, too, of starvation.

To a large extent, Kipling's Law prescribes behavior which we would call instinctive. It specifies, for example, that the jackal may scavenge after other hunters but that the wolves should hunt for themselves, and that the wolf should hunt at night and sleep during the day. But Kipling does not leave the matter at that; his Law ultimately is not just a description of the way animals are, but also a moral suggestion of how they ought to be. It is entirely possible in these stories (indeed, it is entirely *common*) for animals to fail to live up the Law—which wouldn't make sense if the Law represented only instinct. Shere Khan is a gross and chronic violator, he kills humans promiscuously and pollutes drinking water with their blood. The wolf pack reneges on its promise to Mowgli and breaks the Law. The monkey people have so little regard for principle that they are said not even to have a Law.

As a moral system, the Law generally urges restraint and responsibility and the long view, as over against ungoverned selfish impulse. It is deeply conservative, making no provision for democratic improvement, and strictly observing the ideal of hierarchy. "Keep peace with the lords of the jungle," it urges at one point; at another, "Because of his age and his cunning, because of his gripe and his paw, / In all that the Law leaveth open, the word of your head wolf is Law." It shows comparatively little concern for helping or protecting the weak; what little there is in that way comes under the heading of ensuring the perpetuation of species (e.g., taking care of mothers with new-born offspring) rather than the heading of compassion. It is, in short, a system within which those thrive best who are strong, suspicious, purposeful, and proud.

In this hybrid concept of Law—neither purely amoral instinct nor purely moral injunction, but something of both—Kipling has an idea of great value in Mowgli's quest for honor and status. What the Law provides is an ideal of behavior both honorable and practical, which stands apart from mere mob-conformity. If Mowgli is to be vindicated in his war with societies both wolf and human, it is important to have a system of absolutes by which he is right and society is wrong. Kipling separates the ideas of *law* and *society*, rather than treating them as two aspects of social order as most social theorists do. In the Mowgli stories, one chooses between ordinary social life—which is sloppy, unintelligent, and irrational—and life under the Law—which is rigorous, disciplined, and sensible. That he so thoroughly understands the Law of the Jungle and observes it so faithfully proves that Mowgli is stronger, wiser and more honorable than those who rejected him, and proves it, moreover, not according to some eccentric, visionary ideal of his own but according to the very time-perfected principles of life in the jungle. Keeping the Law, in these stories, is a little like obeying the Bible as an unimpeachable authority of rectitude (indeed, the nearest model for the maxims of the Law is the book of Proverbs in the Old Testament); furthermore, this Law is worldly and practical, not at all "religious."

If we were to read all but the last of the Mowgli stories, and stop with "Red Dog," the account of Mowgli's destruction of the barbarous dog pack that invades his domain, we would in some ways have a complete story. "Red Dog" details an apocalyptic blood-feast, the orgiastic climax of Mowgli's need to dominate, and completes the grim story of his rise to power. If the stories stopped here, one fundamental drive—the drive to react against the pain of rejection—could be seen to color the entire value-system and philosophy of the stories, and to help create their characters and shape their plots. With "Red Dog," the demonstration is complete that the world of Kipling's jungle is not just the place of Mowgli's ostracism but the ideal place for avenging it.

But the note of triumph in "Red Dog" is discordant, because of another note in the story, a tone of repletion without satisfaction and the passing of the conditions under which such bloody victories make good emotional sense. The inner circle of Mowgli's friends is in decay in this story.

> Father and Mother Wolf died . . . and Baloo grew very old and stiff, and even Bagheera, whose nerves were steel and whose muscles were iron, seemed slower at the kill. Akela turned from grey to milky white with pure age.

Mowgli mounts his epic battle against the dog pack more out of memory than present inspiration. "Listen now," he says, "there was a wolf, my father, and there was a wolf, my mother, and there was an old grey wolf (not too wise: he is white now) was my father and my mother. Therefore I—" and he makes his oath to fight this one last fight for and with the wolf pack. When it is over, and the most graphic, brutal bloodletting of Mowgli's career has been done, Akela tells him, "All debts are paid now. go to thine own people." Mowgli protests in terms he has used since the humans rejected him years before. "I will never go. I will hunt alone in the jungle." But Akela insists. "After the summer come the rains, and after the rains comes the spring. . . . Mowgli will drive Mowgli. Go back to thy people. Go to Man."

And thus the stage is set for the last story in the series, "The Spring Running," which takes the argument one painful, honest, inevitable step further, and faces Mowgli's need for love and acceptance in a new and necessary form. "The Spring Running" is an odd story, somewhat mysterious to many readers whether child or adult. It is, in more ways than one, "the last of the Mowgli stories," as Kipling says, for it announces, in effect, the finish of Mowgli as we know him; it precisely refutes the whole basis on which Mowgli has built his personality—the fond belief that a soul can survive on an emotional diet of power and dominance alone.

(One other story about Mowgli, called "In the Rukh," was published in 1891, a year before the first of *The Jungle Books*, in a collection of Kipling short stories called *Many Inventions*. It is quite different in tone and subject from the other Mowgli tales, being told from the viewpoint of an English Department of Woods and Forests official in India. In this story Mowgli signs on as a forest-guard with the Englishman's department, marries a native Indian girl, and fathers a child. For the most part the story pictures him at a distance, a godlike woods-creature with mysterious powers over the animals [he has a retinue of four wolves with him], great self-confidence, and a complacent, amused respect for European authority.)

"The Spring Running" is the story of, really, two big crises in Mowgli's life, and the transition into which they impel him. The first of these, and the most obvious, is the crisis of Mowgli's sexual awakening. At the age of seventeen he feels yearnings and excitements which he has never felt before, even though he has witnessed the spring mating season every year, and has been to some extent aware of a change that comes over all creatures at that time. His sexual hunger sends him running through the jungle, a forty-mile lope which takes him, almost involuntarily, into a village of people. "Mowgli," he says to himself, "what hast thou to do any more with the lairs of the man pack?" The answer comes soon enough—he needs women. Messua, the woman who mothered him once before and who may or may not be his real mother, now takes him in again. Her husband is dead, and she has a two-year-old baby. She feeds Mowgli, caresses him, praises his good looks ("Have any told thee that thou art beautiful beyond all men?" she says). Mowgli rests and dandles the baby on his lap and sleeps. The sickness he has felt inside him is momentarily allayed. As he leaves the woman's hut to return to the jungle, he sees a girl walking down a path.

In one way, then, the story is about the place of sex and reproduction in the scheme of life. The Law of the Jungle, preoccupied as it is with the survival of species, would of course require that creatures go forth and multiply; in this respect "The Spring Running" simply shows that Mowgli is not above that feature of the Law.

But the story is also about love, or the need for love, and that is not exactly the same thing. The feelings Kipling writes about here ultimately transcend the simply physical release of mating. Mowgli cannot do as the animals in the story do—disappear into the bushes for brief, intense courtship and mating and then return to the all-male company of Mowgli's circle. Mowgli's fever is sexual, but it is more broadly psychological, too, and finally even philosophical, for it forces Mowgli to question the authenticity of his values. It requires that he leave the jungle and return to human society more or less permanently.

On consideration, one can see rather exactly the nature of the second crisis Mowgli is undergoing. As to the first crisis, the emergence of sexual appetites, we may grant Kipling's notion that this is a natural occurrence for a seventeen-year-old. But the second crisis is more appropriate, perhaps, to a man about the age of Kipling himself when he wrote the story—thirty years. Mowgli, the story tells us, has for some time been the undisputed master of the jungle. "The Jungle-People, who used to fear him for his wits, feared him now for his mere strength, and when he moved quietly on his own affairs the whisper of his coming cleared the wood-path." He is like a man who has made a great success in his career and found that his success is unsatisfying. (Kiping, when he wrote these stories, had already risen to world renown as a brilliant young writer—had known the feeling of being held in almost superstitious awe by the literary world.) The very idea of defining oneself entirely through the power and respect he commands does

not sit easily in Mowgli's mind any longer. He is irritable, unsure of himself—
a fact suggested in an incidental exchange with Bagheera: The panther has
gotten kittenish with the mating-urge, and Mowgli rebukes him.

> "I say, *is* it well for the Black Panther so to mouth and cough and howl and
> roll," he scolds. "Remember, we be the masters of the jungle, thou and I."
> "Indeed, yes, I hear, man-cub," says Bagheera. "We be surely the masters
> of the jungle! Who is so strong as Mowgli? Who so wise?"
> There was a curious drawl in the voice that made Mowgli turn to see whether
> by any chance the black panther was making fun of him.

He has started to sense that the dignity of his position is not unimpeachable,
and that there might be viewpoints from which his eminence could look
hollow.

Mowgli tries in half a dozen ways to describe the new feeling that has
invaded him. He says:

> It must be I have carelessly eaten poison. By night and by day I hear a double
> step upon my trail. When I turn my head it is as though one had hidden
> himself from me that instant. . . . The Red Flower is in my body, my bones
> are water—and—I know not what I know.

He finds himself washed with gentle, uncontrollable emotion. "A large warm
tear splashed down on his knee, and, miserable as he was, Mowgli felt happy
that he was so miserable. . . ."

Clearly, Mowgli is not in the grip of snorting animal lust; he feels rather
a mellow, languid desire for gentleness and love and nourishment. His new
feeling is tied to all the warm, yielding, lonely, softening feelings which, in
his proud and defiant rise to power, he has learned to deny himself. What
Mowgli needs is not release of physical tension but a change in his essential
life. He has "a new stomach in him," as he thinks; he has "changed his skin,"
as Kaa puts it, and "having cast the skin, we may not creep into it afresh."
Mowgli is realizing the conflict between his past delight in exerting his will
over the animals and his new yearning for love. The sexual impulse which
transforms the animals in the mating season represents, for him, a counter-
principle to his exertion of power, a rebuke to that power, a force more
urgent than the desire to dominate which has been the basis of his whole
identity. Mowgli wishes, in short, to break out of that enclosed, defiant,
paranoid circle of force and self-assertion which his early sorrows have taught
him to build and fortify.

The old pride and proofs of self-worth are not immediately forgotten, of
course. There is pain in Mowgli's dim new realization, because submission
to the demands of love is, in some very serious respects, a betrayal of the
old heroic code by which Mowgli has learned to live. To feel as Mowgli
feels—lonely and sorry for himself and in need of warmth and caresses—is,

by the old code, to feel a loss of dignity and honor. Mowgli must reconcile himself to this as best he can. As he takes his leave of his warrior-friends, they assure him that this new departure is no shame, no repetition of the humiliating exclusions he suffered years before. "Man goes to Man at the last, *though the jungle does not cast him out*," Kaa says. "The jungle does not cast me out then?" asks Mowgli. "Nay, look up, Little Brother," says Baloo. "There is no shame in this hunting." Shame there may not be, but there is a come-down, an unsettling sense of vulnerability and of mortality, of letting down the barriers which Mowgli has learned to maintain.

"The Spring Running" is a story more about an ending than a beginning. It leaves us with only the loosest idea of what will become of Mowgli when he reaches the man-village. We expect that he will get married—and Kipling says elsewhere that he does, both in "In the Rukh" and at the end of " 'Tiger-Tiger!' " Presumably he will make some accommodations, temper the stern and critical view of humanity which he brought to the village years before in "Mowgli's Brothers." (Pitched in its different key, "In the Rukh" shows that Mowgli will continue to run afoul of human superstitions and will still be skeptical of human values and customs, but he will acknowledge the legitimacy of society's claims on him anyway.) He comes now not in flight from something—the faithlessness of the wolves—but in search of something—the love of a woman. We know that Mowgli has reached an end to the life lived entirely in reaction to the ostracism suffered in his boyhood. His days of proving his manhood to those who would deny it are coming to a close.

"Four things greater than all things are,— / Women and Horses and Power and War," Kipling wrote elsewhere, with the bravado one finds in much of his fiction and verse. "The Spring Running" is one story where the heroic fantasy comes down to earth, and the claims of Women are felt to outweigh those of Horses and Power and War. Here Kipling tests the mystique of honor and defiance against the claims of love and domesticity, and it is honor that has to yield. The deep message here is that hostility and resentment can make a personality formidable and strong in certain ways, but vulnerable, too, and incomplete. The larger values of love and home and generation lie outside its boundaries. It may be surprising to find such an idea advanced by Kipling the notorious drum-banger and saber-rattler, but there it is.

The Mowgli stories are, then, something larger and more conscientious than an outsider's fantasy about the glories of being outside. Kipling and Mowgli fabricate and achieve their dream of proving the insiders wrong—but then, in the end, face the fact that such proofs are made at the cost of important feelings. "The Spring Running" is not some half-intended afterthought to the Mowgli saga; it is its inevitable culmination. Mowgli began his days seeking love and acceptance, and he returns to the village in the end, still seeking.

25

BEATRIX POTTER

The Tale of Peter Rabbit and *The Tale of Squirrel Nutkin*

Beatrix Potter (1866–1943) may be thought of as a kind of literary naturalist for children. Born into a well-to-do middle-class English family, she was educated largely by her governess. She never complained of her lack of more formal education and said she was glad no school had rubbed off her originality. As a girl, she was somewhat lonely, being an only daughter (she had a younger brother), and she enjoyed her many pets, her drawing lessons, her journal, trips to London art galleries, and her summers in the Lake District.

In 1893 she wrote to the young son of her former governess and in the letter described and illustrated the adventures of Peter Rabbit. In 1901 she borrowed the letter, enlarged the story, added to the drawings (black and white), and sought a publisher. After several publishers refused the book, she had 250 copies privately printed. Then Frederick Warne and Co. offered to print the work with illustrations in color. Published in 1903, *Peter Rabbit* proved an instant success, and Beatrix Potter was encouraged to pour forth during the next fifteen years over twenty more books, including such classics as *The Tailor of Gloucester*, *The Tale of Squirrel Nutkin*, *The Tale of Benjamin Bunny*, *The Tale of the Two Bad Mice*, *The Tale of Mrs. Tiggy-Winkle*, *The Tale of Tom Kitten*, *The Tale of Jemima Puddle-Duck*, *The Roly-Poly Pudding*, and *The Tale of Mr. Tod*. After her marriage, Beatrix Potter slackened her writing of children's books and took up farming, which she engaged in so successfully that she was able to bequeath 4,000 acres in the Lake District to the National Trust.

Beatrix Potter was shy with adults but was a great friend to children and animals. She once rescued a rabbit from a neighbor's snare, and to her loving observation of many creatures and landscapes the delicate water-color illustrations in her books attest. She said that she also enjoyed "taking pains" over her writing; she rewrote her stories again and again, and she said that she read the Bible "if I feel my style wants chastening." Her works are minor monuments to the high quality of a chastened style in both verbal and visual arts.

The Tale of Peter Rabbit tells the archetypal story of a venture out from the security of home to a dangerous and forbidden place. This place, as in much pastoral romance, is the green world, site of vital growth and of the hero's initiation toward maturity, the crossing over from Innocence to Experience. Peter, of course, does not know all this, and to treat the tale as a full-scale myth or romance epic would be to ignore its scale and corresponding charm. In the details of Beatrix Potter's storytelling and in the deft observance of her illustrations lies the special appeal of this children's classic.

Readers of *Peter Rabbit* have long noted Beatrix Potter's family-role stereotyping: The rabbit children live with their mother; the girls have rabbit names, the boy is Peter; the girls are good, the boy is naughty; the girls stay close to home, the boy has adventures; the girls gather food, Peter steals it. Peter's mischief is thus partly legislated from the outset by his position in the family. His trip to the garden is terrifying in one sense, but the tale is hardly cautionary. Though Peter loses his clothes, cries, almost gets trampled, comes home exhausted, and is made to drink medicinal tea, the child-reader is fascinated by and attracted to Peter rather than repelled by him. For one thing, Beatrix Potter's humor intervenes on Peter's behalf. Mr. McGregor is a comic antagonist who not only looks silly in his beard, specs, and old-fashioned cap but also calls out after a rabbit, "Stop thief!" We have time, after Peter becomes tangled in the gooseberry net, to consider the color, material, and newness of his jacket and buttons. The watering can "would have been a beautiful thing to hide in, if it had not had so much water in it." A mouse cannot answer Peter because of a pea in its mouth. Peter "thought it best" not to speak to the cat. Mr. McGregor's scarecrow is pictured as an absurd failure. The author is "sorry to say" that Peter was not very well. And so on. Child readers may not get all of the humor (such as the "accident" of Peter's father being put in a pie), but they can hardly miss sensing that Peter is in the hands of a comic providence who will make everything turn out all right.

Peter's initial rebellion, moreover, comes perilously close to being defended by the author. As his mother buttons tightly around his neck a jacket that Peter obviously hates, she says: "Now run along, and don't get into mischief. I am going out." Any child with an ounce of spunk will accept the invitation implicit in these remarks. Potter's tale is about as "cautionary" as a pirate or outlaw film giving two hours of illicit adventure and a minute of repentance.

Potter, like Grahame and Barrie, works in the direction of re-domesti-
cating children's literature in contradistinction to such authors as Lewis
Carroll, Mark Twain, Robert Louis Stevenson, and Rudyard Kipling who
pushed children's literature toward the more nearly savage and tragic. Rabbits and toy bears are accepted by small children as comfortable familiars.
Rabbits are easily domesticated and Potter's drawings in *Peter Rabbit*—
emphasizing the toddler-like largeness of heads and stomachs and switching
from clothes to no clothes—continually suggest that crossing the line from
natural rabbit to house rabbit is not difficult. The frontispiece, which forecasts
the ending of the story, immediately signals to the child viewer that sympathy
as well as humor is directed at Peter. Snug in a very comfortable bed, he
has enough spirit (even at the end of his ordeal) to resist his mother's dose
of medicine. That we see only his ears and paws makes us laugh both at
him and at his exasperated mother.

The illustrations in the first part of *Peter Rabbit* reinforce the notion that
Peter is set apart from his three sisters by dress, expression, and physical
position. Peter seems to prick up his ears at mention of the garden, and the
warning against mischief is obviously directed at him. We see Mrs. Rabbit
going off to get food, just as the children do. The detail of mentioning
precisely what Mrs. Rabbit bought hints that child listeners deserve to know
some of the business of their parents. Note also the democratic apportioning
of the buns: one apiece for each child and adult.

Then, just as the mother goes out in search of food, so do her offspring,
but swiftly we are made to observe in that search a polarity of "good little
bunnies" against "very naughty" one. Not "good" versus "bad"; Peter's
transgressions do not extend that far. Yet he is not to be considered "little"
or a "bunny," either. His evident delight in testing the forbidden delicacies
of Mr. McGregor's garden is nicely captured in Potter's depiction of his
double-stuffed fists, raised-back head, half-closed eyes, and jauntily-crossed
feet. This is a youngster who takes full pleasure in his mischief. Peter's
satiated rotundity is stressed in the illustration that makes him look large,
especially when it is compared to his suddenly diminutive helplessness facing
Mr. McGregor. There the illustration humorously suggests the shock of
mutual surprise and a moment of stillness before the chase. Soon, Potter
shows both Peter and Mr. McGregor in comical attitudes of flight and pursuit, and in the next three pages she traces the descent of Peter to reflective
misery as he loses his accoutrements of civilization and gives himself up for
lost. Thereafter he alternates between passive stillness and bursts of getaway
activity.

Mr. McGregor's more violently intended ministrations in applying the
sieve and his own foot to Peter are made to seem less violent by the composition of illustrations and wording of text. Peter looks rather sleek and
graceful as he jumps away, and one notes his rabbity energy and his full
form in contrast to the partially shown weapon of his enemy. In each drawing

Potter scatters three things in an artful symmetry of flight, and the text assays internal rhymes that suggest providential control of the violence: "intended to *pop* upon the *top* of Peter"; "tried to *put* his *foot* upon Peter."

The action slows down and the text fills up as Peter enters a more reflective phase of his adventure, asking for help, becoming "puzzled," and learning quietly to avoid the danger of the cat. We see Peter watching the cat, then Peter watching Mr. McGregor, and then the three sparrows watching Peter exit under the gate. The last garden picture yields three blackbirds gazing inquisitively up at the scarecrow while another blackbird perches perkily on the cross piece. The incongruous scarecrow does not work, and we know why: The birds in the garden are the kind who can "implore" Peter to "exert" himself. Mr. McGregor's views of animal nature and intelligence are obviously crude and ignorant.

The final three illustrations in *Peter Rabbit* stress the cautionary element of the book as they depict Peter lying exhausted in his cave, then confined to bed while his sisters stay up, then absent entirely as his sisters complacently spoon up bread and milk and blackberries for supper. But Peter by his confinement to bed perhaps adds a kind of uncomplaining martyrdom to his heroic gyrations in the garden.

Rumer Godden conceived a fictitious correspondence between Beatrix Potter and the editors of a publishing company who wished to revise *Peter Rabbit* for beginning readers. This "correspondence" is designed to provoke amusement over the varying standards and purposes among producers of children's books. It so happens that at least one "revised" version of *Peter Rabbit* is now on the market, and one could profitably amuse oneself by comparing the original story and illustrations to the new in the light of Rumer Godden's analysis.

The Tale of Squirrel Nutkin, the "tale of a tail," Potter's myth of origins as to why squirrels chatter rudely at us, is a good deal more ambitious and complicated than is *Peter Rabbit*. The tale contains more riddles than Nutkin's rhymes contain: In what sense will it turn out to be a tale about a tail? (we don't find out until the end); why does Nutkin tell riddles?; why is he rude to Old Brown?; why doesn't he gather food?; is he challenging Old Brown's power to "own" the island in terms of controlling who eats and is eaten there?; is Nutkin a figure of fun or free will or pride?; is Old Brown a species of ravenous mortality whom Nutkin instinctively exposes as unable to put a broken egg to rights or drive a sunbeam from a kitchen or quiet the roaring in the wind?; is Nutkin reduced on the final page to an angry loss of language, of the power to control his tale? However we may look at the strange battle between over-voluble Nutkin and the silent, menacing Brown, Potter's arts of economy and suspense drive us on fascinated to the end.

Squirrel Nutkin is an eater of nuts, made from nuts, akin to nuts, just as his brother, Twinkleberry, twinkles from or like berries. "Kin" can be a diminutive suffix. Nutkin is "little Nut," and he's a little nutty. Nutkin is also our nut-kin.

The main point of any "tale about a tail" must concern some threat to the tail, and so it behooves us to ask, all through the story, just what Nutkin's tail "associates with," as the psychologists say. Nutkin uses his "tail for a sail" as the other squirrels do (catching up the wind's energy), but eventually he loses his tail. Is it an emblem of his energy or perhaps his pride? Is it (of course) phallic in some way? Do the illustrations help us decide? Such questions may hasten us too quickly into the heavy middle of the story. Is it better, perhaps, to pretend an inductive method whose predeductions remain instinctive?

The story begins in the present tense—"This is a tale about a tail"—but it shifts in its first sentence to past tense for the next verb: "a tail that belonged to a little red squirrel," as if the shift to past tense may be significant. The tail once belonged to Nutkin but no longer does. Margins between present, past, and future are crossed several times in the story. The third paragraph shifts back to present tense: "there is" an island—always there in some sense? Is "Old Brown" an eternal presence, a never-ending story, holding onto the tail of the tale and keeping it in his power? Nutkin will challenge Old Brown ever more insistently with riddles about the limits of authority, but finally Nutkin is imagined as any future squirrel one might meet who chatters nonsense syllables in rage at riddle challenges thrown his way. Crossing margins or shores to take sustenance from the far side is dangerous, just as communicating a challenge to another side is dangerous. This is a story of the riddle as to where things like tails and tales properly end.

Potter's illustrations are wonderfully suggestive. Many are humorous in obvious and not so obvious ways. The squirrels use tools of rafts and oars and sacks and fishing poles. Old Brown at first seems just an owl with a crude tree-home. But as the story goes on and Nutkin loses more and more of his manners (as Peter Rabbit lost his clothes), the squirrels seem to revert more and more to merely animal nature whereas the house of Old Brown becomes more and more civilized. We even see him sitting in an elaborately carved chair eating honey with a spoon! Yet his fierce and Olympian silence consumes even more, consumes both the pertinent and impertinent offerings of the squirrels, the whole tale.

All of the squirrels other than Nutkin seem to be exponents of a ceremonial, in some ways religious and propitiatory, way of life. Though squirrels are herbivores, these squirrels are portrayed as catching sacrificial offerings of mice, mole, and minnows. Old Brown promptly eats their offerings (isn't that the third mouse's tail drooping out of Old Brown's mouth as Nutkin taunts him with the cherry riddle?), and he acts out the inscrutable ferocity of an ancient god. From this point of view, Nutkin might be viewed paradoxically as a kind of latter-day Promethean who champions the causes of

poetry and pleasure as ends in themselves until made to suffer the consequences. Nutkin is plainly obsessed with Old Brown as himself the riddle
of authority, a force that simply is itself, self-contained and betraying no use
for words which always put one thing in terms of another.

The denouement is really quite terrifying. The squirrels have worked in
the fashion of Genesis for six days. They come on "Saturday," "for the last
time," to give the great god Brown "a last parting present." Nutkin positively
dances like a dervish in a flurry and fury of increasingly impertinent challenges to the Owl. All of Nutkin's three riddles tell Old Brown that the
powers of authorities like him are helpless to deal with elemental problems
such as mending eggs, driving sunbeams away, and turning the wind. Old
Brown, in other words, is no God (his name, in fact, riddles over the word
"owl" contained anagrammatically within it), so why must the squirrels
kowtow to him? Or so one reading of Nutkin's challenge might go. And
Nutkin is right. But neither is Nutkin an elemental force such as the
wind is. When, in his hubris, Nutkin forgets that fact, makes "a whir-
ring noise to sound like the wind," and jumps onto Old Brown, he
makes sacrificially the point that his riddles have already made theoretically. Or, to put it another way, he feels impelled to test the truth of
his thought. Living a "life of allegory," he forgets what a real owl can do
to a real squirrel. And his punishment for that forgetting makes him
shun the metaphysical round forever.

"This looks like the end of the story; but it isn't." Having edged close to
a surprisingly violent dimension of her story, Potter eases up and gracefully
dismisses Nutkin, practically with a suspended sentence, with a slap on the
tail and some nonsense words. Readers are reinvited to think of the tale as
a neat device for rehearsing some clever chestnuts of riddles for children by
setting them in a narrative line. That a good deal more may have been at
stake need detain no one.

Both *Peter Rabbit* and *Squirrel Nutkin* tell of boys who refuse to participate
in the food-gathering work of their clan and who prefer to challenge authority
through selfish and somewhat atavistic behavior. The stories seem to disapprove of this behavior. High diction phrases such as "excessively impertinent" suggest that the narrator's view is not from the child's eye but from
the adult's. Yet the birds implore Peter to exert himself toward escape, and
Nutkin's narrator appears self-consciously to intervene to release Nutkin
from the Owl's deadly grip. Nutkin's riddles, moreover, give him a density
of language that competes with the fancy vocabulary of grown-ups. Still, at
the end, he is stripped of that language just as surely as Peter Rabbit is
stripped of his blue coat and buttons. With part of our hearts we applaud,
perhaps, the daring of the two lads; they follow their process to remarkable
lengths of individuation. But, underneath, the tales are deeply cautionary:
The expression of all that boyish energy and challenge rouses a violently
retributive response from male power in the world. Life becomes a losing:

no dessert, no more happy riddles. The stories bend us through the double bind of much trenchant narrative: Yes, enjoy your adventure while you can, and push it to the farthest, but at the end be prepared to take your medicine, lose your tail, and have nothing left but a stamp of your foot to your impotent shouting, "cuck!"

26

LAURA INGALLS WILDER

Little House on the Prairie

What is *Little House on the Prairie* about? Is it the author's memory of a year in her childhood? No, Laura Ingalls was not yet two years old when her family left the little house in the big woods. She couldn't personally remember, and later admitted she couldn't, any of the events in this second (third written) of the Little House books. All was taken from memories of Pa and Ma, of Laura's older sister, Mary, and of others. Beyond that fact, Laura shows from the first paragraph of the book that she is not interested in writing actual history, for she says there that Baby Carrie made the trip from the Big Woods, and Baby Carrie had not yet been born. Laura says in the same paragraph, furthermore, that "they never saw that little house again" when, in truth, they were back in that house the next year. But, if her authorial intent was not to record the events of her childhood with precise historical accuracy, if *Little House on the Prairie* aims at goals other than amassing correct dates, names, places, and faces for one segment of our westering history, then what are we to make of the book? Again, what is it about?

The curve of the author's life may give some hints, some places to look for an empathic spirit, a local genius, of interpretation. Laura Ingalls was born near Lake Pepin, Wisconsin, on February 7, 1867. Her mother and father were farming and working folk whose families had moved in the 1830s and 1840s slowly westward from Connecticut and New York, settling on farms in Ohio, Indiana, Illinois, and finally Wisconsin where Pa and Ma met and married in 1860, about four years after Ma had passed her teacher's exam at the age of sixteen. In May of 1868, Pa bought, without seeing it, some eighty acres of land near Rothville, Missouri, and in the summer of 1868, the family (accompanied by Ma's brother Henry and his wife Polly) journeyed by covered wagon to their new property. A year later, the Ingalls family pulled up stakes and pioneered west onto the Kansas prairie, stopping near Walnut Creek, thirteen miles from Independence, in land long held by Osage Indians. Here Pa built the little house on the prairie, and here in August of 1870 Baby Carrie was born. The Osage were offered a new treaty by the United States government to buy their land if they would abandon it, and in September the Indians moved out. Early the next year, Pa and Ma decided to move back to the little house in the big woods in Wisconsin.

It was on the way "home" to Wisconsin that Pa jumped in a stream to guide the fording horses and that the chimney fire started in a house the family had occupied temporarily. Many of the events in Laura's first book, the one about the little house in the big woods, took place during the family's second stay there, lasting until 1874. In that year, the family moved to Plum Creek in southwestern Minnesota, two miles from Walnut Grove. After grasshoppers ruined the harvest, the family moved into Walnut Grove where Laura's brother was born in 1875. He died the next year as the family was moving to Burr Oak, Iowa. There Pa worked in a hotel and at a mill and did odd jobs. After Grace Ingalls's birth, in the next year, 1877, the family's debts piled up. Ma and Pa decided to return to Walnut Grove. The family lived in the town for two years while Pa worked at a wide variety of jobs. Then Pa received the message that his brother-in-law could find him a job working for a railroad company in Dakota territory. His westering spirit hankered after the opportunity, and he promised Ma that he would never ask to move again if only she would agree to this one last trek. In 1879, the year that Laura's older sister Mary became blind, the family moved to Silver Lake, Dakota territory, where they helped the next year to build the little town of DeSmet. There they stayed.

Laura taught school beginning in 1882. She married Almanzo Wilder in 1885, and, after several years of unsuccessful farming near DeSmet (with a sojourn in Florida), the Wilders moved in 1894 with their daughter, Rose, to a farm near the Ozark town of Mansfield, Missouri. There they fared well for the rest of their lives. Pa died in DeSmet in 1902. Laura was at his bedside. Ma died in 1924. Laura did not return. In the period 1911 to 1924, Laura was an editor and article writer for the *Missouri Ruralist*, and she contributed to other papers as well. From 1919 to 1927, as Secretary-Treasurer of the Mansfield Farm Loan Association, Laura managed millions of dollars of loans to Ozark farmers. In 1930, she began writing *Little House in the Big Woods* in memory of Pa. The book's success prompted her to write seven more books over the next decade, books tracing out the curve of her youth and marriage. After Mary, Grace, Carrie, and finally Almanzo died, Laura lived out her eighties in the Mansfield farmhouse. She died in 1957 at the age of ninety.

When asked about her books, Laura Ingalls Wilder tended to describe them in terms of the moral values such as courage, independence, integrity, and humor that they promoted. Readers of *Little House on the Prairie* may find explicit and implicit praise of such values in the narrative, but readers may also find that praise embedded in a wonderfully tangled matrix of family romance, of aesthetic and religious regard for the western landscape, of care for just how things are made and used, and of surprising and haunting stylistic subtleties. The style, for example, seems to be simple, filled with a child's formulas and views: the clean grass, the glittering stars, the empty prairie, snug covers, to complain is naughty, it's shameful to cry, children should be seen and not heard, all's well that ends well. The very names "Pa" and "Ma" show that these adult characters are supposedly looked at from a child's point of view. The sentences are mostly simple in their syntactic strings of subject-verb-object patterns. But then, on the other hand, the style isn't really a child's style. Its poetic vocabulary exceeds the range of three- or four-year olds when it employs such phrases and terms as pale, thin dark; vast lake; wind was mourning; the more-traveled way; jagged cliffs of bare brown earth; immense; contentment; Providential. And the thematic, refrainlike attention to the enormous sky, the strange and empty silence, the feeling of being small and lost in so much space, may well seem self-consciously beyond the verbal apprehension of a little child. Yet the style works. It is the style of a writer who confessed to a "fascination" with writing, who said "you will hardly believe the difference the use of one word rather than another will make until you begin to hunt for a word with just the right shade of meaning" (Zochert 212). The style works as the best pastoral always works, by paying fresh attention to what the senses tell us, by viewing that which is difficult through innocent eyes, by finding the value of the hearth and of civility in experiencing their absence, by noting an art that nature makes.

Finally, to yield oneself to the full power of Wilder's writing may require one to consider the possibility that some of its energy and depth and emotive significance may come from her fierce search for her own reality and esteem as she hints at her rivalry with Mary who is ever "afraid" or "good" when Laura is "excited" or lively with "naughtiness"; or her rivalry with Ma who is so concerned for manners and security that she will not allow herself to share Pa's and Laura's instinctive restlessness and westering spirit; or as Laura shows Pa's great force and his love of life directed her way, her way over and over, until Pa and Laura become the center, the bond, of the book. If there are darkly beautiful underthemes in *Little House on the Prairie*, if Laura wants Pa as strongly as she wants the black-eyed Indian baby or wants to ride "bare naked in the wind and sunshine" to meet her maker and the elements of life itself, if the story takes us and moves us beyond common reality, then we are happily entitled to affirm once again the surpassing poise and power of children's literature as a mode of writing often valued, as children are often valued, for its imagined brightness but more often valuable, as children should be, for an honest interplay of light and dark.

27

JACK LONDON

The Call of the Wild

The Call of the Wild, published in 1903 when Jack London was twenty-seven and since read by world-wide millions, old and young, is easily criticized as escapist fantasy. The book's hero, the huge dog Buck, is first presented as a pampered favorite child and as a product of civilization's finest comforts, comforts swiftly made to seem paltry things. Buck lives in the "sun-kissed Santa Clara Valley," in the soft and civilizing Southland. His home offers both protection from the world (the house stands "back from the road, half hidden among the trees") and selfconscious pride of exalted place in the world. Buck carries himself in "right royal fashion."

> During the four years since his puppy-hood he had lived the life of a sated aristocrat; he had a fine pride in himself, was even a trifle egotistical, as country gentlemen sometimes become because of their insular situation.

Buck, plainly enough, is due for a lesson. Kidnapped and taken north, he learns that he has been "an unduly civilized dog," but he soon loses "the fastidiousness which had characterized his old life." Buck adapts, as a sled dog in the Yukon, to a ruthless struggle for survival. He learns to shed his domesticated self and to seek backward, atavistically, through wilder and wilder generations of forbears until he becomes, ultimately, the primordial wolf. The lesson, it would seem, for grownups and youth alike, is to slough off one's conventional self or civilization and to liberate for action one's true savage being.

How and why did Jack London develop such a critique of corrupt civilization? And what did he really mean by it? Born into a peculiarly insecure family in a peculiarly insecure time and place, Jack London (1876–1916) sought, almost from the beginning and all during his brief life, a paradoxical combination of inner strengths and external props, of self-esteem and social adulation, a combination whose tensions and contradictions he never resolved. London's mother was a piano teacher and spiritualist medium who had run away from home at sixteen, surfacing in San Francisco in her thirties. His father may well have been the orphaned, roving, free-thinking, much-married astrologer who abandoned Jack's mother during her pregnancy. She quickly remarried, and Jack took the name of his stepfather. The family settled and unsettled in an assortment of homes, farms, and boarding houses in and around Oakland, and Jack later gave romantic and somewhat contradictory accounts of working long hours to help support the family while also becoming an oyster thief and a roisterer around San Francisco bay.

At the age of seventeen, London apparently sailed on a seal-hunting ship to coasts of Japan and Siberia. He returned to the depression of the mid–1890s and traveled to the eastern United States at the time of protest marches by Kelly's and Coxey's "armies." Jailed for vagrancy, riding the rails, associating with out-of-work laborers and homeless tramps, London increasingly professed a commitment to socialism though he also espoused a version of social Darwinism and, at least on an individual level, a belief in the survival of the fittest.

Back in Oakland, he attended high school for a time and later attended the University of California at Berkeley for less than a year. A short but furious spate of rather mannered poetry and fiction writing produced no publications, and London set off with his stepsister's husband for the Klondike in 1897. With various parties he made his way to Dawson, staked some claims, but never worked them, and returned broke to Oakland in 1898. Again, London turned to journalism, hackwork, and story-writing. In the Yukon winter, he had spent long hours studying the sensuous, kinesthetic style of Kipling, and he used this style to good effect. After some months of effort, he found his Yukon stories winning acceptance in magazines, and in 1900 Houghton Mifflin published a collection of his tales which won London wide recognition. In the same year he married Bess Maddern. Soon London had two daughters, a crowd of friends, and literary fame promoted primarily through two other tale collections, an account of social conditions in proletarian London, and the *The Call of the Wild* (1903), an instant best-seller which was reprinted many times in illustrated and children's editions.

During the remainder of his brief life, London continued to pour forth a prolific stream of vivid, virile stories and novels appealing to the popular tastes of the day. He sometimes wrote for boys' magazines, and some of his stories such as "To Build a Fire" and novels such as *The Sea Wolf* are still much read by youth. It should be noted that London's often-simplistic and far-fetched plots, crude characterization, and general unsubtlety earned him his share of detractors though his works have been translated into so many foreign languages that he ranks as the most popular American author internationally.

London seems to have written, often, primarily to make money. He regularly wrote a thousand words a day, rarely waiting for "inspiration." He made and spent lots of money and, despite his professional dedication to sustained writing, lived a restless and perhaps generally dissatisfied life. As a socialist, he ran twice for Mayor of Oakland but received few votes. As an investor, if not capitalist, he dabbled in shabby (and mostly unprofitable) get-rich-quick schemes. He lectured daringly on behalf of socialism at Yale, Harvard, and elsewhere, but he also espoused a species of Anglo-Saxon race supremacy and exaltation of the so-called Nietzschean "blond beast." He made friends quickly but left many of them behind. He divorced his first wife and cheated on his second though he seems to have kept yearning for and attempting more mature contact with both women. He loved boxing and wrestling and manliness, but he died from overdoses of many drugs he had used for years. It is easy to see that, given his background, constitution, and experience, everything he did was in one view natural, the product of respectable reasons or causes. Yet he seems also to have experienced life as a field and drama of contradictions. His life and works give ample and compelling testimony, moreover, to the power and universality of the contradictions Jack London so relentlessly explored.

An account of *The Call of the Wild* as escapist fantasy (a fantasy with obvious links to the child-hero romances of Mark Twain, Robert Louis Stevenson, and Rudyard Kipling), though fair to the book in a sense, fails, nonetheless, to suggest its considerable complexity. For what Buck learns and becomes, as he struggles inward to the axis of his reality, amounts finally to contradiction. "The meaning of the stillness, and the cold, and dark," on the one hand, is "woe," and Buck learns "what a puppet thing life is," yet he learns, on the other hand, that "there is an ecstasy that marks the summit of life," and he becomes at moments "mastered by the sheer surging of life . . . the perfect joy of. . . everything that [is] not death."

The contradiction in Buck (and, perhaps, in Jack London as well) between life as a woeful "puppet thing" and life as "ecstasy" may seem to diminish when we note that Buck feels the woe in his relatively few moments of wolf-singing, those lyrical withdrawals from unselfconscious action, whereas the "ecstasy comes when one is most alive, and it comes as complete forgetfulness that one is alive." Ecstasy as forgetfulness, as anti–self-consciousness theory, emerges as London's response to the pains of waking life, particularly life that cannot be enclosed by working or hunting. Buck finds that his fellow sled dogs, who are gloomy and morose, sour and sullen, when passive, become "utterly transformed by the harness." "The toil of the traces seemed the supreme expression of their being," and so Buck becomes

> gripped tight by that nameless, incomprehensible pride of the trail and trace—
> that pride which holds dogs in the toil to the last gasp, which lures them to

die joyfully in the harness, and breaks their hearts if they are cut out of the harness.

Only in the Arctic snow and cold, by implication, moreover, are men and dogs forced to work so hard for sheer survival that all else can be forgotten. At night, Buck drops instantly to sleep in "the sleep of the exhausted just." Buck finds, however, that work in and of itself, even in the North, is not enough to guarantee the loss of pained self-awareness. Not only does the work become excessive, mechanical, and finally meaningless, but the work that Buck and the others are doing is part of a civilizing process in the North, a process that attracts products of the Southland such as Charles, Hal, and Mercedes. This "nice family party" that has come from the states, as London is careful to note, seems "manifestly out of place" in the rough Klondike region. Because they do "not know how to work themselves," at least in the unselfconscious way that has brought delight to Buck, and because Mercedes remains "occupied with weeping over herself," all chance of ecstatic "forgetfulness of living" becomes obliterated. The dogs are forced to observe and take part in a nightmare of bungling and cruelty. "By this time," says London, "all the amenities and gentlenesses of the Southland had fallen away from the three people." Yet Mercedes, the one woman in the book, continues to seek the comfort and chivalry of the South. Insisting upon them, she nurses "a special grievance—the grievance of sex." Helplessness is "her most essential sex-prerogative," and so she rides upon the sled, "a last lusty straw" to the burden of the animals.

London, at this point in the story, appears well on his way to establishing a wonderfully oversimplified dichotomy of values. The sun-kissed South and its civilization become associated with softness, effeminacy, dependency, self-consciousness, and selfishness. The North and its frozen wilderness are associated with harsh struggle, masculine strength, independence, and forgetfulness of self. One may add the dichotomy in London's allocation of spiritual values: Buck hails from Santa Clara, his father was a Saint Bernard, his mother "a Scotch shepherd," and so on; whereas the men of the North "cursing horribly" with "barbarous oaths" consistently call the dogs "devils," and London describes dog eyes "diabolically gleaming," the pack's "hell chorus," a rabbit a "wraith," the North's "eerie," "ghostly" aspects, and Buck near the end as truly "the Fiend incarnate." It would follow, then, that Buck, seemingly launched on a journey from Southern values to Northern ones, would drive steadily on toward an ever more alienated and savage existence. London could have managed that by having Buck escape from the incompetent trio from the States and then slowly recover his strength on his own. But it is a tribute to this author's often-unrecognized complexity, his openness to contradiction, that Buck should be made to succumb first to the lure of John Thornton's "love" amid a fresh consideration of Southland values.

Buck comes to Thornton in the spring, when the "ghostly winter silence" has been momentarily banished by rising sap, young buds, newly active crickets, woodpeckers, squirrels, and "wild fowl driving up from the south in cunning wedges." The allures of warm sun, rest, play, feminine attention, and the like are all suddenly allowed back into the story. When a maternal Irish setter approaches, Buck finds himself "unable to resent her first advances," and she cleans him "as a mother cat washes her kittens." With the feminine element safely reduced to a motherly, ministering role, Buck is free to conceive a "love that was feverish and burning" for Thornton and his "rough embrace." This love seems, London admits, "to bespeak the soft, civilizing influence," but he will not let the matter rest there. Buck, he says, is no longer a "dog of the soft Southland," for he is in touch, irredeemably, with his primordial wolf self. He knows there is "no middle course. He must master or be mastered," and so Buck responds to the imperious call of the wild, the "blood longing" that defines him, ultimately, as "a killer, a thing that preyed, living on the things that lived, unaided, alone. By virtue of his own strength and prowess, surviving triumphantly in a hostile environment where only the strong survived."

Instead of being forced to adapt for survival in a hostile wilderness which he has been made to enter, Buck now leaves, of his own volition, the comfort and security of Thornton's hearth; his blood longingly seeks out and creates for him the wild environment necessary for his self-expression. When he returns to Thornton's camp, he cannot stay long because a "restlessness" assails him, and he is "haunted by recollections" of his wolf kin. London appears to argue that a rugged individualism is not only our best response to a harsh life thrust upon us against our will but is also the truest response to our inner alienated nature.

Yet again the contradictions appear. For Buck is not really a total loner: After Thornton's death, he becomes the leader of a wolf pack. If only, London seems to plead, those who cannot submit to or who lost the possibility of civilized, domestic affection and comfort might find a society of their own "half-friendly, half-savage" kind. Still the sense of contradiction surfaces in Buck as he returns each summer to Thornton's deserted camp where "here he muses for a time, howling once, long and mournfully, ere he departs." Even there, however, London cannot leave the issue, but must go on to insist finally that Buck "is not always alone." Throughout the long winters, Buck leads his fellow wolves, and sings another song, "a song of the younger world, which is the song of the pack."

Contradiction. Are we invited, at the last, to leave our fellows or to join them? To shun love or to seek it? To deny a middle way between dependence and independence or to long for one? To such questions, readers must frame their own diverse responses. *The Call of the Wild* provides no simple answers but raises a host of teasing possibilities. Therein lies, surely, one secret of its wide and lasting appeal.

28

E. B. WHITE

Charlotte's Web

Although it is only a bedtime story, *Charlotte's Web* expresses as poignantly as anything E. B. White (1899–1985) ever wrote his bright and whimsical but fundamentally melancholy sense of life. In this story of Wilbur a pig—lonely, vulnerable, good-hearted, and decent but incapable of making the world conform to his wishes—White created a consoling fantasy in which a small porcine Everyman survives and triumphs over the pathos of being alone. White was writing for children here, but he expressed the same attitude toward life and death that he expressed in his writing for adults. He may have been having fun with *Charlotte's Web*, but he was not joking.

Charlotte's Web was published in 1952. Twelve years earlier White had written an essay on freedom which provides a valuable commentary on the story's essential meaning.

> Intuitively, I've always been aware of the vitally important pact which a man has with himself, to be all things to himself, . . . to stand self-reliant. . . . My first and greatest love affair was with this thing we call freedom. . . .
>
> It began with the haunting intimation (which I presume every child receives) of his mystical inner life; of God in man; of nature publishing herself through the "I." This elusive sensation is moving and memorable. It comes early in life: a boy, we'll say, sitting on the front steps on a summer night, thinking of nothing in particular, suddenly hearing as with a new perception and as though for the first time the pulsing sound of crickets, overwhelmed with the novel sense of identification with the natural company of insects and grass and night, conscious of a faint answering cry to the universal perplexing question: "What is 'I'?" Or a little girl, returning from the grave of a pet bird, leaning with her

elbows on the windowsill, inhaling the unfamiliar draught of death, suddenly seeing herself as part of the complete story. Or to an older youth, encountering for the first time a great teacher who by some chance word or mood awakens something and the youth beginning to breathe as an individual and conscious of strength in his vitals. . . .

This is the beginning of the affair with freedom (*One Man's Meat* 208–9).

That is to say, sometime early in life, every child experiences a mildly mystical sense of his participation in a vast natural order as a separable, individual part. This experience provides the true basis for his sense of himself, the indispensable first part of the answer to the question, "What is my self?"

But more than White's explicit point, notice the particular atmosphere with which he dramatizes the moment of insight into the link between the self and the cosmos: a boy sitting alone, musing aimlessly, not thinking of anything; or a girl whose pet bird has died, feeling for the first time the nearness of death; or a student making his first acquaintance with a skilled teacher. These situations, for White, contain the intuited clues, the intimations of the depths of one's inner life. They all take place in one's youth; White presumes that all children experience them in some form. They are abstracted, unsocial moments of personal isolation. In two of the three, the child is alone, and in the third—the youth who meets for the first time with a powerful teacher—the experience is again essentially a lonely one, not a reciprocal transaction but a receiving of "some chance word or mood" from without, impinging, for once, on the youth's sensibilities. This realization of one's self in the universe, then, has something to do with the impact of language—the chance word of a teacher; it has something to do with idleness and aimless musing; and it has something to do with the thought of death.

Charlotte's Web is the consolation White offers to the child who has lived and continues to live in the presence of the beautiful but rather forbidding and unsociable personage, freedom, and in the lonely realization of one's individuality. He approaches the task by creating a character and a set of circumstances that dramatize the anxieties of that situation.

Wilbur is the runt of his litter, rescued from infanticide and befriended by Fern. But then, after an interlude during which Fern mothers him, he is sold to an alien farm where he is the only pig in a barnyard full of animals with their own affairs to attend to. Food and shelter are provided for him, and he has no purposeful activity. His life is one of utter idleness. At the age of only two months, he complains to himself, he is tried of being alive. Being the only pig on the farm, being the only creature without a family (except for Templeton the rat, who devotes himself to an outlaw's life of getting and hoarding, a lifestyle that makes no sense for Wilbur), and having been overfed on the loving attentions of Fern, Wilbur is lonely, unendurably so. Finally, he is threatened with death. Mr. Zuckerman, his new owner, plans to butcher him in the early winter—a prospect of which a rather callous old sheep notifies Wilbur. Wilbur is terrified. He hurls himself on the ground, screaming that he does not want to die.

White thus establishes Wilbur in a desperate existential situation: He is bored, he is starved for affection, and he is scared of dying. These are precisely the psychic problems attendant on the haunting intimation that one is ultimately alone. Wilbur's loneliness is the emotional counterpart of the philosophical perception that between oneself and others lies an unbridgeable gap. Since on this level one becomes the sole measure and standard of his own world (becomes all things to himself, as White puts it) everything depends on his being fulfilled. Boredom is simply that enervating sense that this is not happening. One comes to believe that nothing he does really matters. Doing novel things can allay this feeling temporarily, but novelty wears out. To find significance that appears permanent, the individual must find a context larger than himself to give purpose to his actions. Without it, one is prey to the debilitating state of mind in which the only important question is "Am I being fulfilled?"

In this state of mind, the thought of death has a keen edge. The person whose sense of himself is governed by a feeling of communality—of being most importantly a member of a tribe or a family or a people or a cause—can see his own death as less than absolute. To one who lives in and for himself, death must be the ultimate terror, the end of all that matters. Indeed, the thought of death in this situation often combines thoughts of ultimate boredom and ultimate loneliness. Death appears as a vast emptiness, where no one else is and where there is absolutely nothing to do. White once evoked this view of death in an essay on visiting the grave of his dog:

> I do not experience grief when I am down there, nor do I pay tribute to the dead. I feel a sort of over-all sadness that has nothing to do with the grave or its occupant. Often I feel extremely well in that rough cemetery, and sometimes flush a partridge. But I feel a sadness at All Last Things, too, which is probably purely selfish, or turned-in, emotion—sorrow not at my dog's death but at my own, which hasn't even occurred yet but which saddens me just to think about in such pleasant surroundings (*Points of My Compass* 49).

Wilbur of course is not a philosopher meditating on alienation and mortality; on the contrary, he is an eager and gregarious child wishing to live and to be loved and happy. White is the philosopher; through Wilbur he addresses the anxieties that a child in a modern, fragmented culture might feel. White says, in effect, "Once upon a time there was a youngster who was bored, lonely, and afraid of dying." The story which follows, like a fairy tale, soothes these anxieties.

To disarm boredom, White offers a vision of a rich and various world, a world filled with dramatic experiences such as winning a prize at the county fair, riding the Ferris wheel, taking dizzying swings on the big rope in the barn, sledding, listening to stories, making new friends. Even without such events, the world of *Charlotte's Web* resembles Mr. Zuckerman's barn—full of splendid ordinary things: tools and equipment and farm machinery and scraps and clutter and odds and ends—a place good for nesting in, for poking around in, for playing in. In this world the variety of experience is practically inexhaustible.

> Life in the barn was very good—night and day, winter and summer, spring and fall, dull days and bright days. It was the best place to be, thought Wilbur, this warm delicious cellar, with the garrulous geese, the changing seasons, the heat of the sun, the passage of swallows, the nearness of rats, the sameness of sheep, the love of spiders, the smell of manure, and the glory of everything.

And of course there is Charlotte, the articulate spider who knows so much and is glad to tell Wilbur all sorts of things—the meanings of words and the ways of spiders and the events of her past. Once Charlotte puts in her appearance, Wilbur is free from boredom forever.

The book speaks just as soothingly to the fear of loneliness. When Wilbur voices his complaint, and cries out that he is young and friendless and depressed by the rain and devoid of any happy prospects whatsoever, there comes an answer. A small voice that Wilbur has never heard before issues out of the darkness, rather thin but comforting. "I'll be a friend to you," the voice says. It is of course Charlotte, the perfect friend: confidante, instructor, protector, mother. A tacit message of the book is this: If you feel lonely, do not despair; look for love and companionship, and you will find it.

The book's answer to the fear of death is a bit more complicated but nonetheless firm and unambiguous. The book says that if you (like Wilbur) are panic-stricken at the thought that you may suddenly and horribly die, be assured that clever, solid, reliable adults (like Charlotte) will see to it that this does not happen. Children may feel vulnerable, but they need not fear the worst, for grown-ups can protect them. When Wilbur screams that he doesn't want to die, Charlotte promises him that he won't have to. In a strict sense, of course, she is lying; but she is telling a truth true enough for Wilbur, because what she really means is that Wilbur, the young pig, will not die; death is for the old, not the young. And by the time you are old, you (like Charlotte, dying alone at the fairgrounds) will accept and perhaps even welcome death. By then you will have lived out your life, wearied yourself in the fulfillment of your mortal purpose, and you will be ready for the sleep of death. By then death will be seen as one of the elements in the wholesome natural cycle of existence; dying in season will create no special terror. The old don't mind dying, White's argument runs, and since it will be a long time before you are old, you need not worry about it now.

In the center of this consoling fantasy is Charlotte, the radiantly perfect adult—completely reliable, completely considerate, completely competent, completely right. In availing himself of her services, White has engaged in an act of fantasy, of wishful thinking. The world of modern individualism has sweepingly outlawed the idea of the sage who knows the answers. White's hero Thoreau, for example, was strident on this point.

> "I have lived some thirty years on this planet, and I have yet to hear the first syllable of valuable or even earnest advice from my seniors. They have told me nothing, and probably cannot tell me anything, to the purpose. Here is life, an experiment to a great extent untried by me; but it does not avail me that they tried it." (Thoreau 11)

There speaks the true individualist—and there speak most of the classic children's authors, the Mark Twains and Lewis Carrolls and James M. Barries and Hans Christian Andersens, to whom adulthood is seldom much more than a stultification of the genius and vitality of childhood. In the face of this august company sits White's Charlotte, an adult who has actually lived and learned, and who uses her wisdom to save the child Wilbur. She embodies a very old-fashioned notion ("Hear, my son, your father's instruction, and reject not your mother's teaching; for they are a fair garland for your head, and pendants for your neck," Proverbs 1:8–9); but in White's handling she is a figure of fantasy, for she is there not because the world has really provided a way for her to exist, but because Wilbur (and White and the reader) needs her to be there.

In White's writing for adults, the experts or sages are usually threatening, irrationally headstrong creatures whose way it is best to stay out of. Only in his fantasy writing, where spiders talk lovingly to pigs and spell out words in their webs, can someone like Charlotte exist. She is needed there; and need, rather than reality, is the operative principle in fantasy.

It may seem perverse to lay such stress on fantasy in *Charlotte's Web* when compared with other more patently fantastic stories like *Alice in Wonderland* or *Peter Pan*. In the fantasies of Carroll and Barrie, the prospect of growing up and growing old holds terrors which send the authors' imaginations into spasms of rejection. Adulthood in *Alice in Wonderland* is a mixture of mystery and madness; in *Peter Pan*, it is a dull round of routine through which flirts the ghost of serious sexuality. Next to these stories, *Charlotte's Web* stands forth as a wise and fatherly discourse acknowledging the sadness of mutability and mortality, but reassuring the reader all the same.

White's book acknowledges that when people grow up they change, and the change is not entirely for the better. The little girl Fern, who begins as Wilbur's devoted friend and protector, grows up, and loses interest in Wilbur. Early in the story, when Fern's mother is worried about the girl's spending so much time "alone" in the barn, wise old Dr. Dorian assures her that the company of animals is healthy enough. He even avers that animals may talk, may have spoken to him on occasion, and that he missed hearing their remarks because he wasn't paying attention. "Children pay better attention than grown-ups." By the end of the story, Fern, who no longer comes to the barn, has stopped paying attention. She has found a boyfriend named Henry Fussy. In this way White acknowledges that one of the things that will draw one away from childish concerns is the awakening of sexual interests. At the height of Wilbur's triumph, just as he is to be awarded the special prize at the fair, Fern runs off through the midway crowd, looking for Henry.

The book acknowledges, too, that people die. Charlotte dies, tired and alone. The account of her death is the only undisguisedly sad scene in the novel. But White stresses that it is right for Fern to grow up and lose interest and for Charlotte to die. These events are natural parts of life's order. Even more important than this, psychologically, is the fact that, lovable as they may be, Fern and Charlotte are not Wilbur. Fern changes, and Charlotte dies, but Wilbur is allowed to live a long life without the permanent changes or trauma of maturation. He finds interest outside himself (primarily in Charlotte and the endless succession of her descendants who live with him in the barn) without the burdens of real responsibility for them. (He never, for example, has to arrange their destinies in the way Charlotte has arranged his for him.) He finds love without the complications of sex or parenthood (the nearest thing to reproduction he experiences is the adoption of the little spiders). Essentially he is allowed to remain a child for life: "Mr. Zuckerman took find care of Wilbur all the rest of his days." Strictly speaking, he never even has to die. That phrase "all the rest of his days" is as close as White comes to suggesting Wilbur's death. Since Wilbur is the character with whom the reader is invited to identify, and since to him none of the problems of boredom, loneliness, maturation, or death proves insoluble, the plot serves to assure the reader that, though sad things do happen, they don't exactly happen to him.

The story soothes and consoles in even subtler ways. Its abundant humor and White's famous crafted style mute its sadness and control a troublesome sentimentality. When the going gets sticky, either by becoming too painful or cloyingly sweet, the narrator steps back rhetorically and reminds us that the story is, after all, only a story. It can be viewed with an aesthetic detachment we could not afford if its events were happening to real characters we really cared about.

In this first chapter, for instance, when Fern learns that her father intends to kill the runt of a new litter of pigs and frantically intercedes on its behalf, the potentially ghastly episode ends with a very E. B. White-like speech from the father: "Fern was up at daylight, trying to rid the world of injustice. As a result, she now has a pig. A small one, to be sure, but nevertheless a

pig. It just shows what can happen if a person gets out of bed promptly."
Thus the scene is drained of some of its intensity, and made safe for con-
sumption. Wilbur's brush with death becomes a little example of the world's
injustice, his salvation something that "can happen if a person gets out of
bed promptly."

Or, for another example of how White sweetens his material through tone,
consider Templeton the rat, the story's nearest thing to a villain. Templeton is
predatory, selfish, pugnacious, and dirty—in most ways, the antithesis of the
love and generosity the story celebrates. But White makes him funny and even
a little likable by implicitly assuring us that, for whatever harm he may intend,
he is finally harmless. In the chapter "Summer Days," which deals with the
hatching of a brood of goslings, the narrator says this about him:

> Both the goose and the gander were worried about Templeton. And with good
> reason. The rat had no morals, no conscience, no scruples, no consideration,
> no decency, no milk of rodent kindness, no compunctions, no higher feeling,
> no friendliness, no anything. He would kill a gosling if he could get away with
> it—the goose knew that. Everybody knew that.

Thus is Templeton neutralized; White's tone makes Templeton safe: He has
no "milk of rodent kindness." And everybody knows that. Templeton is an
irascible local character, not a real menace.

The final paragraph of *Charlotte's Web* is a masterpiece of semi-sweet,
semi-serious humor, expressing melancholy sentiment without tears: "Wilbur never forgot Charlotte. Although he loved her children and grandchil-
dren dearly, none of the new spiders ever quite took her place in his heart.
She was in a class by herself. It is not often that someone comes along who
is a true friend and a good writer. Charlotte was both." The play of tone
here is vintage White: wry, amiable, softly arch. It is sad that Charlotte is
gone forever, but it's funny to think of her as a good writer, since her entire
published canon has consisted of five words in her web.

In an important way, this is exactly the right epitaph for her: a true friend
and a good writer. What, after all, has been Charlotte's service to Wilbur?
She has never touched him, never fed him, never sheltered him. She has
talked to him, sung to him, and written advertising copy for him. Their
contact has been purely verbal. One of the clearest marks of *Charlotte's
Web* as the fantasy of a lonely, yearning imagination is the importance it
places on language as the means through which spirit is laid against spirit.
The highest and best love, in this book, is that which expresses itself through
words, and words only. Language is pure, a process in which "all animal
heat and moisture may have a chance to evaporate," as Thoreau approvingly
puts it (98). Wilbur has talked to Charlotte, she has talked to and for him,
her descendants converse with him—in the ambience of Wilbur's idyllic
barnyard, these have found the best kind of friendship. When hearts make

contact through language alone, they do so without invading each other's privacy. Approaching each other through the formal channel of words, they soften the pain of individuality without positively intruding. Hence, the truest friend must be a good writer. And that, of course, is Charlotte.

AFTERWORD

Children's Literature and the Siren Call of Child-Romance

Oh how I long to travel back
And tread again that ancient track!

The words of Henry Vaughan in "The Retreat," his searchings there back toward his "angel infancy" and its "bright shoots of everlastingness," speak, surely, to and for all of us. At one time or another, our deep longing to return to the place from where we came, to rediscover our origins, is evoked by thoughts of childhood and its perennial promise, which Edward Gibbon terms "the warm desires, the long expectations of youth." Our wish to return home, to "retreat" in Vaughan's sense, tends often to be celebrated as a momentary impulse of nostalgic yearning suitable for brief lyrical expression. What happens when the impulse is extended into narrative form and drawn out from wishful yearning to imagined actuality? Traditionally, the return home has been an important part of the dominant mode in world fiction, the romance. As the *Odyssey* follows the *Iliad*, romance has tended to follow tragedy by providing release and redemption from finalities of estrangement and death; foreign war turns out to be but a portion of life, the outer darkness. Odysseus returns home. So does Apollonius of Tyre. So do many heroes, like Gawain, or lovers, like Aucassin and Nicolette, in medieval romances. So do several principals in Shakespeare's great dramatic romances. From classical, medieval, and renaissance romance, the pattern of the return home stretches in a steady line through the novels of Fielding, Smollett, and other eighteenth-century authors; the gothic, historical, and other romances of many nineteenth-century writers, including Scott, Cooper, and Dickens; and on into this century where it still plays a part in writing not only of the popular romancers but even of novelists such as Saul Bellow and John Updike and playwrights such as T. S. Eliot and Bertolt Brecht. In the classic Odyssean pattern, moreover, to "travel back" is to travel forward, for the concluding focus tends to take in the new generation: Telemachus, Miranda and Ferdinand, the baby in Brecht's *Caucasian Chalk Circle*. Romance heroes return from island, cave, or desert place to pass on the torch of generation. In traditional romance, it seems, one treads again that ancient track for a vision of everlasting progeny.

Some of the very greatest works of children's literature—*The Snow Queen, Alice's Adventures in Wonderland, Treasure Island, Huckleberry Finn, The Jungle Books, Peter Pan, The Little Prince*—take the romance form of quest-journey and ultimate return home. The returns in these works differ, however, in meaning and spirit from the returns in the sorts of mature romance just described. None of the child protagonists returns to tread again that ancient track in much delight. None projects a way clear to domestic felicity and joy in ongoing generational continuity. Perhaps partly because the adventures may be impelled by authorial longings to re-enter childhood, these child-romances are distinguished, in fact, by their general indifference, mistrust, and even antipathy toward worlds of home, civilization, parents, and grown-ups.

Though conventionally separated in diverse categories of fantasy and realism, the child-romances not only reveal, upon consideration, remarkable affinities in doubts they cast on the return home and the maturation process associated with it, they also reveal affinities in the very structure and content of each adventure. All begin with a loss or separation from parents and home that carries with it implied criticism of life at home. Simply for a child to leave its family behind and embark upon extended adventures of its own implies some disruption of the normal protective relation. The initial wandering may stem from several sources. Huck Finn treats us to a thorough-going critique of the stifling routine foisted upon him by the Widow Douglas and Miss Watson and of the terrifying imprisonment forced by his own father. His impulse to escape seems at first the impulse of any natural creature to escape bondage, but the subsequent exploration and criticism of society's genteel veneer and inner savagery widens out into awesome dimensions. Huck does eventually return to the world of Tom Sawyer's relatives with its stale security. Yet the return to domesticity cannot be permanent. Huck lights out for the territories.

Antoine de Saint-Exupéry's *Little Prince*, too, opens with a thorough lambasting of adults and their ways. Grown-ups, we are told and shown repeatedly, fail to understand children, love, life itself. The child-prince leaves his planet largely because of frustration concerning his Rose-love. After the series of satiric encounters with foolish and greedy grown-ups, he comes to the sacred desert place, scene of death and redemption, where he learns about the principle of Taming from the fox and teaches the fatherly narrator to yearn, after the prince "dies," for his return.

In James Barrie's *Peter Pan*, similarly, the orphaned hero of obscure parentage disdains any extended contact with worldly reality and teaches us to long for that isle of Neverland where, as Barrie insists, we can beach our coracles no more. Plainly the tendency in child-romance is to disparage civilization and its discontents. In Rudyard Kipling's *Jungle Books*, Mowgli, too, is orphaned, at least temporarily, from a world of foolish greedy adults who deserve to have the Jungle let in on them. When Mowgli, in "The Spring Running," returns to his people, presumably under the call of sex to found a family, the event is a tragic close, not a hopeful beginning. His animal friends croon in the Outsong of "the dawns, when thou shalt wake / To the toil thou canst not break / Heartsick for the Jungle's sake." As in *The Little Prince* and *Peter Pan*, we are made to feel that the end of childhood is the end of everything.

Alice begins her adult-mocking adventures at least partly out of boredom generated by her older sister's pictureless book. To grow is to gravitate into a world without images. When Alice returns above ground, it is to a scene of "dead leaves," "dull reality," and anticipated nostalgia for "the simple and loving heart of childhood." Again, at the end of the second adventure, Carroll invites us to mourn the passing of childhood through a retrospective lament for the way in which "Echoes fade and memories die: / Autumn's frosts have slain July." It is a world of the "melancholy" maiden's "unwelcome bed," as Carroll so pathetically puts it in the *Looking-Glass* dedicatory poem which admits the "shadow of a sigh" trembling through the story.

In Hans Christian Andersen's *Snow Queen*, Kay and Gerda, who were initially led on their adventures by Kay's "masculine" growth toward the mathematical world of icy reason, finally return home not to maturity but to be "children, children at heart." Many of Andersen's tales, of course, carry this anti-maturational theme.

Plainly one deep-set instinct of the literary imagination which fosters child-romance is to deny that return home to completion through regeneration which is often promoted in mature romance. It may be that choice of a child-protagonist is dictated partly by the desire to recapture a pre-adolescent innocence, a desire which helps account for the aura of wistful regret over lost childhood so prevalent in children's literature. From a practical standpoint, certainly, once a child is chosen as protagonist-voyager, then the propagatory instinct for the return home is not easily asserted unless much time elapses. Yet the writer of child-romance who eschews the motive of return home to found or head a family, to participate in ongoing life, must either suggest some other motive for the return or else make the journey its own reward, in which case the very desire to return may be minimized if not eliminated. When we examine the child-romances from this perspective, we see that they do indeed tend to promote the value of the voyage or journey as an end in itself. It is play or game which tends to concentrate upon and live within a detached world of rules and laws.

Of the child, said John Earle, "he plays yet, and is not come to his task of melancholy." In child-romance, the sense of play as end in itself, an excursus from progenitive time, is very strong. In order for the child's quest to become an endless detour from the business of life, from getting on with life, the romance world needs only to take infinite interest in seemingly self-sufficient play. Huck most admires Tom Sawyer for his impeccable sense of "style," and Tom's notion of style, as is repeatedly shown, often runs counter to getting things done, counter to life-objects such as freeing the slave, Jim, to return to his family. Peter Pan, similarly, pursues "Good Form" as an end in itself, even giving Captain Hook advantages in fight. "Bad Form" in these works tends to be the adult's desire to achieve some end, beyond the game, or to use or misuse the game to the adult's advantage. We thus have on the one hand great emphasis upon games and their rules in the *Alice* books, ceaselessly-intoned Laws of the Jungle in the Mowgli stories, and in *Treasure Island* intent concentration upon bargains, truces, map-following, rules of ship conduct and of piracy, and the evils of rule-breaking. On the other hand, we have the persistently disruptive behavior of adults who try to change rules, disrespect the law and violate it, break their word, and generally display "Bad Form." It is as if the writers thought their way back into childhood, empathized with the child's attempt to absorb life in patterns of play, but then had honestly to repeat the child's frustration (often admittedly comic) at trying to incorporate more and more breaches of pattern into the game. The most serious breaches of all come, of course, when the play-adventures are interrupted by returns to family and procreative time.

Successful child-practitioners of the game, such as Peter Pan and Tom Sawyer, are likely to strike us as, to use Barrie's term, "heartless," that is, they seem peculiarly aloof from the sorts of human concern that would sacrifice the game to some further end. Alice leaves the White Knight to become Queen; Mowgli pursues the Jungle Law even to the injury of man; the Little Prince shocks the pilot with his lack of concern over the problem of how to get out of the desert; Jim Hawkins rather smugly sermonizes the atheist Israel Hands and, after shooting Hands, quickly gets on with the game. Displaying the same absorption in style and form as tends to be displayed by the books in which they appear (consider how many great children's authors are unusually devoted stylists), the heroes of child-romance often suggest that the game is more important than the people playing it, or even that the game need not, because it cannot, try to enclose the full range of human desires and freedoms. They lure us to an esthetic Neverland where form and style—the simple good manners sought in Winnie the Pooh's world, the cosy etiquette of Mole and Ratty—can solve everything, can order life, because the Neverland is essentially static, timeless, uninvaded by the need to found families or to participate in history. Child-romance celebrates in this sense a lost world that must remain lost forever.

Entry into the special or lost world of child-romance is often gained by dramatically birth-like traumas, as if the authors would imagine rebirth into lands of far away, far past. Often the child will emerge from confining spaces and dark tunnels to a swimming freedom in flight or upon amniotic waters. One thinks of Alice emerging from the tunnel soon to swim in her own salt tears, or Wendy and her brothers borne in free flight from the confining night of their nursery to the ocean scene of Neverland, or Andersen's Gerda and Little Mermaid leaving home through water-journeys, or the Hobbit and companions issuing from dark caverns in caskets upon the flood, or Tolly in Lucy Boston's *Children of Green Knowe*, first seen journeying through the flooded night and thinking of Noah's ark, or Jim Hawkins cast from the dark confinement of his mother's inn to the vast sea-journey, or even Huck Finn, who escapes the parental cabin to the river, the flood on Jackson's Island, and the snake that threatens there as if from Genesis. But while the authorial impulse to conceive and give birth to these children may at first be celebratory, dazzling us with playful danger and serious joy, the celebration slowly fades and evolves toward nostalgic lament as the child-figures face the grey prospect of maturation. Such child-romance tends to produce an elegiac mood at its close when the children are denied the sorts of returns that promise lovers' meetings or the joys of parenthood. Even where, as in *Peter Pan* and the *Jungle Books*, the prospect of generational continuity is opened up, the mood remains, as we have seen, nostalgic for eternal childhood. And even works such as *Treasure Island* which seem to have no particular bias against maturity depend in part for their effect upon adulation of the free child-state which worships *this* life over against the adult-state which is all too aware of the predestined dark. The heroes of child-romance live wonderfully, if sometimes selfishly, for the moment. When Huck's "conscience" tells him how "sinful" it is to help his slave-friend, Jim, he says, "All right, I'll *go* to hell!" In pursuing only his own concerns like a child, Long John Silver seems cheerfully to brave damnation.

One would be but a foolish didacticist to count the strain of child romance against adulthood, its fear of maturation, as a blot upon its value. We may momentarily enjoy, in the manner of Ulysses, the siren call for detour everlasting. We may glimpse the Neverland and move on. We might then agree with Randall Jarrell in his poem "Thinking of the Lost World," who said upon seeing his child-shape that he reached out to it empty-handed, traded his emptiness for its emptiness, but then held in his own hands, in happiness, "Nothing, the nothing for which there's no reward." Yet that nothing is also a something which, if we reflect upon it, may teach us to not submerge ourselves too fully in our lives' socially productive uses or functions but to cherish each self-justifying childhood and the beauty of its play, its irreplaceable form.

In the Twelfth Book of the *Odyssey*, Odysseus pursues his course home-ward from Circe's realm. To pass the isle of the Sirens, he must be bound to the mast of the ship. Still, he listens to their song and even for the moment believes in it, for he calls to his mariners for release. The Sirens promise great delight and great wisdom, especially wisdom of mortality and the underworld. Some say they were once companions of Persephone. They failed to save her from the lusts of Hades (those mortal and season-producing lusts), were turned into birdlike women, and were consigned to their island of enchantment. Odysseus and his companions are committed to the return home. Were they to submit to the Sirens, they would learn of and experience a death that is no part of ongoing life. At home they may die into progeny. Yet the song of the Sirens is clear and sweet. It promises a freedom from care denied to fathers and citizens. It celebrates a self-enclosed beauty of retreat, one that might lure us out of time. It is a high wonder of the imagination.

BIBLIOGRAPHY

Primary Sources

Alcott, Louisa May. *Little Women, or, Meg, Jo, Beth and Amy*. Boston: Roberts, 1868.

Andersen, Hans Christian. *The Complete Fairy Tales and Stories*. Trans. Erik Christian Haugaard. New York: Doubleday, 1974.

———. *Danish Fairy Legends and Tales*. Trans. Caroline Peachey. London: Pickering, 1846.

———. *The Fairy Tale of My Life*. Trans. Horace E. Scudder. 1871. New York: Paddington, 1975.

———. *Hans Christian Andersen's Stories for the Household*. New York: McLoughin, 1893.

Asbjörnsen, Peter, and Jörgen Moe. *Popular Tales from the Norse*. Trans. Sir George Dasent. Edinburgh: Edmonston & Douglas, 1859.

Barrie, James. *Margaret Ogilvy*. New York: Scribner's, 1897.

———. *Peter and Wendy*. London: Hodder and Stoughton, 1911.

———. *Peter Pan*. 1911. Harmondsworth: Puffin-Penguin, 1968.

———. *The Plays of J. M. Barrie*. 1928. New York: Scribner's, 1948.

Baum, L. Frank. *The Wonderful Wizard of Oz*. Chicago: George M. Hill, 1900.

Beaumont, Marie Le Prince de. *The Young Ladies Magazine*. Trans. anon. London: J. Nourse, 1760.

Boston, Lucy M. *The Children of Green Knowe*. New York: Harcourt, Brace, 1955.

Carroll, Lewis. *Alice's Adventures in Wonderland*. London: Macmillan, 1865.

Collodi, Carlo. *The Adventures of Pinocchio*. Trans. M. A. Murray. London: Unwin, 1892.

Craik, Dinah Maria Mulock. *The Little Lame Prince*. New York: Harper, 1875.

Dickens, Charles. *A Christmas Carol*. London: Chapman & Hall, 1843.

Grahame, Kenneth. *The Wind in the Willows*. London: Methuen, 1908.

Griffith, John W., and Charles Frey, eds. *Classics of Children's Literature*. New York: Macmillan, 1981, 1987.

Grimm, Jacob and Wilhelm. *German Popular Stories*. Trans. Edgar Taylor. Vol. I. London: C. Baldwin, 1823. Vol. II. London: J. Robins, 1826.

Harris, Joel Chandler. *Uncle Remus: His Songs and Sayings*. New York: D. Appleton, 1880.

Hoffmann, Heinrich. *Struwwelpeter*. Trans. anon. Leipzig: F. Volckmar, 1848.

Jacobs, Joseph. *English Fairy Tales*. London: D. Nutt, 1890.

Kipling, Rudyard. *The Jungle Books*. London: Century, 1894. New York: Harper & Brothers, 1894.

Lear, Edward. *A Book of Nonsense*. London: Thos. McLean, 1846.

———. *More Nonsense*. London: Frederick Warne & Co., 1888.

London, Jack. *The Call of the Wild*. New York: Macmillan, 1903.

MacDonald, George. *Dealings with Fairies*. London: Strahan, 1867.

Newbery, John. *Mother Goose's Melody*. Boston: N. Coverly, 1812.

Perrault, Charles. *Tales of Mother Goose*. London: Sambur. 1729.

Potter, Beatrix. *The Tale of Peter Rabbit*. London: Privately printed, 1900.

———. *The Tale of Squirrel Nutkin*. London: Frederick Warne & Co., 1903.

Ruskin, John. *The King of the Golden River; or, the Black Brothers*. London: Smith, Elder & Co., 1851.

Saint-Exupéry, Antoine de. *The Little Prince*. Trans. Katherine Woods. New York: Harcourt, Brace, 1943.

Spyri, Johanna. *Heidi; Her Years of Wandering and Learning*. Trans. Louise Brooks. Boston: DeWolfe, 1884.

Stevenson, Robert Louis. *Treasure Island*. London: Cassell & Co., 1883.

Tolkein, J. R. R. *The Hobbit*. Boston: Houghton Mifflin, 1937.

Twain, Mark. *Adventures of Huckleberry Finn*. New York: Harper, 1884.

———. *The Adventures of Tom Sawyer*. London: Chatto & Windus, 1876. Hartford, CT: American Pub. Co., 1876.

White, E. B. *Charlotte's Web*. New York and Evanston: Harper & Row, 1952.

———. *One Man's Meat*. New York and London: Harper & Brothers, 1942.

———. *The Points of My Compass: Letters from the East, the West, the North, and the South*. New York, Evanston, and London: Harper & Row, 1962.

Wilder, Laura Ingalls. *Little House on the Prairie*. New York: Harper, 1935.

Secondary Sources

Avery, Gillian. *Nineteenth Century Children: Heroes and Heroines in English Children's Stories: 1780–1900*. London: Hodder and Stoughton, 1965.

Baring-Gould, William S., and Ceil Baring-Gould, eds. *The Annotated Mother Goose*. New York: World, 1967.

Basile, Giovanni Battista. *The Pentameron*. 1636. Trans. Sir Richard Burton. London: Kimber, 1952.

Baughman, Ernest W. *Type and Motif Index of the Folktales of England and North America*. The Hague: Mouton, 1966.

Bettelheim, Bruno. *The Uses of Enchantment: The Meaning and Importance of Fairy Tales.* New York: Knopf, 1976.

Bredsdorff, Elias. *Hans Christian Andersen: The Story of His Life and Work 1805–1875.* New York: Scribner's, 1975.

Brundvand, Jan Harold. *Folklore: A Study and Research Guide.* New York: St. Martin's, 1976.

Chesterton, G. K. "The Ethics of Elfland." *Orthodoxy.* New York: Dodd, 1908.

Commire, Anne, ed. *Yesterday's Authors of Books for Children.* 2 vols. Detroit: Gale, 1977.

Darton, E. J. Harvey. *Children's Books in England: Five Centuries of Social Life.* 2nd ed. Cambridge: Cambridge University Press, 1958.

Doyle, Brian. *The Who's Who of Children's Literature.* New York: Schocken, 1968.

Dunbar, Janet. *J. M. Barrie: The Man Behind the Image.* Boston: Houghton Mifflin, 1970.

Dundes, Alan. *The Study of Folklore.* Englewood Cliffs: Prentice-Hall, 1965.

Edmonson, Munro S. *Lore: An Introduction to the Science of Folklore and Literature.* New York: Holt, Rinehart, 1971.

Egoff, Sheila, et al., eds. *Only Connect: Readings on Children's Literature.* 2nd ed. Toronto: Oxford University Press, 1980.

Freud, Sigmund. "On the Relation of the Poet to Day-Dreaming." Tran. Joan Riviere, et al. *On Creativity and the Unconscious.* Ed. Benjamin Nelson. New York: Harper & Row, 1958.

Gardner, Martin. *The Annotated Alice.* New York: World, 1961.

Geduld, Harry M. *Sir James Barrie.* New York: Twayne, 1971.

Godden, Rumer. "An Imaginary Correspondence." *Horn Book Magazine* 38 (1963): 197–206.

Gray, Donald, ed. *Alice's Adventures in Wonderland.* New York: Norton, 1971.

Green, Roger Lancelyn. *Tellers of Tales: British Authors of Children's Books from 1800 to 1964.* New York: Watts, 1965.

Haviland, Virginia. *Children and Literature: Views and Reviews.* Glenview: Scott, Foresman, 1973.

Hürlimann, Bettina. *Three Centuries of Children's Books in Europe.* Trans. Brian Alderson. Cleveland and New York: World Pub. Co., 1959.

Karpe, M. "The Origins of Peter Pan." *Pscyhoanalytic Review* 43 (1956): 104–110.

Larrick, Nancy. *A Parent's Guide to Children's Reading.* 5th ed. Philadelphia: Westminster, 1982.

Lewis, C. S., ed. *George MacDonald: An Anthology.* New York: Macmillan, 1960.

———. "On Three Ways of Writing for Children." *Of Other Worlds.* Ed. Walter Hooper. New York: Harcourt, 1966. pp. 22–34.

Locke, John. *Some Thoughts Concerning Education.* 1693. Ed. R. H. Quick. Cambridge: UP, 1902.

Meigs, Cornelia. *A Critical History of Children's Literature.* Rev. ed. New York: Macmillan, 1969.

Opie, Iona and Peter. *The Classic Fairy Tales.* London: Oxford University Press, 1974.

———. *The Lore and Language of Schoolchildren.* Oxford: Clarendon, 1959.

———. *The Oxford Dictionary of Nursery Rhymes.* London: Oxford University Press, 1951.

Paine, Albert B., ed. *Mark Twain's Letters*. 2 vols. New York: Harper, 1917.

Propp, V. *Morphology of the Folktale*. Rev. ed. Austin: University of Texas Press, 1968.

Smith, James Steel. *A Critical Approach to Children's Literature*. New York: McGraw-Hill, 1967.

Smith, Lillian H. *The Unreluctant Years: A Critical Approach to Children's Literature*. New York: Viking, 1967.

Starkey, Penelope Schott. "The Many Mothers of Peter Pan: An Explanation and Lamentation." *Research Studies* 42 (1974): 1–10.

Stott, Jon C. *Children's Literature from A to Z*. New York: McGraw-Hill, 1984.

Sutherland, Zena, et al. *Children and Books*. 6th ed. Glenview: Scott, Foresman, 1981.

Thomas, Katherine Elwes. *The Real Personages of Mother Goose*. Boston: Lothrop, Lee, 1930.

Thompson, Stith. *Motif Index of Folk Literature*. 6 vols. 2nd ed. Copenhagen: 1955–58.

——. *Types of the Folktale*. Helsinki: Folklore Fellows Communications No. 184, 1961.

Thoreau, Henry David. *Walden*. 1854. New York: New American Library, 1960.

Thwaite, Mary F. *From Primer to Pleasure in Reading: An Introduction to the History of Children's Books in England to 1914*. 2nd ed. London: Library Assn., 1972.

Tolkien, J.R.R. *Tree and Leaf*. Boston: Houghton Mifflin, 1965.

Zipes, Jack. *Breaking the Magic Spell*. Austin: University of Texas Press, 1979.

——. *Fairy Tales and the Art of Subversion*. New York: Wildman, 1983.

Zochert, Donald. *Laura: The Life of Laura Ingalls Wilder*. New York: Avon, 1976.

INDEX

About the Authors

CHARLES FREY, Associate Professor of English, University of Washington, is the author of *Shakespeare's Vast Romance: A Study of the Winter's Tale* and co-editor of *Classics of Children's Literature*. He has published numerous articles on literary subjects, as well as poems and reviews.

JOHN GRIFFITH, Associate Professor of English, University of Washington, is co-editor with Charles Frey of *Classics of Children's Literature*, and author of articles and contributed chapters on a variety of topics in American literature, modern poetry, and children's literature.

DATE DUE